CW00543687

LIBERATION OR CATASTROPHE?

Liberation or Catastrophe?

Reflections on the History of the
Twentieth Century

Michael Howard (Spring 2007)

hambledon
continuum

Continuum UK
The Tower Building
11 York Road
London SE1 7NX

Continuum US
80 Maiden Lane
Suite 704
New York, NY 10038

www.continuumbooks.com

First published 2007

British Library Cataloguing-in-Publication Data
A catalogue record for this book is available from the British Library.

ISBN 1847251595

Typeset by YHT Ltd, London
Printed and bound by Cromwell Press Ltd, Trowbridge, Wiltshire, Great Britain

Contents

Foreword

The contents of this book were mainly written in the last decade of the twentieth century, when retirement from full-time teaching made it possible to reflect at leisure over the events that I had studied or experienced during the past fifty years.

I ended a previous collection with the words 'I would rather be living in the year 1989 than 1939 – or any date between the two'.[1] This was true enough. The first decade of the century had seen a storm gathering in Europe that broke in 1914 and took the rest of the century to blow itself out, in wars that engulfed the entire planet. These in turn gave rise to ideological conflicts that ended with the triumph of liberal capitalism in every developed society; certainly in the West. My own world had survived intact and me with it, though at times it had seemed a very close-run thing. A little mild triumphalism did not seem out of order.

This understandable euphoria did not make me believe, as it did some of my friends across the Atlantic, that we had reached 'The End of History'. In my earlier writings I had admitted to a Hegelian belief in the historical dialectic, whereby the solution to every problem produces in its turn further challenges; together with a more controversial Kantian conviction that in facing and overcoming fresh challenges mankind has at least the opportunity for moral improvement. So I should not have been surprised to find that the liberal capitalism that seemed so triumphant in the West regarded with such smouldering resentment in the regions suffering from the social upheavals it had caused; and that such resentment should find expression, not in traditional inter-state conflict, but in horrific acts of terrorism directed against the most secure and prosperous regions of the developed world. Clearly History was not dead: it may have taken a brief holiday, but was now back on the job. *La lutta continua*, and it is probably very good for us that it should. At the very least it compels us continually to re-examine our own beliefs, and our will and capacity to defend them.

The last section of this book thus consists of lectures that should be judged less as dispassionate essays in academic analysis than as inevitably

[1] *The Lessons of History* (Clarendon Press, Oxford 1991), p. 5.

partial contributions to an ongoing political debate. Some of their judgements have been falsified by events, and others may yet be in course of time; yet writing as I do at the beginning of 2007, I still cannot see the Anglo-American intervention in Iraq of 2003 as anything other than a massive political misjudgement whose consequences may prove as catastrophic as did the Austrian invasion of Serbia in 1914, provoking another storm of comparable length, if not destructiveness.

I

Introductory

St Edmund Hall 1998

The Enlightenment and its Enemies: Reflections at the close of the Twentieth Century

When I held the Regius Chair of Modern History at Oxford I often wondered about this concept of 'Modern'. Has it any intrinsic validity, or was it just a synonym for 'recent'? I came to the conclusion that it had a distinct meaning, though not quite that assumed by the founders of the Chair in the eighteenth century, who considered that it should include everything that had happened since the fall of the Roman Empire. For me the concept 'Modern' makes sense if it begins with the Enlightenment of the eighteenth century. It defines a world in which we have ceased to rely either on tradition or on divine revelation as guides to thought and action, and trust instead to human 'reason' as a tool to unlock the secrets of the universe and teach people how to do things and how to behave; a Copernican revolution that has placed man, rather than God, or the gods, at the centre of the universe. 'Modern History' is the story of the consequent development, first of thinking and then of political and social relations, increasingly accelerated as scientific discoveries resulted in technological change; the process, in fact, now generally termed 'modernization', which has transformed the conditions of life for most of mankind and continues to do so with undiminished speed. Jan Christian Smuts once stated memorably that 'mankind has struck his tents and is on the march.' It has been a march of accelerating velocity that as yet shows no sign of reaching a destination.

In Europe and North America in the late seventeenth and eighteenth centuries the philosophers, themselves the children of the process, absorbed and disseminated the ideas of the Enlightenment. A new nation, the United States of America, was to be created on the basis of those ideas. Another, France, was torn apart by them, and its wounds have not yet entirely healed. In the nineteenth century came the economic and social transformation of the West as the technology developed from scientific enquiry filtered into the mechanisms of production and communication, transforming traditional agrarian into urbanized, industrial societies. Finally, our own century has seen that process extended to the rest of the world. Today social patterns and practices that endured perhaps for millennia have been uprooted in a single generation; while in our own older, already industrialized societies, the impact of endlessly new technical change continues to break up social patterns almost as soon as they are formed. We are hardly allowed a single night's rest before we have to break camp again at dawn and renew our march.

Karl Marx was one of the first people to understand that this transformation of means of production, from agrarian to industrial, was the underlying explanation for the instability of his age, and we all owe much to his insights. But when he and his followers turned to from economic analysis to political prescription, they abandoned conclusions based on scientific thinking in favour of aspirations based on moral judgements and romantic acts of will. The aspiration, to replace the chaotic jungle of early capitalism by a more just and stable social order, was in itself a noble one; it would hardly have appealed to so many of the best and the brightest of thinkers and political leaders throughout the world if it were not. But Communism was not, as Marx claimed, so much an attempt to continue the revolution in human affairs initiated by the bourgeoisie, as one to check, if not indeed to reverse it: to refashion the world in order to recreate that sense of community, of *Gemeinschaft*, that had been shattered by the alienation wrought by industrialization; to restore to mankind a lost sense of dignity and order and mutual responsibility; an order based on an idealized vision of the 'proletariat' that bore a close resemblance to the Rousseauite concept of the noble savage. It was the bourgeoisie, as Marx himself recognized, who were the true revolutionaries, the heirs and transmitters, for better or worse, of Enlightenment rationality; people who ruthlessly followed the light of Reason wherever it led, at whatever cost to human relations and the fabric of society. These were the demons in the Marxist eschatology. Only if the bourgeoisie were eliminated, wiped off the historical map, could the destructive processes unleashed by the Enlightenment be brought under control, the terrifying flux be stemmed, and a new, stable order be found comparable to that which mankind appeared to have lost.

So the nineteenth century in Europe saw the exponents and followers of the Enlightenment – increasingly defined as 'liberals' – attacked on two fronts: by the members of the old order which they sought to replace, and by those who sought to create another kind of order; one they believed to be based on scientific and rational Enlightenment principles, but far more stable and benign than any that had gone before.

The former, the conservatives and reactionaries, have had a bad press from liberal historians, understandably. But we have to understand that perhaps the most fundamental, and certainly the most shocking result of the Enlightenment was the *secularization* of society; the replacement of divine authority by the power of human reason, thus undermining the legitimacy of all hitherto existing social hierarchies and political authorities. Of course the ruling elites hated it, and where they still exist they still do. But they were not the only ones. Religion was not the opium of the people; it was their meat and drink, an entire life-support system, especially for those – still the great majority – who lived in the countryside. Protestant countries accommodated themselves more easily to modernization than did Catholic, but in Southern Europe – to say nothing of Latin America – the Catholic Church had barely come to terms with the Enlightenment even by the twentieth century. France, Spain and Italy remained deeply divided, the Church fighting a desperate rearguard action against the erosion of its authority that the onset of industrialization and urbanization seemed to bring so inexorably in its wake.

It was not only *croyants* and conservatives who felt like this. At the beginning of the twentieth century nostalgia for a lost past seems to have permeated the whole of European culture. Think of those bucolic idylls of English musicians and poets of the Edwardian age with their revivals of folk-music and their yearning for blue remembered hills. Think of the longing for a vanishing age that throbs through the music of Mahler and his con-temporaries. Think of the spread of *völkisch* ideas in Germany, of the *Wanderjugend* and their communings with nature. This all blended uneasily with the science-based optimism that also characterized the dawn of the twentieth century, a century in which publicists confidently and not unreasonably expected that human life would be yet further transformed for the better by the miracles of electricity and flight. In contrast to the cheerful optimism of H.G. Wells and his like, we find, at a very much deeper level, the cultural despair charted for us by Fritz Stern.

But in Western Europe at least, the role of the old lost rural *Gemein-schaften* had been largely subsumed by nation-states; themselves perhaps 'imagined communities', as Benedict Anderson has memorably suggested,[1] but ones effectively ingrained in the minds of their citizens. Nationalism drew much of its strength from this nostalgia for a past which historians refurbished when they did not actually invent it. It was a past always per-meated by regional images (those *German* forests! those *English* hedgerows! those *Scottish* moorlands! those *Bohemian* rivers!) even though most of those whose minds were shaped at school by these images, and who were encouraged to die for them, may never have been outside the slums of Essen or Birmingham or Glasgow in their lives.

[1] Benedict Anderson, *Imagined Communities: Reflections on the Origin and Spread of Nationalism* (Verso, London 1991).

But nation-states, as Ernest Gellner reminded us, were both the result and the condition of modernization. Their power and indeed their very existence were made both possible and necessary by the improvements in communications and literacy which they in their turn did so much to encourage and develop. Nowhere were the contradictions of the nation-state sharper than in Germany, where a feudal order still clung to their privileges and life-style, largely supported by a *Mittelstand* alarmed by the growth of an urban working class that increased exponentially with the expansion of industries created by the enormous lead gained by German scientists and technologists over their rivals. The German paradox is beautifully depicted in a mural in the hall of the Deutsches Museum in Munich, that monument to modern technology, depicting its opening ceremony in 1910. In the foreground is Kaiser Wilhelm II, fully caparisoned in his uniform as Colonel in Chief of the Death's Head Hussars, sur-rounded by an equally gorgeously uniformed suite of courtiers and princes. Tucked away in the background, almost invisible in their sombre frock-coats, are the world-famous German scientists and engineers whose activ-ities were leading the world into the new century. But none the less they were good *Germans* and anxious to prove in their several ways that this was so. So equally were the industrial working classes, moulded in childhood by their schoolteachers and in adolescence by their drill-sergeants, whatever Marxist beliefs may have been held by their political leaders. National loyalties overrode class differences, and in 1914 the peoples of Western Europe had no doubt what they were fighting for. They were fighting for their *countries*; those communities into which they had been born, which had provided the structure of their lives, and which now sent many of them to their deaths.

Some thirteen million men died in the First World War, and an entire world died with them. In some ways we could say that, although the sen-timents that inspired those who fought on either side owed little to the Enlightenment – indeed, owed far more to the ideals of the Counter-Enlightenment that we shall consider in a moment – it was that war which saw the ultimate triumph of the Enlightenment in Europe. Only rational, bureaucratic, effectively modernized states could fight such wars, with weapons scientifically designed to inflict maximum destruction. The rem-nants of the old feudal order, with its ideology of warrior heroism on the battlefield and deference to an aristocratic hierarchy off it, were swept away. Rock-pools lingered on in Eastern and South-East Europe for another generation but in the West the sons died on the battlefield, as was appro-priate to their aristocratic calling, while the privileges of their fathers were taxed out of existence. Much of the old order, as Arno Meyer has shown us, survived intact until 1914.[2] Little was left, at least in Western Europe, four years later.

But if the old order died in the First World War, something else, far more powerful and sinister, was born; the 'rough beast' of Yeats's apocalyptic poem, which was to dominate Europe for the middle decades of the century and, in spite of all that happened to it since 1945, remains alive, and in places flourishing, in many part of the world.

It is perhaps significant that it is a beast without a name. The sobriquet 'Fascism' that was attached to it by its Italian progenitors is too trivial to describe its full implications. As for 'National-Socialism', that is far too benign. Its enemies were to condemn it in terms that reflected their own preferences and prejudices. Marxists termed it 'reactionary', but they could not have been more wrong. It was a force quite as revolutionary, and far more effectively so, than their own communism. Liberals condemned it as undemocratic, and assumed that it was imposed and sustained by a terrorist minority over a submissive but resentful majority only too anxious, once given the chance, to overthrow their leaders and show themselves good 'enlightened' democrats; a view superficial at best, totally mistaken at worst. The strength of the beast, alas, lay, and still lies in its *populism*: it is willed by a significant number, if not an actual majority, of the people. The roots of Fascism (as I suppose we must call it) lie deep in the hearts and minds of men.

Neither liberals nor Marxists had foreseen the emergence of Fascism. Both children of the Enlightenment, they assumed rationality in political thinking. But the whole point of Fascism is that it was *irrational*; indeed, counter-rational. Isaiah Berlin explored its cultural roots in his studies of the Counter-Enlightenment, with its attacks on the superficiality of rationalism and the inadequacies of individualism, its stress on the collective, the community, the *Volk*; ideas that elevated the concepts of ethnic and racial solidarity, *Blut und Boden*, over those of individual and human rights. Such concepts could not be rationally argued; they could only be *felt*. The appeal of liberal and Marxist ideas had always been to educated minorities; but the peoples of Europe had not fought the First World War for such abstractions as democracy and human rights. They had fought for the communities that had nurtured them, whose values were hallowed by prescription and embodied in their nation: for God, still, for King, still; but everywhere for country, for *patrie*, for *Vaterland*.

Even among the victorious powers that sense of traditional community

---

[2] Arno Meyer, *The Persistence of the Ancien Régime: Europe to the Great War* (Croom Helm, London 1981).

legitimized by prescriptive authority was weakened by the ordeals of war. For the defeated it had been almost destroyed. Within a few years the economic promises and political slogans of 'enlightened' liberal capitalism were shown to be equally empty. What was left? Communism, certainly; but the promises made by Communism, so attractive to some, appeared as threats to many more. But now there was also Fascism; and Fascism promised what so many lost souls in that era craved, whatever their social class; membership in a new, powerful, protective *community*; not at some time in the indefinite future, but at once: now.

The community they promised was of a kind that many men had experienced during the First World War and grown to love, although it is not nowadays fashionable to say so. The positive experiences of an Adolf Hitler or an Ernst Junger were probably far more typical for the majority who served in the armed forces of their countries than those of such liberal intellectuals as Wilfred Owen and Siegfried Sassoon. In the army they had found a new kind of community, a *Kameradschaft* forged in the heat of discomfort and danger. Even in England, where a civil society of interlinked communities had survived the war almost intact, Ex-Servicemen's Associations provided a new and continuing focus for an entire generation. In post-war Germany there was nowhere else for them to go: that was the initial appeal of the Nazi Party. This movement, with its uniforms and its banners, its ceremonies and its hierarchy, above all its designated enemies, once more provided meaning for their lives. And note that designation 'The Movement' – *das Bewegung*. This lay at the root of all Fascism. It was the *dynamic* that mattered, the *action*: not the programme or the goal. Come march with us, invited the Nazi anthem, the *Horst Wessel* song, and join our ranks: *in unser Reihen mit*. No destination for the march was, or needed to be given.

This was the mood that Hitler both captured and embodied. Historians have squabbled over whether he had 'a programme' or not. In my view he did; but for his followers – perhaps for Hitler himself – the programme was secondary. There was never a final 'goal' to be achieved. If anything, the programme existed to justify the Movement, rather than the other way round. That was something that rational statesmen, whether they were Stalin or Neville Chamberlain, never really understood. One could not negotiate rational outcomes with a Movement. Nor could it be destroyed, like some Latin-American dictatorship, by a military coup, as good liberals hoped and some still believe. Its roots had dug far too deep and far too successfully into the psyche of the German people.

Why the German people? Was there something special about their genetic or socio-political inheritance that made them more vulnerable to Fascism than anyone else? Could it have happened anywhere? Of course it could. Xenophobia, an inclination to violence, a pleasure in humiliating others, the desire to find security from a hostile world in one's own group or tribe or gang with it own initiation processes and symbols and necessary enemies, all these are features common to all mankind (though not of course woman-kind) as schoolboys know very well. We are all born Fascists, and have to be expensively educated out of it. And when all the structures of civil society painfully built up over generations disintegrate, whether through sudden catastrophe or gradual erosion, it is to those habits that we naturally return. It was indeed its very Protean quality, its lack of any coherent intellectual structure, that gave Fascism its widespread appeal. To conservatives of all classes it emphasized traditional, tribal values and anti-modernism. To the deprived and discontented it offered an alternative to revolutionary social-ism – *national* socialism, which could embrace anyone and everyone. Above all it appealed to the young with promise of an exciting present, a glorious future, and a career wide open to the talents. What could liberal democracy offer in return?

But it must be said that the Germans were particularly vulnerable to the disease in a way that other European peoples were not. If the United States was the incarnation of the Enlightenment, Germany was a kind of labora-tory for the Counter-Enlightenment. For them the Enlightenment was French, foreign, *welsch*, introduced by the aristocracy in the eighteenth century and enforced by French bayonets in the nineteenth. Its very inter-nationalism made it superficial. Led by their own intellectuals since the days of Herder, if not indeed of Luther, the Germans had been taught to look to their roots, their language, even their music for a deeper kind of truth than anything the rationalists of the Enlightenment had to offer; a *Kultur*, as they liked to put it, as opposed to a *Zivilisation*. The Germans in the nineteenth century embraced the science and technology of the Enlightenment, but fought hard to resist its eroding effects on their society, clinging to their national symbols and myths and if necessary, inventing new ones. Many, perhaps most Germans, and certainly most German intellectuals, saw the First World War as a battle for cultural survival against the converging forces of Russian barbarism and, far more subversive, the decadent *Zivili-sation* of the West, embodied no longer by French aristocrats but by the materialist societies of the Anglo-Saxon world. This belief was taken over in its entirety by the Nazis and provided the bedrock of their own philosophy. Armed as they were with all the military technology and bureaucratic rationality of the Enlightenment, but fuelled by the warrior-values of a culture based on a largely invented past, it is not surprising that the Ger-mans held the world at bay through two terrible wars.

Fascism was ultimately defeated by the two powers that embodied the two divergent strands of the Enlightenment, who then confronted each other during the second half of this century. For the West in general and the United States in particular, the Enlightenment was, and remains, a continually unfolding process, led by free human thought and enquiry, with results that may be painful, are usually unfair, but are ultimately beneficial to mankind; a process requiring continual judgement, discrimination, and reconciliation of apparently conflicting values; an unceasing, necessary if often painful dialectic. Government exists to make this dialectic possible, not to direct it.

But for Marxist-Leninists the Enlightenment had revealed, once and for all, scientific certainties; certainties preserved by the Party, an intellectual priesthood, and where necessary enforced by the secular arm. This certainly had the advantage of creating, or re-creating, a community that, so long as one played by the rules, provided security of a kind; the security provided by every dogmatic church. But unlike those made by other churches, the claims made by communism were empirically verifiable. They promised that present sufferings would be rewarded, not in another world, but in this one; and after a couple of generations it became very clear that they would not. The competition between the liberal West and the Communist East was purely secular, to provide wealth, health, and happiness. The West won that competition hands down. The first two, health and wealth, were easily quantifiable; the last, happiness, was misleadingly believed to be so, in terms of consumer goods of a kind and in quantities unimaginable even in the earlier part of the century. Socialists sneered at this as 'consumerism', but it was what people wanted, and what the West showed itself able to provide. Communism collapsed as all creeds collapse when their elites lose faith. Thus the century ends with the Western Enlightenment triumphant. According to Francis Fukuyama, following those two great British historians Sellars and Yeatman in their work *1066 and All That*, History should now come to a full stop.[3]

The trouble with this view is that it is oxymoronic – unkind people might go further and call it moronic. The Enlightenment cannot come to a full stop. It is continually dynamic. It released sources of energy comparable to those trapped within the atom, which once released endlessly multiply by a process of continual fission. The process cannot be arrested. The story of the past two centuries has been that of vain efforts to resist it. The 'reactionaries' of the nineteenth century fought a rearguard action to prevent their

[3] Francis Fukuyama, *The End of History and the Last Man* (The Free Press, New York 1992).

entire world being uprooted: their epitaph in this country has been mov-
ingly written by Evelyn Waugh. But in the twentieth century those who
hoped to arrest this juggernaut took the offensive and tried to destroy its
agents, the bourgeoisie; the people whose ruthlessness, energy, inventiveness
and entrepreneurial talents were transforming the world.

In Europe, especially Eastern and Central Europe, these trouble-makers
could be readily identified with the Jews, hated since the Middle Ages as
aliens within closed communities and identified in the nineteenth century as
the spearheads of economic disruption. So long as they were around, so
their enemies believed, there could be no stability, no homogeneity in
society; hence the attractiveness to fanatics – and not only to Germans – of a
Final Solution. Elsewhere the whole economic class of entrepreneurs,
whether urban or rural, could be more easily identified and destroyed. In
Russia in the 1920s and 1930s; in China in the 1940s and 1950s; most
horribly in Cambodia in the 1960s and 1970s; everywhere we find attempts
to restore or create stability in society by eliminating the educated classes,
the entrepreneurs, the intellectuals who by their ideas, skills and activities
seemed likely to destroy it.

Has this process now come to an end? Will the dissemination of bourgeois culture be placidly accepted in what we still call 'The Third World'?
And can it be guaranteed to produce perpetual peace and stability, eroding
class and national and ethnic conflict, in our own societies in the West?

In the Third World it must be said that the prospects are not good. The
impact of industrialization is having much the same effect as it had in
Europe in the early nineteenth century. In Asia, Africa and Latin America,
new means of production are destroying traditional communities based on
an agrarian economy whose social hierarchy or tribal structure was legitimized by religious beliefs; much as they destroyed them in Europe a
century ago. Everywhere urban populations have increased far beyond the
capacity of the economy to absorb them, creating masses of uprooted
peoples desperate to escape to wealthier lands, and ripe for fanatical milit-
ancy if they cannot escape. The only answer that the West can offer is
homoeopathic – the hope that science and technology will in time cure the
problems that they have themselves created. But the cure worked in the
West largely thanks to the existence of a safety valve, the United States, to
which millions of those 'huddled masses' could and did emigrate and
become part of a thriving new economy. Now the West, alarmed at the
effect of such an influx on its own social stability, is battening down its
hatches. A decade or so ago Marxists had good hopes that this immiseration
might lead to the revolution and the consequent triumph of communism of
which they had been cheated in Europe a century earlier, but the implosion

of the communist world has disillusioned them. What is there now left, if liberal capitalism continues to result in misery for the masses, except some form of Fascism?

As for the West, we know our situation far too well to believe that the Enlightenment has yet solved the problems it has created and that history for us has come to an end. André Gide said something to the effect that 'to free oneself is only the beginning. The real problem is to know how to live in liberty'; a discovery being made today by the populations of the former communist countries. A prison is also a kind of a home. In the West, intellectuals may have become used to living in the godless world explored by Schopenhauer and Nietzsche in the last century, Heidegger and Sartre in this. But the social effects are only now beginning to be widely felt, of a world in which people are left entirely free to create and live by their own values, with neither traditional authority nor religious beliefs to guide them. We do not worry too much so long as, for most of the population, liberal capitalism continues quite literally to deliver the goods, in quantities and of a quality undreamed of by our forebears. But if liberal capitalism were to fail, as has its rival communism, we know what would be the likely alternative.

So we face a new century with the assurance that History has not come to an end, which is good news for historians. We also know, if the last century has taught us nothing else, that there is no escape, either to a recreated past, however much it may be sanitized by the repellent sobriquet 'Heritage', or to a Utopian future, the promise of which allows us to inflict untold suffering on those still living. The past century had been a record of vast, of terrifying mistakes, which I hope we now know better than to repeat. We have to use the knowledge that we have to deal with the problems which that knowledge has itself created, accepting that every solution will only create further problems. We must steer between the Scylla and Charybdis that caused so many catastrophes during the past century – hubris and despair. Whatever happens, the next century will be a very interesting one indeed.

The Twentieth Century:
Liberation or Catastrophe?

In 1900 the world was 'Eurocentric' to an extent that it had never been before, and certainly no longer is today. By the end of the nineteenth century the peoples of Europe – their merchants and financiers, their soldiers and sailors, their scientists and engineers – had created a single global system of communications through which they had been able to extend their military, economic, and cultural power. European cities, financed by European capital and built by European architects, had sprung up throughout the world. The United States was beginning to develop its distinctive models that the Europeans themselves were trying to imitate; but even for the Americans – especially the American East-coast elites – Europe was still the fount of culture and ideas. Elsewhere in the world peoples might ignore European cultural hegemony, but none offered an alternative. Some, like the Japanese, assiduously copied it. Others, like the Indian nationalists, reacted against it. But even those who did react against it had to acquire the weapons of the enemy if they were to resist successfully: whether those weapons were machine guns, or the battleships with which the Japanese destroyed the Russian fleet at the Battle of Tsushima, or the printing-press, or the wealth-creating mechanisms of European capitalism, or the ideas of liberty, self-government and the rule of law propagated by the Western democracies, or those of revolutionary socialism spread by the disciples of Karl Marx. European, or, increasingly, Atlantic hegemony seemed inescapable; the hegemony, that is, of the white races.

We can thus usefully discuss the ideas of European elites as those of a world ruling-class – or of people who believed themselves, with good reason, to be a world ruling-class, with all the privileges and all the responsibilities which that status carried with it.

These elites were not all of one mind. Many of the older generation retained the genial optimism of the mid-nineteenth century, itself the child of the Enlightenment of the eighteenth century, and believed in the inevitability of Progress; progress based on the liberation of Reason from superstition, of Science from tradition, of popular self-government from tyranny, above all of the mass of mankind from hardship, poverty, suffering and disease through the ever-broadening application of science and technology. They had on the face of it every reason to suppose that this would be so. In their lifetime they had seen the world they had known as children transformed by a technological revolution based on steam and iron, that had built railways and factories and ocean-going liners; opening up the countryside by linking it with world markets for its produce and its labour; pulling their surplus population into great cities or sending them further afield to found new nations overseas. They had seen advances in medicine and hygiene that had decimated infant mortality, increased life-expectancy and gradually ameliorated the condition of the poor. They had seen the plagues that had once ravaged Europe become things of the past; and the tropical diseases that had made white settlement impossible throughout great tracts of the world were in their turn being conquered.

Now, at the turn of the century, a second era of technological transformation seemed to be opening with the advent of electricity and the internal combustion engine. In the 1890s it was the infinite promise of the first as a source of cheap and universal power that caught the imagination. Already city-centres and the houses of the well-to-do were being lit by electric light. At the Paris Exhibition of 1900 an entire pavilion was dedicated to displaying the potential of this new and magic force, symbolized by the cinematograph of the appropriately named M. Lumière. Signor Marconi would mark the last year of the old century by bridging the Channel with his 'wireless' telegraph, and open the new, three years later, by doing the same for the Atlantic. Already the world was beginning to shrink to the size of a village, making the benevolent dominance of European ideas through European technology yet more absolute.

The automobile took rather longer to make its impact: in 1900 it was still a toy for the rich, and another ten years would pass before Henry Ford with his Model T made it available to the masses. Still, the process was well under way whereby mankind was to turn its back on what had been its main means of transport and traction for the past thousand years – the horse. Everywhere stables were gradually being turned into garages, coachmen into mechanics. Horsed vehicles were beginning to disappear from city streets. The world of which the horse had been the centre began to disappear – an entire culture, an entire social hierarchy, not least an entire countryside. Even among those city-dwellers who would most benefit by it, the revolution in transport was shadowed by a nostalgia for what they felt they were losing; a nostalgia that was to permeate so much English verse and so much English music for a generation to come.

But the optimists saw only the bright side. Whatever might be lost, mankind as a whole could only gain from the huge new opportunities opened up by science and technology. Powered flight – the brothers Wright got their heavier-than-air machine briefly airborne in 1903, but Count Zeppelin and others had already made long flights in dirigible balloons – was seen from the beginning as a mixed blessing, as H.G. Wells very quickly indicated in his vision of a future War in the Air. As for the implications of the discovery of the electron by J.J. Thomson in 1897 and of radium by the Curies a year later, the development by Max Planck of the Quantum theory in 1900 and by Albert Einstein of the theory of relativity, discoveries that were to revolutionize mankind's understanding and control of the universe, only specialists as yet understood their significance, and very few even of those their long-term implications. Half a century was to pass before these were, for better or worse, to make their full impact on society with the development of the computer and, more sinister, that of nuclear weapons. But meanwhile there was plenty to be going on with; ever-improving standards of living, of education and knowledge, of opportunities and comforts which had hitherto been within the reach only of a tiny minority of mankind. In the coming century, so the optimists believed, these benefits would be universally extended, first within all classes of their own societies, and then throughout the entire world.

But there were also those who, while sharing with the optimists their belief that progress was inevitable and desirable, did not believe that it would necessarily be peaceful, or indeed that it should be. These can be roughly divided into the disciples of one or other of those two giants of the mid-nineteenth century, Charles Darwin and Karl Marx.

Marx had taught, following the Hegelian concept of the Dialectic, that progress had been made throughout history by conflict, and in particular class conflict. He gave full credit to the bourgeoisie of the nineteenth century for their role in destroying the old stagnant feudal economy and the dominance of the landed classes, but saw within the womb of capitalism the growth of a new class, the industrial proletariat, who would in their turn revolt against the old order and introduce a classless society in which all the benefits of the new industrial age would be equally shared. It is true that the expectations of bloody revolution that had been so general in mid-century Europe had faded as economic growth had (in defiance of Marx's prognosis) made possible the improvement of working-class standards of living. Perhaps more important, mass overseas emigration had unexpectedly defused many social tensions; but none the less the class-struggle was being waged as bitterly as ever, and everywhere in Europe massive strikes were to rise in a crescendo throughout the first decade of the new century. Within the British Labour Movement Marxists may have been an insignificant minority, but that did not inhibit the growth of militant trades-unionism. In Continental Europe all socialist parties were explicitly Marxist. Where, like the Social Democrats in Germany, they were not revolutionary, it was because they had learned how to work very effectively within the parliamentary system and were in consequence seen by the possessing classes as presenting even more of a threat. In Britain wise concessions from above and moderate leadership from below had avoided the polarization of society that increasingly characterized Germany, France, Italy and Spain; but even in Britain the future of working-class liberation and universal brotherhood to which socialist leaders looked forward, and which was symbolized at Labour Party meetings by the singing and waving of the Red Flag, was looked on by the possessing classes with something like dread.

More numerous among the possessing classes were the admirers of Charles Darwin. Few, probably, of Darwin's self-styled disciples fully understood his subtle theory of evolution through 'survival of the fittest', but many thought that they did, and believed that it was as valid for human society as it was for the world of nature. 'Progress', so Darwin had taught – or was generally believed to have taught – had not been peaceful at all, but the result of continual struggle, in which only the strongest and 'fittest' species had survived. So why should mankind be any different from his ancestors? Would not the strongest, fittest, and most adaptable peoples triumph in the unending struggle for survival? Had this not been so in the development of their own capitalist economies, when the weakest had gone to the wall? Had it not been so in the struggle for dominance among the powers of Europe, from which Great Britain had emerged so triumphantly successful? And had it not been so in the whole pattern of imperial expansion and world conquest? Indeed for many this creed was linked with an equally widespread belief in the inherent superiority of the white races, especially the Teutonic; a superiority that had enabled them to spread their dominion throughout the globe. The appalling results of the implementation of this creed by Adolf Hitler a generation later, and the intellectual absurdity of those publicists like Houston Stewart Chamberlain who tried to propagate it, must not blind us to the degree to which at the beginning of the century this belief in inherent racial superiority was widely taken for granted, especially within the Anglo-Saxon world. Apart from anything else it seemed both to explain and to justify the existence of the British Empire.

But would the white races maintain their superiority indefinitely? Might not their very progress in civilization, the growing ease of life for the ruling classes, the stunted, unhealthy street-life of the urban masses, lead to degeneracy and decay? Would not long peace sap their vitality? The *fin de siècle* was obsessed with the idea of degeneracy and decadence: the horrified interest in the Oscar Wilde case, and the widespread satisfaction at the verdict, speaks volumes for the inner insecurities of the ruling classes in late-Victorian England. But even more alarming was the miserable performance of the British Army in the Boer War, and the 'Black Week' of defeat with which the century closed. Not only had the British Army shown itself apparently incompetent to deal with another 'civilized' enemy, but the reservists and the militiamen who were called to the colours proved to be miserably 'unfit'; a condition that further official enquiries showed to be only too typical of the population as a whole. In spite of all the splendours of the Diamond Jubilee, the prospects for Britain at the turn of the century looked distinctly unsettled. There were those who proposed a kind of race-renewal of the British people by settling the 'street-bred peoples' of over-crowded British cities in the wide-open spaces of the colonies and binding them to the motherland in a single great Empire – a view that grew in popularity as it became clear, at the dawn of the new century, that the supremacy on which the British had prided themselves for a hundred years was now under challenge from a truly formidable Teutonic rival across the North Sea. Within a few years a yet more alarming threat was to appear when an Asian people, the Japanese, used European techniques of war, combined with a quite un-European spirit of heroic self-sacrifice, to defeat a European enemy in their successful war against the Russian Empire. The awful question began to be asked: would the twentieth century belong to the white races at all?

In addition to these groups there was one that rejected the whole idea of 'progress', whether it came about peacefully or as the result of conflict, and which regarded the whole course of European history since the French Revolution as catastrophic. In Central and Eastern Europe there was still an *ancien régime*, consisting not only of the aristocratic landowning classes but widespread groups associated with them, who regarded industrialization and democratization itself as the enemy; literal and self-confessed 'reactionaries' supported throughout Europe by the still immense power of the Catholic Church, the incipient liberalism of whose hierarchy had hardly penetrated into the rural parishes of France, Italy and Spain. In the great Empires of the Habsburgs and the Romanovs – even within that power-house of modernization, Imperial Germany – the aristocracy was not only still immensely rich and enjoying, within their own estates, unchallenged feudal power, but their position close to the imperial throne gave them often a controlling influence over the policies of their governments. In France, it is true, they had withdrawn from active politics, but the Dreyfus Affair gave them the opportunity to display the contempt in which they held the Republic and all the values it professed. In Italy the Enlightenment had barely penetrated south of Florence, while in Spain a civil war grumbled that was to erupt with horrible violence three decades later. For these people, and those in all ranks of society who shared their traditional values – chivalric honour, hierarchical loyalty, religious devotion, reverence for the past – the prospects held out by the twentieth century were nothing short of horrible. One finds some echoes of their views – including the anti-Semitism that usually characterized them – among such Catholic intellectuals in this country as Hilaire Belloc; but they had to await a further generation for their most eloquent, if somewhat posthumous defender: Evelyn Waugh.

This dread of a future that promised nothing but catastrophe, the destruction of 'civilization as they knew it' was only deepened by the work of those who claimed to speak for the future: the artists of what came to be known as the 'Modern' movement. Hitherto the term 'modern' had been applied to the culture of the Enlightenment; the thinking and styles that turned their backs on the dominance of the medieval Church and trusted human reason as the surest guide in truth and taste. This was entirely compatible with a judicious use of classical models; indeed the 'modern' age was usually dated to the Renaissance, and in academic history syllabuses it still is. But now artists began to turn their backs on everything that had happened *since* the Renaissance with a perversity that could only appear as deliberately malicious. Certainly innovation in the arts had been coming thick and fast in the last decades of the nineteenth century – Impressionism, post-Impressionism, Symbolism, *Art nouveau, Jugendstil* – but each new style grew out of the last, and not too fast for the educated layman to keep up with it. But now artists began to glory in their discontinuity, in their rejection of all traditional models, in their role as an *avant-garde* marching boldy into the future with little concern whether anyone followed them or not. Such painters as Mondrian and Picasso and Kandinsky, such composers as Webern and Schönberg and Stravinsky, such architects as le Corbusier and the craftsmen of the Bauhaus, explicitly rejected the traditions of the past, adjusted their outlook to the new and unprecedented world being opened up by science and technology, and regarded their works of art as political manifestos. The new century, they proclaimed, was the moment to make a clean break: now mankind must look to a future – a future, so Marinetti and his fellow Futurists declared, that would be exhilarating, violent, dedicated to speed, action, colour, and the destruction of the rubbish of the past.

If apprehensive conservatives wanted further evidence of national degeneracy, this *avant-garde* seemed to provide it. Such conservatives included not only the self-confessed reactionaries I have described, but whole swathes of country-dwellers and the middle classes, who saw their values challenged by something they barely understood, and in so far as they did understand it, they hated. It was after all a *déraciné* petty-bourgeois inhabitant of Vienna, Adolf Hitler, who was one day to mount a mocking exhibition of 'Degenerate Art', which contained many of the finest masterpieces of the twentieth century; and his taste was very widely shared.

How on earth did societies that contained such irreconcilable views hold together at all? For hold together they did, with a degree of social cohesion that was to be amazingly demonstrated when, fourteen years later, they were to plunge into the greatest war the world had ever seen.

It may indeed have been the very strength of these fears and these antagonisms that account for the most remarkable feature of Europe at the dawn of the twentieth century; its ferocious and atavistic *nationalism*. For in 1900 the Nation-State reached its apogee. Throughout the nineteenth century the power and reach of national governments had become increasingly intrusive, as improved communications enabled them to increase their control over their citizens; first to tax them, then to conscript them into their armies, then to educate them for the new industrial age, then to assume responsibilities, hitherto left to the Church or private charities, for their health and welfare. That growing intrusion of the state would hardly have been politically possible unless the old, tenacious, personal loyalties that had held European states together since the sixteenth century, the sense of obligation to a ruling dynasty in whose name all these things were done, had not been powerfully reinforced, or indeed sometimes replaced, by a broader sense of belonging to a *nation*: a country, a *Vaterland*, a *patrie*. As the power of the state increased, so there increased with it the capacity to inculcate this sense of nationhood; not only through schools, but through military parades and ceremonies, through flags and symbols, through songs and anthems, and through monumental neo-Baroque architecture. Historians created patriotic myths and where necessary lexicographers developed distinctive languages out of peasant dialects. The person of the monarch, where there was one, was converted into an ikon, the embodiment of the Nation. In France, where there was not such a monarch, the Army took his place. In Britain the convenient coincidence of three great national events within five years – the Diamond Jubilee, the funeral of Queen Victoria and the coronation of Edward VII – made it possible to create, not just an entirely new tradition of grandiose ceremonial around the person of the Monarch, but to redesign the core of London on a scale appropriate to an Imperial capital city. Even more hideous memorials erected at the same time in Vienna, Berlin and, above all, Rome, show that the British were not unique in their literally monumental bad taste.

It would be misleadingly simple to see all this in Marxist terms, as a deliberate programme by the ruling classes to bamboozle the masses and keep them in line. In fact, nationalism was a response to deeply felt social needs. Certainly it provided the old ruling classes with the opportunity for transmitting all those chivalric values of service, subordination, honour, and respect for the past that appeared so threatened by the modern age. National sentiments usually found expression through the imagery of bogus feudalism, especially in Germany. But nationalism was a middle-class rather than an aristocratic phenomenon, an urban rather than a rural one. It gave to city-dwellers a powerful and much-needed sense of identity, linking them with the dignity and permanence of a past they feared they had lost. It drew deeply on the kind of nostalgia I have already described, but it also provided a sense of mission, function, purpose that appealed to the adventurous young. Its appeal reconciled all but the bitterest reactionaries and the most dogmatic socialists. It was, quite literally, a cause to die for. Indeed, how could Nations prove their greatness in the future – indeed, their very fitness to survive – except by the means that had served them so well in the past: by war?

They were soon to have their chance. In 1914 the peoples of Europe, not excepting the *avant-gardistes*, accepted war, sometimes welcoming it with almost hysterical enthusiasm. Some fought to vindicate traditional values, some to liberate themselves from a shabby and worn-out past. Both succeeded. The result of the subsequent wars was to destroy for ever the world hegemony of the European elites. Liberation, or catastrophe?

3 *Univ. of Liverpool 1996*

The Shifting Balance: A Changing Britain in a Changing World

It requires little imagination to picture the horror and amazement with which an Englishman of 'the upper classes' who was in his prime a hundred years ago would regard the state of his country, and its position in the world, if he were to revisit it today. His own world was, to all appearances, one of certainties and order. The Britain that he would have known was racially homogeneous. It was governed by an elite to whose status, and *mores*, the rest of society was deferential. It was a world of strict religious observance, if not necessarily of deep religious beliefs. The social position of the ruling class was buttressed by a dominant state Church. At the apex of society, its position sanctified by that Church, was a Monarchy that had never before in its history enjoyed such respect and affection. Britain was still the wealthiest power in the world, although her position was under challenge from her German neighbours and her American cousins. Above all, she was the centre of the greatest empire the world had ever seen, whose power and extent would be celebrated with massive pomp and ceremony in the Diamond Jubilee of Queen Victoria in 1897. It was said at the time – I think by the Master of Balliol – that to be born an Englishman was to have drawn a winning ticket in the great lottery of life. That was certainly true of those fortunate enough to have got into Balliol. Not many did. But even those who did not felt a Gilbertian pride in 'being an Englishman' – unless of course they were Scots, Welsh, or Irish, or a woman; and the lower down they were in the social scale, the more strongly they may have felt it.

Today all that has gone. At home we have a society where, if it is not yet entirely classless, no respect is paid to ancient wealth and lineage. The very survival of the monarchy is in question. The aristocracy do their best to keep a low profile, and the great houses from which they once governed the country survive, at best, as museums. The moral certainties that are supposed to hold society together have disintegrated. The country has become totally secularized, and the churches have dwindled into sects. Abroad the status that Britain enjoyed as a great global power has evaporated with the dissolution of the Empire and the dwindling of the Commonwealth. The respect in which we were once held on the continent of Europe – even if it was a respect often tinged with cordial dislike – has gone as well, to be replaced by an exasperation among our European partners sometimes little removed from contempt. How on earth, our *revenant* might well ask, has all this come about? Did we in fact *lose* the two World Wars?

Before trying to answer his question let us first reverse the process and transport ourselves back a hundred years. How comfortable would any of us have been in the Britain of 1900, even if we had been born into the tiny minority that had drawn the winning lottery tickets? Could we have adjusted ourselves to the serene triumphalism, the conviction of racial superiority, the contempt for 'lesser breeds without the law' that was bred into the ruling classes at their public schools? We might have welcomed the apparent social stability, but how happy would we have been with the huge inequalities of wealth, and the near-destitution in which a high proportion of the population – by some estimates, nearly one-third – were still condemned to live? We would certainly have been shocked by the incidence of infant mortality and infectious diseases, and the misery in which so many of those who did survive had to pass their lives. Admittedly today a time-traveller from 1900 could still find areas of misery and deprivation comparable to those of his own time, where whole families seek relief from lives of total despair in drugs, drink and crime. But he would have also to note the prosperity of the countryside, the huge, neat, well-tended suburbs, the cleanliness of the inner cities, and for the great majority of the population a standard of diet, health, comfort and well-being – to say nothing of opportunities for entertainment and travel – unimaginable in his own day for anyone save the very, very rich.

Moreover, if our time-traveller was in the least intelligent and well read, he would have discerned the extent to which the stability of his own social order had already been undermined; the moral foundations by Nietzsche and his followers, the intellectual foundations by Darwin, the social foundations by Marx. The image of a peaceful rural 'England' projected by so many poets – and which they went on projecting for the first two decades of the coming century – were hard to reconcile with the reality, at the turn of the century, of a complex, largely urbanized British society torn by industrial strife. Abroad the foundations of British power were far from secure, as the Boer War was humiliatingly to reveal. A few clear-sighted prophets, the young Rudyard Kipling foremost among them, had realized this even in the midst of the Diamond Jubilee celebrations, warning that all the pomps of yesterday might, if people were not careful, soon be one with Nineveh and Tyre.

By 1900 indeed Britain, though respected for her Empire, was virtually friendless in the world; in productivity she was being fast overhauled by Germany and the United States; and her Empire looked far from secure. It was threatened on two continents by her old enemies, France and Russia; while a new and far more dangerous adversary, the newly united Germany, was showing herself increasingly hostile to a Britain whose global dominance seemed the principal obstacle in the way of her own achievement of the status of a world power. The Royal Navy was still formidable, but would be able to remain so in face of German competition only by expensive and continuous modernization, paid for by taxes that would bite deep into the wealth and status of the landed aristocracy. As for the army, it had been shown by the Boer War to be effective only as an imperial gendarmerie, and attempts to enlarge it by calling up militia and reservists had revealed a level of physical unfitness and lack of education in the population as a whole that in itself seemed almost enough to disqualify Britain from being a serious military power in the coming era of mass industrialized warfare.

So at the beginning of the new century responsible British statesmen regarded the future, not with complacency, but with well-merited foreboding. In world affairs isolation, however splendid, was obviously not enough. Some hoped that the scattered resources of the Empire might be so knitted together as to constitute a true world economic and military power capable of facing down all opposition, but the colonies of settlement, soon to be styled 'Dominions', made it clear that, however friendly their feelings might be towards a country that most of their peoples still regarded as 'home', they would not again submit themselves to political direction from London. Safety could lie therefore only in a policy that Britain in her Victorian heyday had almost forgotten; the neutralization of foreign threats by a policy of 'balance'; the enlistment of allies against the continental power whose emerging ambitions seemed most dangerously to threaten British security. So as German policy appeared increasingly menacing, Britain was drawn more closely into continental politics, mending fences with her former enemies France and Russia, in order to preserve a balance on which her own peace and prosperity ultimately depended.

But simultaneously the British government had to concern itself with another and equally urgent balance: that between expenditure on her external security, and that on the welfare of her own people.

That concern had never been absent in the nineteenth century, though it had long been largely a matter for private charity. As the franchise slowly increased and the balance of society tilted from an agrarian to a largely urban population, it became a matter of political concern as well. In 1906 there came into office a Liberal administration with a radical wing, for whom social welfare was to be an overriding priority. The revelations of the

Boer War and the social enquiries it set on foot, added a defence dimension to the issue that gained it a considerable measure of cross-bench support. By 1913 the percentage of GNP spent on the social services had doubled from some 2% to 4% – slightly more than military expenditure for the same year. In the following five years of the Great War military expenditure naturally soared, and both taxation and indebtedness with it. But also, as a direct consequence of that war, the franchise was extended to embrace the entire adult population, female as well as male; voters for whom their own welfare and that of their families was an understandable priority, whether in the form of low taxes for the middle class or social insurance against the arbitrary fluctuations of the market system for the working classes. After the war military expenditure could be and was axed, remaining until the mid-1930s well below 4% of GNP. Expenditure on social welfare, however, never fell between the wars below 10%. Even that was not enough to avert the miseries of the great slump, among which the generation grew up who voted Labour at the end of the Second World War in the determination that such a situation must never be allowed to recur.

Can it be said therefore, *post hoc propter hoc*, that Britain's decline in world influence abroad is the direct consequence of the growth of social democracy at home, which has increasingly tilted the balance away from military towards domestic expenditure? Superficially such a case can be made. I shall leave aside for the moment the argument that there was a systemic failure of British governments over a century or more to invest in the growth of the economy, emphasizing financial stability at the cost of industrial development, so that the military and the social services had to compete for shares in a gradually shrinking cake. The promise of growth always seems the way out of all fiscal dilemmas. But it is questionable whether higher military expenditure at any level could for long have sustained the position which Britain occupied at the turn of the century, as a 'Great Power'.

Ideally a Great Power is one that can take on any combination of rivals and defeat them, but Britain has never been that. The naval supremacy on which British power rested at the end of the nineteenth century was ultimately the result of the inability or the unwillingness of her main European rivals, land powers with major problems of territorial defence, to challenge her. Once a major continental power, Germany, did begin to pose such a challenge, Britain had to seek continental allies as she always had in the past, and rely on them to do the bulk of the land fighting for her. Her 'greatness' rested not on military strength as such, but on economic resources built up over two centuries when Britain led the world in trade and industrial production. When in the First World War the weakness of her continental allies compelled her to convert those resources into military effectiveness and raise a continental-sized army, she found herself facing bankruptcy within two years. Even then it took the combined resources of the British, French and Russian Empires, together with a promised commitment from the United States greater than any of them, to break what a German historian has called the German 'Grasp for World Power',[1] and her contribution left Britain economically and emotionally exhausted.

The balance was preserved, but only just. When the American resources which had tipped the balance were withdrawn, Britain found herself once more required to sustain it together with greatly weakened European allies against a Germany whose economic potential was still intact and whose ambitions were unappeased; and this at a time when public opinion, for the first time electorally unleashed, was showing itself deeply hostile to the possibility of future war, or any expenditure to fight one.

It is easy to condemn the selfishness and short-sightedness of the British electorate between the wars, and the statesmen – Ramsay Macdonald, Stanley Baldwin, above all Neville Chamberlain – who represented them. But even if those statesmen, in defiance of public opinion, had transferred resources from domestic to military expediture on a vast scale, they could still have not maintained Britain's position in the world. The Empire itself was now security-consuming rather than security-producing. The rise of a predatory and hostile Japan put the whole of the Far East at risk. Britain's new acquisitions in the Middle East only gave further hostages to fortune. Repeatedly the Chiefs of Staff made it clear that under no imaginable circumstances could Britain cope with a combined threat from a revived Germany, a hostile Japan, and any third adversary threatening communications through the Middle East. It was not so much competition from domestic demand that made military expenditure impossible on the requisite scale. It was the capacity of the economy as a whole, and of industry as a whole, to sustain it, even if the entire country had been placed on a wartime footing. When ultimately this did happen, in the spring of 1939, bankruptcy was certain within two years, whether war came or no, and whether Britain 'won' it or no. The problem that British statesmen faced between the wars was not how to win another major war: it was how to avoid one, whether by appeasement, deterrence, or a mixture of the two. Given the fact that Hitler actually *wanted* to fight one, it is hardly surprising that they failed.

When war did come Britain survived and was ultimately victorious,

[1] Fritz Fischer, *Griff nach der Weltmacht: die Kriegszielpolitik des Kaiserlichen Deutschland 1914–1918* (Droste Verlag, Düsseldorf 1961).

thanks not to her own military prowess but to alliance with two continental powers, Russia and the United States, whose intervention had been quite unpredictable but whose combined strength dwarfed anything that Germany and Japan could put into the field. Those allies exacted their price. That of the Soviet Union was the assertion of dominion over Eastern Europe, which created a new problem of balance. The United States was concerned to create a world political and economic structure that it could dominate, and in which there would be no room for a British Empire. But the British people themselves exacted a price for the losses and hardships they had endured. They were concerned, not with the consolidation of British power abroad, but with the preservation and extension, in a 'welfare state', of the social gains that had been achieved under the 'siege socialism' of the wartime years.

The British emerged from the Second World War battered and justifiably proud of themselves, but suffering from two illusions. One was that Britain was still, in her own right, a Great Power. The other was that her economy would be able indefinitely to support the costs of the welfare state that they set about establishing in 1945.

The first illusion was understandable. There was not much competition in 1945 for Great Power status. Germany and Japan were prostrate. France and the rest of Western Europe were dependent on the mercy or generosity of the triumphant Allies. British forces were restoring order in the Empire, and even if India, the jewel in the Crown, was shaking loose, the rest remained apparently intact. Successive British governments, Labour as well as Conservative, took it for granted that it should remain intact. The term 'Superpower' was coined by an American political scientist, William Fox, in 1944, and he included Britain in that category as a matter of course. It was a status that called almost automatically for the acquisition of an independent nuclear capability.

There were certainly two very difficult years, when financial stringency compelled Britain to amalgamate her occupation zone of Germany with that of the United States, to hand over to the Americans the task of maintaining stability in Greece and Turkey, and to wash her hands of responsibility for Palestine; all questions that a Labour Government quite naturally regarded as secondary in importance to the consolidation of the welfare state at home. But once the Cold War set in in 1948, the old warm relationship with the United States was restored. NATO was created under Anglo-Saxon leadership with Britain again sitting, as of right, well above the salt.

By the early 1950s, indeed, the British seemed to have recaptured a mood of self-confidence almost unparalleled since the end of the previous century. The two objectives for which their governments had been striving for so long – objectives which to many appeared incompatible – seemed to have been achieved. At home they had established a welfare state that was a model for the world. Abroad Britain was incontestably a Great Power, second in the West only to the United States. She looked on European aspirations to unification with patronizing if somewhat sceptical approval, without any idea that she might take part in them herself. As Churchill himself explained, the claims of 'the special relationship' with the United States, and of the newly enlarging Commonwealth (to say nothing of the sterling area) made this out of the question. Britain would maintain a balance between the three circles of Europe, the Commonwealth, and the 'special relationship' and, hopefully, draw strength from them all. Domestically the British public basked in a series of nostalgic movies in which such stars as John Mills and David Niven celebrated, albeit with gentlemanly understatement, British heroism in the war. The press hailed the accession of Queen Elizabeth as the beginning of a new Elizabethan age, and at the time of her coronation in 1953 there was in the air a distinct whiff of the kind of hubris that had manifested itself at the time of the Diamond Jubilee. It was to be followed, equally swiftly, by nemesis.

* * * * *

The Suez fiasco will continue to fascinate historians anxious to explain how it was that a country like Britain, guided as it was by statesmen and officials whose experience of the world was unparalleled and under the leadership of a statesman, Anthony Eden, whose expertise in foreign affairs was unrivalled in the twentieth century, could have stumbled into so humiliating a catastrophe. But any explanation must take into account the implicit belief – one very comparable to that prevalent sixty years earlier – that Britain had all the resources she needed to sustain her status: that she had, as it were, sufficient economic and military capacity in the bank to meet any demands made on it by a life-style appropriate to a Great Power. In the case of Suez, the financial analogy is all too apt. Within days, if not hours, it became apparent that the entire British economy still depended on a support that the United States refused to provide for an enterprise about which she had not been consulted and of which she did not approve. When she made her disapproval explicit, Britain found herself helpless.

In fact the immediate damage to British interests was remarkably limited. Her diplomatic skills at least enabled her to retain a footing in the Middle East, and restore the relationship with the United States on which her capacity to exercise influence ultimately depended. But she was able to do so only through a virtual acknowledgement of that dependence and its acceptance as the keystone of her foreign policy. Unfortunately after Suez it was no longer possible to claim that what the British lacked in power they made up for in wisdom; that they could, in Harold Macmillan's much quoted analogy, play the part of sagacious Greek advisers to the naive American Romans. For Washington, Britain became one more European ally, and not necessarily the most important.

The long-term consequences were more far-reaching.

The connection between political action and cultural attitudes is a complex one that historians have hitherto been reluctant to explore, but neither is fully intelligible without the other. In the second half of the 1950s the culture of the British people began to change quite dramatically. The change was well summarized by the poet Philip Larkin, when he observed that sexual intercourse had begun in 1963, 'between the end of the *Chatterley* ban and the Beatles' first LP'. There was a sudden, drastic revolution in *mores* as the British people, or a new generation of the British people, began to shrug off the standards of their elders and (socially speaking) their betters, and to strike out on their own.

Larkin chose his examples well. In the Lady Chatterley case, the jury ignored the directions of their betters and broke with sexual taboos that had dominated British society for generations. Almost simultaneously, the development of reliable birth-control divorced sexual activity from the family responsibilities to which it had been subordinated in Western societies throughout the Christian era. As for the Beatles, they introduced a new kind of folk-art that turned its back on traditional middle-class forms and introduced instead, as role models, lusty young proletarian males belting out Dionysiac music which shattered, even more completely than had the earlier introduction of jazz, the orderly rhythms that had previously determined the nature of the dance. Men's fashions saw the disappearance of the hat – always a badge of class – and of the military hair-cut of the upper-class officer-and-gentleman that had dominated civilian style for over a hundred years. In women's clothing there appeared a bewildering and almost random eclecticism whose manifestations had only one thing in common – the abandonment of all traditional concept of mature elegance. Altogether it was as if vast and barbaric energies, long held in check, had suddenly burst their bounds. It was a wonderful time to be young, but rather disturbing to be anything else. A sympathetic continental observer, the French philosopher Raymond Aron, remarked that the British seemed to have changed from Romans to Italians in the space of a single generation.

It is at least a tenable hypothesis that there was a direct connection between this cultural transformation and the change in self-image that came over the British, in particular the British elites, in the aftermath of Suez. The virtues and disciplines needed to sustain the responsibilities of a Great

Power were no longer needed. A newly aggressive press thrived on satirizing the pretensions of the old order and mocking the life-style of those who tried to adhere to it. The Empire, a source no longer of power but of expensive responsibilities, was shrugged off with remarkable speed and with minimal domestic debate. Only a few right-wing eccentrics suggested that welfare expenditure should be reduced in order to maintain a military presence east of Suez. As for the welfare state, its benefits were now taken for granted; but as the state of the economy worsened, there set in a scramble to maintain and if possible enhance the domestic standard of living that the Labour government found it impossible to control and which brought the country to the verge of Third-World bankruptcy.

That was twenty years ago. Under strong leadership the country has been able to recover its nerve, and go some way to re-establishing the most important balance of all – that between wealth consumption and wealth creation. But we have a long way to go yet.

*　　*　　*　　*　　*

History, wrote Wystan Auden, may say alas, but cannot help or pardon. Historians describe, and where possible explain. Some historians seek to explain events in terms of long-term trends, economic cycles, the pattern of rise and fall of Great Powers. By any such criterion, Britain has certainly been since the turn of the century in a condition of continual decline brought about by what Professor Paul Kennedy has termed 'imperial overstretch'.[2] But the fate of our country has been shaped by forces far beyond the capacity of British statesmen, or the British people, to control. The growth of national self-consciousness throughout the world – a growth we ourselves did so much to encourage – would anyhow have made it impossible to preserve the Empire, even at a cost in military expenditure that could have been supported only by suppressing democracy at home; and without the Empire, we were, as generations of British statesmen had warned, a European power like any other; one with greater world interests, certainly, but with less in the way of human and material resources than our neighbours Germany and France.

Yet for the British, imperialism had been a passing if powerful phenomenon. Unlike her predecessors France and Spain – to say nothing of Rome – Britain had risen to world power not as a military but as a trading and an industrial nation. It was when she was overtaken in those capacities by the Germans and the Americans that her 'decline' began. The decision to ⌐

---

[2] Paul Kennedy, *The Rise and Fall of the Great Powers* (Random House, New York 1987).

spend two centuries' accumulation of wealth to prevent Germany from achieving a European hegemony, and ultimately to use that hegemony to challenge not only British power, but the values on which European civilization had rested for a thousand years, was one that even today only a few revisionist historians are beginning to question. The acceptance of American hegemony, with all its drawbacks and embarrassments, was based, not on the sentimentality of any 'special relationship', but on a bleakly realistic assessment of the true power balance in the world. Only American support could have brought victory in 1945, and ensured global stability thereafter. The course of events since the end of the Cold War suggests that, whatever efforts we and our European partners may make, it is still only the application of American statesmanship, backed by American economic and where necessary military power, that can preserve a global order in which our own nation can flourish.

And what of our European partners?

I hardly need to rehearse again the mistakes into which we were led after the war, both by the hubris of those who believed that we were still primarily a global power and by the solipsism of those who were obsessed in building up our domestic welfare state; an unholy alliance of right and left who persisted in ignoring what was happening and what might happen in Europe. Of Churchill's 'three circles' between which British policy had to balance, Suez showed that the relationship with the United States was not nearly so special as we had thought, while the fragile structure of the Commonwealth could never bear the weight we hoped to place on it. There was left only a Europe that we joined late, as a supplicant, on terms that we could no longer mould to our own requirements. We have suffered from it ever since.

Today few people believe that we have much of a future outside Europe; but equally few welcome the idea of a Federal Union to which we have surrendered all control over our own destinies. Between the two extremes we have, again, to find a balance. We must learn how, within the framework of the Union, to fight for our own interests with sufficient vigour to gain respect, but without an obstinacy that will marginalize us by antagonizing all our colleagues.

Perhaps the most intractable of these problems is that of a common defence and foreign policy. Few people realize the extent to which, nearly half a century after the establishment of NATO, our defences are already integrated with those of our European neighbours. British armed forces are no longer viable for major operations, except in close co-operation with our allies: arguably, indeed, they never were. But European armed forces command little credibility unless they enjoy the support of the American logistic and communications infrastructure; and military strength is of little value unless it can be exercised in support of an agreed foreign and defence policy. In a group containing two former imperial powers with rival ambitions, several states with a tradition of neutrality, and nations with geopolitical perspectives as different as those of Greece, Norway and Spain, such agreement is hard to come by. The enlargement of NATO to contain several nations from Central Europe will not make it any easier. Whatever the political arguments in favour of such enlargement, it will add nothing to the capacity of Europe to act as a forceful actor on the world scene.

In conclusion, the world has changed over the past hundred years as radically as has Britain herself. Europe no longer lies at its centre, and its destiny is no longer determined by the balance of rivalries between European powers. The collapse of the Soviet Empire, even more spectacular than that of the British Empire, destroyed the global balance, between the Superpowers and their associates, that prevailed after 1945, leaving the Americans as reluctant hegemons, with great power but little will to exercise it. None the less the wealthy nations on the rim of the Eurasian land-mass, both east and west, still look to the United States as the great stabilizer. In such a world Britain can and should still make a unique contribution, based on our world experience, the links still provided by the Commonwealth, and not least the fortunate circumstance that the world is now almost wholly Anglophone. But we can make that contribution only if we can manage what is now the most important balance of all; that between the creation of wealth and its use to create a society where 'security' provides an enduring basis both for productivity and for social cohesion. In achieving this, memories of past greatness and nostalgia for a largely imagined past can play no part. All our pomps of yesterday *are* one with Nineveh and Tyre, and we had better not forget it.

II

The German Wars

4

Yale University 1994

The First World War Reconsidered

The name 'The First World War' was coined a few years after the event by a sardonic and far-sighted journalist, the British Colonel Repington. It is in any case inaccurate: the Seven Years' War of 1756–63, whose decisive battles were fought as much in North America and in the Indian Ocean as they were on the plains of Europe, has a far better claim to that title. Most of those who took part in it – certainly the British – called it simply 'The Great War'; and that sombre spondee, like a tolling bell, seems a far more appropriate description of that huge tragedy. For the French it is *La Grande Guerre*, for the Italians *la Grande Guerra*. But to this general consensus there was a very significant exception – the Germans. In spite of their minimal military and naval commitments outside Europe the war was for them, from the very beginning, *das Weltkrieg*, the World War. Perhaps that in itself tells us something about German aspirations in 1914.

The term 'The First World War' is appropriate in that it suggests – and was, when it was coined, intended to suggest – that the war had left unfinished business and that further wars were bound to follow. This apprehension was very generally shared in 1919. Immediately after the signature of the Treaty of Versailles a cartoon was published showing Wilson, Clemenceau and Lloyd George leaving the conference chamber and saying to each other 'Funny: I thought I heard a child crying'; and sure enough, behind a pillar, there is a little boy crying his heart out, wearing a sash marked 'Class of 1939'.

There are indeed those who would see the two World Wars as a single Thirty Years' War, interrupted by a long truce. There is much to be said for this: I myself believe that at least the campaigns of 1939–40 should be seen as a continuation of the First World War; a war for the dominance of Europe which Germany ultimately won, and which had to be won before Hitler could begin the war that he really wanted, to conquer his *Lebensraum* in the East and create his Thousand-Year Reich. But the First World War is enough to be going on with, and the historian is faced with a mass of questions about it which can be grouped under three headings. First, of course, and most difficult of all, what was the war about? And – not necessarily the same thing – what did the belligerents *think* that it was about? Second, why did it take the form that it did? And finally, what were its consequences; for those taking part and for the world as a whole?

Yale University boasts a cenotaph bearing the moving inscription: 'In Memory of the Men of Yale who, true to her traditions, gave their lives that Freedom might not perish from the Earth; 1914–1918'. For them that war, like all American wars, was one of ideology. Cynics have pointed out that the principal freedom these young men were defending was that of American business-men to trade and make money. But for those who hold the values of the Enlightenment, freedom was and is indissoluble, whether it be freedom to trade or to travel, to speak one's mind or to change one's government; and it must be said that these values were not generally pre- valent in Germany in 1914, nor would she have promoted them if she had won. For British liberals the cause was much the same, though the emphasis was laid not so much on abstract Freedom as on upholding the rule of law, the sanctity of treaties and the rights of small nations. Again, cynics have pointed out that at the time the rule of law upheld the global supremacy of the British Empire, and that for the British the rights of small nations had not included those of the former Boer Republics or indeed the nascent Irish nation. But it can truthfully be said that in 1914 these were matters that lay heavy on the conscience of the Liberal administration that took their country into war to defend the independence of Belgium; and they could legitimately claim that they had restored self-government to the Boers and were attempting in good faith to reach an equally generous settlement with the Irish – so generous indeed that in 1914 they had brought their own country to the brink of civil war.

On the war memorials that you will find in even the smallest village throughout the United Kingdom there are not, in fact, many high-sounding statements about Freedom and the rule of law, but there is one phrase that you will find on nearly all of them: God, King, and Country. It is the same on the more old-fashioned memorials in Germany – *Gott, König und Vaterland*; although under the Weimar Republic the first two words tended to disappear, as they had long-since in post-revolutionary France. There they mourned simply the millions who had died *pour la Patrie*. Country, *Patrie, Vaterland*; these were the 'causes' in defence of which the young men of Europe enlisted, rather than Freedom, Democracy, or the Rule of Law; and these were the communities that mourned them – and still mourn them – long after they were gone.

These monuments, rather than any purely documentary material, should be the starting point for any new generation coming to the study of the First World War, and they tell us a number of things. First, they are monuments of mourning, not of triumph: all of them, even those of the victors, depict the war as a tragedy, rather than as – as is often the case with the Second World War – a triumphant crusade. They emphasize sacrifice rather than achievement. Second, their ubiquity, their presence in nearly every settlement, however small, throughout Western Europe, bears witness to the total involvement of those communities in the war. The lists of names on those memorials, tragically many from the same small number of families, gives the measure of their loss; while those on the walls of elite universities and colleges show the extent to which entire classes were decimated.

But finally, and perhaps most important, those memorials reveal the social solidarity of European society at the beginning of this century; a solidarity that did not survive the war. Only tiny minorities in any of the belligerent countries questioned their duty to serve if called upon to do so, or the legitimacy of the call made on them. 'King and Country' or its equivalent was enough. The most successful recruiting poster of the war, and perhaps of any war, consisted simply of a picture of a uniformed general, Britain's premier war hero Herbert Horatio Kitchener, stabbing his finger and saying 'Your King and Country need YOU!'; a poster later to be imitated innumerable times, however sardonically. That mantra was in itself enough. After a few years, as sacrifices grew and enthusiasm ebbed, that call had to be reinforced by massive propaganda, but in 1914 it tapped deep resources of patriotic enthusiasm throughout Europe; enthusiasm at its most frenetic in the great cities.

France, it must be said, was an exception. Within the last few years there had been a revival of nationalism that led many French intellectuals to greet the advent of war with as much enthusiasm as their British and German counterparts, but it found little echo in the countryside, *la France profonde*. There the experience of war and invasion little over forty years earlier was too fresh in the memories of the older generation, and their children who responded to the call to the colours did so in a mood of stoical resignation rather than patriotic enthusiasm. But respond they did. After all for France, more perhaps than for any other of the Great Powers, there was a clear *casus belli*. Once again their territory had been invaded, this time without the shadow of an excuse. On the eve of the war the socialist leader Jean Jaurès was assassinated by a right-wing fanatic in the belief that he was a pacifist. He was not. He had spent his life fighting for international understanding and the abolition of war, but no one supported more strongly the necessity for national defence. The working classes as a whole took the same line, and France entered the war united in a *union sacrée* such as she had hardly known since the Revolution.

The charge that in 1914 the peoples of Europe were being manipulated by war-mongering elites was scornfully rejected by one witness in Germany.

'The struggle of the year 1914 was not forced on the masses,' he wrote, '– no, by the living God – it was desired by the whole people. People wanted at length to put an end to the general uncertainty. Only thus can it be understood that more than two million German men and boys thronged to the colours for this hardest of all struggles, prepared to defend the flag with the last drop of their blood.'[1] The fact that the name of that witness was Adolf Hitler does not make him any the less reliable: there is plenty of other evidence to bear him out.

It cannot be said that this patriotic enthusiasm – the famous 'mood of 1914' which appeared as strongly in the dynastic states Russia and Austria-Hungary as it did in the 'mature' nations of Western Europe – in itself created the war. Indeed it took the leaders themselves by surprise: it was only a few years since massive 'peace' demonstrations had been held in all major European cities, including Berlin. The French authorities were in genuine doubt as to how many of their conscripts would answer the call to the colours, and the police stood ready to intern left-wing political leaders. The more far-sighted European statesmen realized that, however great the popular enthusiasm, the long-term consequence of the war were incalcul-able, and that it might, in words written earlier in the year by the German Chancellor Bethmann-Hollweg, 'topple many a throne'. But in no country was policy-making crippled, as it was to be so disastrously in France and Britain in 1938, by a public opinion profoundly reluctant to face the need for war. If there were, as there were in every country in Western Europe, groups critical of their government's brinkmanship, they were outshouted if not outnumbered, especially in Germany, by powerful and equally popular forces on the Right who preached that war was necessary as an instrument, not simply of policy, but of legitimate self-assertion, and who would make considerable trouble if it were not so used. The crowds that surged round the royal palace in Berlin on those hot July nights while the issues of peace or war were being debated inside its walls were not urging peace.

So the peoples of Europe – not excepting the intellectuals of Europe – fought because their governments told them to, in causes which, in so far as they understood them, they entirely approved. So what were the causes, or the 'Causes' of the First World War?

It is important to realize in the first place that it was not one war that broke out in 1914 but two, distinct even if closely interlinked. Each was fought over issues about which war, if not inevitable, would have been very

---

[1] Adolf Hitler, *Mein Kampf*, trans. Karl Mannheim (Hutchinson, London 1969), p. 148.

difficult to avoid even if there had been any great desire to avoid it; which, as we have seen, there was not.

The first of those two conflicts might be termed the Third Balkan War, or the War of the Austrian Succession; one fought to determine who was to be master in the Balkans. This war had been threatening ever since the Congress of Berlin in 1878, and an entire generation of European diplomats had successfully devoted their professional careers to preventing it. The second might be called the First German War – or if we take into account the wars of 1866 and 1870, the Third German War; and that was fought to expand or contain the immense latent power of the recently united Germany. Within the same framework of conflict we can find other equally distinct minor wars. For the Italians it was the final act – or intended to be the final act – of the Risorgimento, the struggle to expel the Austrians from the peninsula. For Britain, it provided an opportunity to consolidate her imperial possessions in a great arc round the Indian Ocean, from South Africa to Singapore. For Japan it likewise provided an opportunity for some limited imperial expansion. But none of those opportunities would have arisen except in the context of the great general conflagration ignited by the pistol-shot fired by Gavril Princip in Sarajevo on 28 June 1914.

That pistol-shot precipitated what was at first seen as only the latest in a succession of Balkan crises that had been erupting over the last six years; ever since Austria-Hungary had annexed Bosnia-Herzegovina in 1908, thus upsetting the careful balance established thirty years earlier at the Congress of Berlin. This new eruption did not at first cause any general concern. All the previous crises had been managed successfully, so why not this one? Historians indeed might well ask, not why the First World War began in 1914, but why did it not break out at any point during the previous six years?

Probably no few days in the history of the world has been subjected to such detailed scrutiny as those between 28 June, when the Archduke Franz Ferdinand was assassinated, and 4 August, when Britain declared war; scrutiny not only by historians but by political scientists who saw in the Balkan confrontation a sinister but useful paradigm for the problems of crisis-management in the Cold War. In it they found the situation with which their generation was so familiar: two major powers contesting dominance of a region through satellites they only imperfectly controlled; neither willing to risk war, but neither willing to abandon their stakes and admit defeat at the hands of a dangerous adversary. So long as both major powers understood the situation – and could when necessary be reminded of it by their allies – peace could be kept and crises could be surmounted. So what went wrong?

The new factor in 1914 was that Austria-Hungary had ceased to be part of the solution and become part – indeed the major part – of the problem. Two developments had come together to create an explosive 'critical mass'. One was the process of internal disintegration within Austria-Hungary, as the national minorities in both parts of the Monarchy became increasingly unmanageable. The other was the onward march of a triumphalist Serbia, increasingly a magnet for the South Slavs within the Dual Monarchy, whose territory and military power had been suddenly doubled between 1912 and 1914 as a result of the two Balkan Wars. Each of these problems might have been managed on its own. Without an external threat Vienna and Budapest might have coasted along indefinitely, managing their minorities with a mixture of repression and concession. Even if they could not, the disintegration of the Monarchy, so widely foreseen on the death of the aged Emperor Franz-Joseph, need not have caused a European War. On the other hand a united and confident monarchy might have regarded the rise of Serbia more calmly, and taken more effective steps to deal with it. As it was, the existence of each problem made the other lethal. A war that would destroy Serbian power and, hopefully, unite the Monarchy seemed to the statesmen in Vienna the only way to postpone, if not to avoid, the ultimate disaster.

Certainly the declaration of war was immensely popular in Vienna, not least among its formidable circle of intellectuals. Those young enough – Kokoschka, Musil, von Hoffmannsthal, Wittgenstein, to name only a few – enlisted in the Royal and Imperial Army. Sigmund Freud, too old to enlist, nonetheless, as he put it, dedicated his libido to the service of the monarchy. With all its inadequacies and inequities, none of the subject peoples of the Monarchy – with the possible exception of the Czechs and perhaps a growing number of Croats – wished to see it humiliated and destroyed, and they sang the anthem *Gott erhalten Franz den Kaiser* probably with greater enthusiasm than ever before in their lives.

Nor did literate public opinion in the Russian Empire wish to see their country humiliated. Those optimistic thinkers who believe that the spread of democratic institutions necessarily guarantees international peace should ponder the example of Russia in the late ninteenth and early twentieth centuries. There the growth of representative institutions only increased internal pressures for a 'forward' policy in the Balkans to rescue brother Slavs, first from Ottoman and then from Magyar and German oppression. The record over the past eight years had not been good: repeatedly Russia had first encouraged the Serbs, and then, conscious of her own military weakness, had retreated under German pressure. There may not have been the same enthusiasm for the Serbs in Moscow and St Petersburg as there had been for the Bulgarians in 1877, but Russian 'honour' (a quality better known today as 'credibility') was as deeply involved in their support as that of Britain would be in supporting the Belgians a few weeks later. With Austria determined effectively to destroy Serbia, the Russian government confronted the alternatives of going to war or suffering a further massive humiliation; and that, 'public opinion', as expressed through the press and in the Duma, was not prepared to tolerate.

Whether Austria would have pressed on to the destruction of Serbia without her 'blank cheque' from Germany is still a matter of major controversy; but to my mind those historians (nowadays primarily German) who locate responsibility for the war entirely in Berlin and see the Austrians just as puppets dancing on a German string take too little account of the situation in Vienna. The Austrians needed no urging from Berlin; they might indeed have ignored an attempt to veto their action. But Berlin made no such attempt; and that brings us to 'the German Question'.

Analysis of 'the German Question' has been confused, first by the accusation that Germany was solely responsible for the war – an accusation first made by the victorious allies at Versailles and later to be revived by Fritz Fischer and his associates – and then by the rebuttal, so popular in the 1930s, that she had no greater responsibility than anybody else. But the problem is not whether or not Germany first planned and then deliberately provoked a world war. Rather the question is, first, was Germany set on a course that sooner or later was almost bound to lead to armed conflict with her neighbours? And second, did her leaders act in a way that they *knew* carried a high risk of escalation into a European and – since Britain would almost certainly be involved – a world war?

The answer to both these questions seems to me to be, yes. Before 1914 the German government *had* been behaving in a manner that made war in the long run highly probable. In their eyes – and in those, it must be said, of a large proportion of the German political classes – what we would now term 'war-avoidance' enjoyed a very low priority indeed. Over the Sarajevo crisis the German leadership pursued a policy which they must have known carried a very high risk, not only of European, but of World War. They did this on the assumption that war was bound to come sooner or later, and that, given the growing power of the Russian Empire, the balance of military power was as favourable to them at that moment as it was ever likely to be. Statesmen like Bethmann-Hollweg could thus regard it as a justifiable preemptive war and depict it to the Reichstag as entirely defensive. By so doing Bethmann-Hollweg was able to enlist the support of all parties and created a degree of national unity unknown since 1870. The emotion this engendered was so intense that even the level-headed Minister for War, General von

Falkenhayn, made the amazing declaration 'Even if everything turns out disastrously, it will have been worth it.'

But for many influential German thinkers and political leaders it was not a pre-emptive war at all. It was the dawn of the long-awaited day when Germany could make evident the full measure of her greatness, not only as a European but as a World Power. As she had been able to assert her status as a European Power only by defeating France, so she could break into the ranks of the World Powers that would dominate the coming century only by defeating, and humiliating England. This was being stated by a significant number of German publicists and journalists, and a lot of people, not least in England, had come to believe them.

In 1914 Germany had nothing specific to fight Britain about. Each was the other's best customer commercially, and there were no territorial disputes overseas that could not be – indeed, that had not been – peacefully settled. But Germany had nothing specific to fight *anyone* about. She needed and desired no more territory; economically she was already becoming domi-nant throughout *Mitteleuropa*, a dominance that was ripening into a peaceful hegemony; and she was peacefully and skilfully penetrating the Middle East, with the acquiescence, if not the explicit consent, of a Britain who saw German influence there as a useful counter-balance to that of Russia.

But that was exactly the trouble. Germany was both a satisfied yet at the same time a deeply unsatisfied power. How far the deeply felt need for expansion and self-assertion that is so typical of so much German writing before 1914 was the result of her internal social tensions is difficult to assess. So is the influence of such thinkers as Nietzsche and such intellectual trends as Social Darwinism, with their emphasis on the inevitability and indeed the glory of conflict. These ideas existed in solution, as it were, throughout Europe and indeed the United States of Teddy Roosevelt. But in Germany they were combined in a uniquely explosive mixture. Further, they had no legitimate outlet within the existing political framework. The British, the Russians, the Americans, even the French and the Italians could pursue their 'manifest destinies' within the framework of their own territories or empires without any major disturbance of the existing international system. But land-locked Germany could expand only at the expense of her neighbours, and in so doing destroy a European order that had been peacefully settled for a hundred years. She could not make understandable, limited and negotiable claims for frontier revision. The war-aims that emerged within a few weeks of the outbreak of war in the notorious 'September Programme' with its claims for mastery over the Low Countries and the Channel coast, the perpetual subordination of France and the massive redrawing of frontiers in the Baltic was a programme, not for limited revisions based on principles of ethnic consolidation, but for a New European Order, and one designed to perpetuate German mastery.

To such a challenge the British were bound to react. Even if the Germans had not invaded Belgium, which they very conveniently did, and even if their troops there had behaved impeccably, which it has to be said they did not, it would not have been difficult to persuade even the most liberal and peace-loving Englishman that German power and explicit intentions constituted a threat to the whole structure of international justice and the rule of law. As for the conservative opposition, they believed with equally good reason that the target Germany had in her sights – and had had ever since the beginning of the naval race ten years earlier – was nothing less than the British Empire itself and the oceanic supremacy on which, or so they believed, the independence of the British Isles themselves depended.

There is today a tendency to think that, whereas the Second World War was necessary and fought for serious causes that justified the sacrifices needed to win it, the First World War was not: that it began and continued as a result of mutual misunderstandings and that all who died in it laid down their lives in vain. But that was not the way it seemed to the generation of Englishmen that fought the war. The threat posed both to core democratic values and to national survival by the Germany personified by the grotesque figure of the Kaiser and the philosophy misleadingly labelled as 'Prussian militarism' appeared to them quite as total and as dangerous as that which confronted their children a generation later, and one that no sacrifice seemed too great to avert.

Moreover, as the war went on, the threat became more real, not less. The September Programme makes clear the peace that Germany would have imposed on Europe if 'the Schlieffen Plan' had worked, as it very nearly did. As the war went on and Germany became more desperate and the Right wing tightened its grip on the government, so her objectives became more extreme; so extreme indeed that Bethmann-Hollweg did not dare to state them when challenged to do so by President Wilson in the winter of 1916. The Treaty of Brest-Litovsk, with its programme of sweeping annexations to the East and the virtual destruction of the Russian Empire, was a preliminary blue-print for the objectives in Eastern Europe later to be pursued by the Third Reich. There is no reason to suppose that the terms imposed by a victorious Ludendorff in the West would have been any more moderate. And it was in the shadow of that treaty, we must remember, that the victorious allies drafted the punitive Treaty of Versailles.

If the Schlieffen Plan had succeeded ... Let us not forget that it very nearly did succeed, and if the German generalship had been more enterprising and the French less phlegmatic, it very likely would have done so. If the French army *had* been defeated, Russia would almost certainly have hurried to make peace. Austria would have had her will with Serbia and gained for herself at least a stay of execution; while Germany would have emerged triumphant on the Continent and the Right wing triumphant within Germany. Not a pretty prospect; but would it have been peace? Hardly. Britain would have been beaten off the Continent as she had been during the Napoleonic wars and was to be again in 1940. But she would not have been defeated. She could have been defeated only by measures of naval warfare of a kind that would ultimately bring the United States into the war. It is significant that the German political and military leadership had never thought through the implications of the war with England that had been so widely expected in both countries before 1914. The Army and the Navy had never discussed it together, and neither had raised the matter with the politicians. The Prussian military tradition – and the Germans had no other military tradition – was rigorously ethnocentric. In their book, wars were won by military victories in the field, and that was it. The book in question was Clausewitz *On War*. In that immensely influential treatise, naval and economic warfare are not even mentioned.

So German victories in the field could not have defeated Britain, any more than did those of Napoleon. But more to the point, they could not in themselves – unlike Napoleon's great victories – even defeat Britain's continental allies, France and Russia. After a year the Germans realized this, and set out instead to wear their adversaries down by attrition. This technique was effective enough against the Russians, but it was equally disastrous for Germany's allies the Austrians, whose collapse followed that of the Russians within a matter of months. As for the Western allies, such a strategy was playing into their strength. Admittedly France and Britain made things easier by continuing with their costly and clumsy attacks on the Western Front, but with American resources behind them they had the capacity to exhaust Germany long before they themselves collapsed; and those resources could be cut off only by measures that were almost certain to bring the United States into the war as a full belligerent. Unrestricted Submarine Warfare was for the Germans a desperate gamble revealing the bankruptcy of their strategy. 'It is Germany's last card,' said one of her statesmen; 'If it is not trumps, we are lost for centuries'. It was not trumps. As a result, Germany found herself fighting against odds that virtually guaranteed her destruction.

In her defeat, Germany dragged down the whole of Europe. Within the tightly integrated nexus of interdependent industrial societies, the strategy of attrition is almost as mutually destructive as a strategy of nuclear war.

The German General Staff consciously destroyed the political system of the Russian Empire by subventing the Bolshevik Party and facilitating Lenin's return from exile at a crucial moment during the Russian Revolution; and having sown the wind, they lived in dread of reaping the whirlwind – and they did almost exactly a year later. The Habsburg Empire, which with all its faults had been the major element of stability in Central Europe, disintegrated, and probably the Western allies could not have saved it even if they had wanted to. In Germany itself civil war was averted only by an alliance between the revolutionary government and the conservative military leadership. The decade of instability that followed was to make many Germans of all classes welcome Hitler as their rescuer and leader, not caring very much where he led them. As for the victorious powers, France and Britain, they were left wondering whether victory at such a cost had really been worth it, and determined to avoid ever having to endure such an ordeal again.

*   *   *   *   *

Had it been worth it? If Germany had won, would Freedom really have perished from the earth? We must allow for natural hyperbole, and nobody writing such an epitaph is on oath. But if the United States had stood back and allowed Germany to win the First World War – and without American intervention, it is hard to see how this could have been prevented – both Germany and Europe as a whole would have been a very much nastier place. Ludendorff and his followers of the extreme right wing would have been established solidly in power, and though not all shared Adolf Hitler's fanatical anti-Semitism, their philosophy was intrinsically racist and explicitly anti-democratic. The methods they would have used to suppress liberal and socialist opposition might not have been so brutal as those employed by the Nazi regime, but they would have been ugly and probably effective. The proto-Fascist ideas that were already germinating throughout Europe would have flowered sooner and more prolifically than in fact they did. The defeat of Germany at least gave the cause of democracy in Europe another chance.

5

Queen Mary College
London 1991

War and Peace in 1914

During the early months of 1914 two works were enjoying large sales in England. One was a pamphlet which had first appeared five years earlier under the title *Europe's Optical Illusion* and was now re-issued, much expanded, with the title *The Great Illusion*: by which it has been known ever since. The other was an English translation of General Friedrich von Bernhardi's work, *Germany and the Next War*, which had been published in Germany two years earlier. The first maintained that war was irrational and obsolete; the second, that it was necessary, and imminent. Each was the fruit of a peculiar national cultural tradition; and though each found some sympathizers in the other's country, *The Great Illusion* could only have been written by an Englishman or an American, while *Germany and the Next War* could have been written only by a German; and an Englishman and a German, one is tempted to add, only of that particular generation. Both were essentially ephemeral, addressing contemporary issues in international affairs, but both – or their titles at least – are still familiar to anyone with a working knowledge of European history in the twentieth century. Finally both raised issues that are still relevant in international relations today.

First *The Great Illusion*. The author was one Ralph Lane, but as he was a working journalist on the *Daily Mail* he used his middle names, Norman Angell, as a *nom de plume*. He was a man of firm Cobdenite convictions of a kind that even in 1914 were beginning to look a little old fashioned, but which still probably represented the 'conventional wisdom' in pre-war Britain: the belief, as old as Adam Smith, that free trade made for peace, and that the real interests of all the nations of the world were essentially harmonious. This had been stated so firmly, so frequently and so eloquently by Cobden and Bright and their numerous disciples and had entered so deeply into the assumptions, spoken and unspoken, of the Liberal Party, that we may wonder why Angell found it necessary to restate it, and why he caused such a stir when he did.

The trouble was that the contrary belief, that trade needed both fiscal and military protection against powerful rivals and that nations must be prepared to defend or advance their interests if necessary by war, had been growing in Britain, as everywhere else in the world, over the past two decades. They had been expressed with increasing intensity ever since the beginning of the Anglo-German naval race in 1904. The expression of these views had come to a head with the famous naval panic of 1909, when the productive capacity of the German armament industry became evident and it seemed for the first time seriously possible that the Royal Navy might lose 'command of the Sea'. Britain, according to those who hold these beliefs, was in immediate and mortal danger, and only drastic action could avert it. As a journalist working with the Northcliffe Press, Angell was particularly exposed to such ideas, and he quoted some of the most extreme in his work. From the socialist Robert Blatchford:[1]

> Why should Germany attack Britain? Because Germany and Britain are commercial and political rivals; because Germany covets the trade and colonies, and the Empire which Britain now possesses.

From the liberal journalist John St Loe Strachey:

> If the command of the sea could be taken from us for a week or two these islands and their riches would be absolutely open to the plunderer.

And in particular, from an article in the right-wing but widely circulated *Blackwood's Magazine*, which brought the insights of fashionable Social Darwinism to bear on the issue:

> We appear to have forgotten the fundamental truth – confirmed by all history – that the warlike races inherit the earth, and that Nature decrees the survival of the fittest in the never-ending struggle for existence. ... Our yearning for disarmament, our respect for the tender plant of non-conformist conscience, and the parrot-like repetition of the misleading formula that the 'greatest of all British interest is peace' ... must inevitably give way to any people who covet our wealth and our possessions ... [and who possess] the ambition to strike a swift and deadly blow at the heart of the Empire – undefended London.

It was specifically to counter these views, and especially those on this particular topic – the vulnerability of British prosperity to German military (or rather, naval) force – that Angell wrote *Europe's Optical Illusion*.
  This illusion was the belief that

> military and political power give a nation commercial and social advantages, that the wealth and prosperity of the defenceless nation are at the mercy of stronger nations, who may be tempted by such defencelessness to commit aggression, so that each nation is compelled to protect itself against the possible cupidity of its

---

[1] All these following quotations are from Norman Angell, *The Great Illusion* (William Heinemann, London 1912), pp. 15–17.

neighbours. The author challenges this universal theory and declares it to be based upon a pure optical illusion.[2]

Angell supported his challenge by simple – perhaps deceptively simple – statements of what he saw to be the economic facts:

> If an invasion by Germany did involve ... the total collapse of the Empire, our trade, and the means of feeding forty millions on these islands ... the disturbance of capital and destruction of credit, German capital would, because of the internationalization and delicate interdependence of our credit-built finance and industry, also disappear in large part, and German credit would also collapse, and the only means of resolving it would be for Germany to put an end to the chaos in Great Britain by putting an end to the condition that had produced it.[3]

For similar reasons he believed that 'the exaction of tribute from a conquered people has become an economic impossibility', and that it was equally impossible to 'capture' the trade of a nation by military conquest. National prosperity, he pointed out, did not depend on political or military power: look at the wealth of defenceless Holland and Belgium. Finally, no one could gain any advantage by conquering Britain's colonies and Britain would not suffer from their loss. Indeed she would gain, since she would no longer have to pay for their defence.

The same principle applied more generally. Germany had not gained by the acquisition of Alsace-Lorraine, nor had the French lost by it: wealth continued to be produced and to circulate in the international community in exactly the same fashion as before. The problem was, not that war enhanced or detracted from national well-being, but that people thought that it did. There were, Angell admitted, influential Germans who did believe that the wealth and power of Germany and her inhabitants would be enhanced by the destruction of Britain's, and so long as they held such beliefs, it was necessary to maintain adequate defences. But those Germans, and the British who thought in the same way, were simply *wrong*. It was a creed as out of date as witchcraft. A campaign of public education was therefore needed throughout the world to tackle the problem at its roots and transform public opinion. Once that had been accomplished, arms races and naval panics would be things of the past, and peace would reign throughout the world.

Angell wrote in the commonsensical no-nonsense fashion popularized by Tom Paine, Jeremy Bentham and William Cobbett, and transmitted to a later generation of such distinguished radical pamphleteers as Bertrand

[2] Angell, *Great Illusion*, p. vii.
[3] *Ibid.*

Russell, J.B. Priestley, E.P. Thompson and A.J.P. Taylor. It is the voice of the Enlightenment, straightforward and reasonable, explaining things in a manner accessible to any intelligent child and wryly astonished that anyone could possibly see things differently. Everything, it implies, would be very simple if only people were not so stupid; but patient explanation and education would, sooner or later, put things right.

Angell's arguments were persuasive; but they might not have gained such rapid and widespread currency if *Europe's Optical Illusion* had not caught the eye of that *éminence grise* of the British defence establishment, Reginald Viscount Esher. From his privileged position on the Committee of Imperial Defence, Esher had been increasingly worried by the 'navalist' propaganda from the Conservative back benches that was making the government's task of formulating a balanced defence policy so very difficult, and he saw in Angell's ideas a convenient antidote. He persuaded a philanthropic indus-trialist, Sir Richard Garton, to set up a 'Foundation for the Study of International Polity', whose avowed objective was the propagation of the ideas of Norman Angell, or 'Norman Angellism': as it rapidly came to be called. Under the auspices of the Garton Foundation Angell published further, enlarged editions of *The Great Illusion* and floated a monthly journal, *War and Peace*. 'Norman Angell Societies' sprang up all over the country, which came together in at least one national conference in 1913. In the summer of 1914 the Foundation sponsored a ten-day International Polity Summer School at Jordans in Buckinghamshire presided over by Angell himself. It adjourned on 27 July, and did not have a successor.[4]

The *réclame* enjoyed by 'Norman Angellism' evoked an international controversy. This is conveniently easy to track since Angell embodied the arguments of his opponents (albeit somewhat selectively) in successive editions of *The Great Illusion*, together with his sardonic replies. It cannot be said that he always got the better of his opponents, especially when they were joined by the formidable Cambridge medievalist G.G. Coulton, who subjected Angell's arguments and references to careful analysis and showed that the latter were very much less than scholarly. Some of the critics were straightforward Social Darwinians, who argued that war was not only morally elevating but biologically necessary: it was Nature's mechanism for winnowing out societies unfit to survive. Angell countered them with arguments drawn from Herbert Spencer (though more felicitously expres-sed) to the effect that industrial societies had shown themselves more fit than military societies to survive in the modern age, and the latter were

[4] See J.B.D. Miller, *Norman Angell and the Futility of War* (Macmillan, London 1986).

simply inefficient archaisms. 'The warlike nations do not inherit the earth,' he wrote: 'They represent the decaying human element'.[5]

More formidable were critics such as the American Admiral A.T. Mahan. Angell, argued Mahan, was knocking down a straw man. Nations in the twentieth century did not go to war simply for profit, to balance their books. International conflict was over *power*, especially power over the as yet unsettled regions of the world. The reasons that led nations to extend their power were as much moral as material. People nowadays fought for ideas, not for profits. Further, in the absence of any enforceable legal system, nations had to fight, when all else failed, to vindicate the justice of their cause in an international dispute. 'Nations are under no illusion' wrote Mahan, 'as to the unprofitableness of war in itself, but they recognize different views of right and wrong in international relations against which the only safeguard is armament'. And he quoted an anonymous but level-headed banker as saying 'I do not know what [people] ... go to war about, but I am quite sure it is not about business'.[6]

Angell would perhaps have been wiser if he had admitted that his original thesis had been stated in order to counter one particular fallacy, and needed considerable rethinking before it could claim to constitute a comprehensive theory of war and peace. His ripostes became increasingly evasive, arrogant and irritable. When Mahan and others suggested that Germany might be a dangerous example of a military society, he denied it: 'During the last forty years eight thousand out of sixty million Germans have been engaged in warfare during a trifle over a year, and that against the Hottentots or Hereros. ... The men who really give the tone to the German nation', he wrote in 1914, 'have never seen a battle, and never will see one'.[7] It was a very rash prophecy indeed.

*   *   *   *   *

Let us now turn to General Friedrich von Bernhardi. After a distinguished military career Bernhardi made his reputation as a military thinker with a massive study, *On War Today*. As was not unusual with retired military officers of that generation – one thinks of our own General J.F.C. Fuller – Bernhardi ended up in the arms of the extreme Right; in his case the *Alldeutscher Verband*, the Pan-German League, a body whose strident militaristic propaganda was becoming increasingly notorious throughout Europe. For several years Bernhardi and his associates in the League had

[5] *Great Illusion*, p. x.
[6] A.T. Mahan, *Armaments and Arbitration* (Harper, New York 1911), pp. 126, 152.
[7] Norman Angell, *Prussianism and its Destruction* (Heinemann, London 1914), p. 143.

been worried by what they saw as the dangerous spread of pacifism in Germany; a sentiment which, he wrote (paraphrasing the sentiments of the historian Heinrich von Treitschke), 'has rendered the most civilised nations anaemic and marks a decay of spirit and political courage such as has often been shown by a race of Epigoni'. The same phenomenon had been worrying Mahan and the English Social Darwinians, and much of what Bernhardi wrote in *Germany and the Next War* can be easily paralleled from the Anglo-Saxon authors quoted by Norman Angell. To choose a few of his typical sentences:

> War is a biological necessity of the first importance, a regulative element in the life of man that cannot be dispensed with, since without it an unhealthy development will follow, which excludes every advancement of the race, and therefore all true civilisation.

> Without war, inferior or decaying races would easily choke the growth of healthy budding elements, and a universal decadence would follow.

> The possibility of war is required to give the national character that stimulus from which these sentiments spring, and thus only are nations enabled to do justice to the highest development of civilisations by the fullest development of their moral forces. ... From this point of view, efforts to secure peace are extraordinarily detrimental to the national health.

So, he concluded, 'reflection ... shows not only that war is an unqualified necessity, but that it is justifiable from every point of view'.[8]

There was, I repeat, nothing in this likely to shock or surprise pre-war Englishmen, where right-wing pundits had for the past ten years been saying very much the same. But Bernhardi went a great deal further than that. He was not concerned simply to counter the arguments and activities of the German peace movement. He felt impelled to write as he did by what he, in common with many nationalistic Germans, saw as the humiliation they had suffered in consequence of the Agadir affair in 1911; when an attempt by the German government to force a crisis and intimidate France had failed, largely in consequence of the firm stand taken by Britain. Germany, so Bernhardi believed, had then missed an excellent opportunity to go to war, and she must not do so again.

Statesmen, wrote Bernhardi, should not only not shrink from war; they had the duty to make it when a convenient opportunity arose. Germany had risen to greatness because her leaders had done exactly that. Both the first and the second Silesian Wars had been initiated by Frederick the Great, and

[8] Freidrich von Bernhardi, *Germany and the Next War* (Edward Arnold, London 1912), pp. 10, 12, 17, 21, 23.

every one of the three great wars of German Unification had been not only initiated but manufactured by Bismarck. 'The military success and the political position won by the sword laid the foundations for an unparalleled material prosperity'. Bernhardi pointed out: 'It is difficult to imagine how pitiable the progress of the German people would have been had not these wars been brought about by deliberate policy'. More recent examples such as the Japanese attack on the Russian Empire in 1904 pointed in the same direction. 'The lessons of history', he concluded, 'thus confirm the view that wars which have been deliberately provoked by far-seeing statesmen have had the happiest results'.[9] And 'the verdict of history will condemn the statesman who was unable to take the responsibility of a bold decision, and sacrificed the hopes of the future to the present need of peace'.[10]

Bernhardi had no doubt that German statesmen were now confronted with that responsibility. England was clearly determined to hinder any further expansion of German power. So

> since the struggle is ... necessary and inevitable, we must fight it out, cost what it may. There is no standing still in the world's history. All is growth and development. ... it is tantamount to retrogression when we are contented with our present place among the nations of Europe. ... we must have the courage to strive with every means to attain that increase of power which we are entitled to claim.[11]

The attainment of such an objective, Bernhardi admitted, 'would certainly clash with many old-fashioned notions and vested rights of the traditional European polity'. The validity of existing political treaties would have to be re-examined – especially those relating to neutrality, and in particular the neutrality of Belgium. 'The concept of permanent neutrality is entirely contrary to the essential nature of the State, which can only attain its highest moral aims in competition with the other States'. But in general:

> We must remain conscious in all eventualities that we cannot, under any circumstances, avoid fighting for our position in the world, and that the all-important point is, not to postpone that war as long as possible, but to bring it on under the most favourable conditions possible.[12]

In one respect Bernhardi agreed with Norman Angell. His policy could be effective only if a crash programme was initiated to influence public opinion. 'We must', he wrote, 'rouse in our people the unanimous wish for

[9] *Ibid.*, pp. 37, 39.
[10] *Ibid.*, p. 48.
[11] *Ibid.*, pp. 102–3.
[12] *Ibid.*, pp. 109–11.

power together with the determination to sacrifice on the altar of patriotism, not only life and property, but also private views and preferences in
the interests of the common welfare. Then alone shall we discharge our
great duties for the future, grow into a World Power, and stamp a great part
of humanity with the impress of the German spirit'.[13] The Pan-German
League was to be no less active than the Garton Foundation in trying to
convert the public to its way of thinking – and unfortunately, rather more
effective.

Angell and Bernhardi were not so much conducting an argument as
inhabiting totally different universes of discourse. For those who thought
like Bernhardi, Angell's approach exhibited all the trivial superficiality of
what the Germans called 'Manchesterism'; a creed which reduced the role of
the State to that of a stockmarket, as Treitschke had put it, and international
relations to matters of pounds, shilling and pence. For Angell on the other
hand, Bernhardi's philosophy, in so far as it consisted of more than discredited Social Darwinism, was simply nonsense. It was misty Teutonic
verbiage, not susceptible of rational analysis, and the arguments were hardly
worth countering. What *was* national power, Angell might have asked, if it
was not the capacity to enhance the physical well-being of the common
man? And if it could not be shown to do that, why possess it? But Angell
never directly took issue with Bernhardi. He relied on Bernhardi's own
countrymen to deal with him, as he was dealing with the arguments of his
own right-wingers who wrote in *The Nineteenth Century* and *Blackwood's
Magazine*. People simply had to be disabused of such false notions. Given
enough international conferences and journals and summer-schools, sooner
or later this would come to pass. 'We are saying to the statesmen', Angell
explained to his summer-school in July 1914, 'we know quite well that you
cannot reduce your navy because of public opinion; but in five years we are
going to bring you a new public opinion'. It might, he agreed, take rather
longer to convert the public in France and Germany, but he hoped 'in ten
years the spread of our ideas will have brought about the possibility of co-
operation between the Great Powers'.[14]

Unfortunately the two sides were not playing on a level field. In Britain,
Angell's views commanded a wide measure of support. They were deeply
rooted, not only in the optimistic rationalism of the Enlightenment, but in
the traditions of Nonconformity that still provided the main strength of the
Liberal and Labour parties and in which anti-militarism had always played a

[13] *Ibid.*, p. 113.
[14] Quoted by G.G. Coulton, *The Main Illusions of Pacifism* (Bowes & Bowes,
Cambridge 1916), p. 170.

prominent part. The Peace Movement had, since the days of Cobden, been part of the mainstream of British political life. In Germany, the opposite was the case. The first Hague Conference in 1899 had indeed stimulated a certain amount of pacifist activity, largely under the guidance of Bertha von Suttner and the delightfully eponymous Alfred Fried. Large 'peace' demonstrations were organized by the Social Democrats in the years before the war. But although these were enough to alarm and annoy the Pan-German League, they were emphatically not part of the German political mainstream. The government and governing classes were openly hostile to them, and even the Social Democrat leader Eduard Bernstein had to tell Alfred Fried 'Forgive my candour, (but) "Pacifism" is really an unfortunate word – it seems too foreign to Germans'.[15] Angell's own teaching evoked none of the sympathetic interest in German universities with which it was heard in British. His visit to Göttingen in 1913 provoked a hostile mass rally, and at Berlin the protests against his presence culminated in a full-scale riot.[16] The prospects for a 'Norman Angellist' crusade, in pre-war Germany, were not at all good.

It might be not unfair to suggest that sympathizers with Angell's viewpoint were as marginal to German political life as were such full-blooded militaristic Social Darwinians as Professor J.A. Cramb of London University in pre-war Britain. Cramb indeed, an eccentric figure who overtly espoused the doctrines of Treitschke, frankly welcomed and endorsed the teaching of Bernhardi. Germany, he wrote ecstatically in 1914, 'is the greatest and most heroic enemy ... that England, in the thousand years of her history, has ever confronted. ... These two empires [are] both the descendants of the war-god Odin, and yet, because of that, doomed to this great conflict'.[17] Even the most extreme right-wing nationalists among Cramb's compatriots must have found such even-handedness disconcerting.

Until the outbreak of war, Angell ignored the difference between the two cultures. He saw rather a single transnational confrontation between two viewpoints, militarism and 'Norman Angellism'. 'The fight for ideals can no longer take the form of fights between nations', he wrote in the 1914 edition of *The Great Illusion*, 'because the lines of division on moral questions are within the nations themselves and intersect the political frontiers ... the moral and spiritual struggles of the modern world go on between citizens of the same State in unconscious co-operation with corresponding groups in

---

[15] Roger Chickering, *Imperial Germany and a World without War* (Princeton University Press, Princeton 1975), p. 384.

[16] Angell, *Great Illusion*, p. 180.

[17] J.A. Cramb, *Germany and England* (John Murray, London 1915), p. 69.

other States, not between the public powers of rival States'.[18] But to equate Professor Cramb and those who thought like him in England with Bernhardi and his influential supporters among the German ruling classes was to make a profound mistake.

Quite how profound became clear in the late summer of 1914. There are still – or until recently there were still – German historians who discounted Bernhardi as an irresponsible and atypical publicist, whose views reflected neither official policy nor public opinion. But Germany's attitude during the Sarajevo crisis, her actions on the outbreak of war, and more important still, the manner in which she conducted that war seemed to provide *prima-facie* evidence to the contrary, which the British public found entirely convincing. The invasion of neutral Belgium, and Betthman-Hollweg's shuffling defence of it in the Reichstag, the brutality of German reprisals to Belgian civil resistance – brutality all too well documented, however much it may have been exaggerated by allied propaganda – fitted too well into the pattern Bernhardi and his master, Heinrich von Treitschke, had prescribed for the conduct of German policy for it to be regarded as coincidental.

Further, when friendly liberal intellectuals in Britain and France suggested that Germany's policy did not reflect the attitude of the German people as a whole, but should be blamed on the 'militarism' of the dominant Junker ruling class, leaders in German scientific, academic, literary and artistic circles rushed to deny it. In October 1914 they issued an 'Appeal to the Civilised World' (*Kulturwelt*) containing over 93 signatures, including those of Max Planck, Max Reinhardt, Gustav von Harnack, Paul Ehrlich, Wilhelm Röntgen, Engelbert Humperdinck, Wilamowitz-Mollendorf and Gustav von Schmoller.[19] This indignantly denied that German troops had committed any atrocities anywhere, but accused the allies of unspeakable deeds. 'In the east the earth is saturated with the blood of women and children unmercifully butchered by wild Russian troops and in the west dum-dum bullets multilate the breast of our soldiers'. The appeal failed of its purpose. Western, including neutral, observers commented that these distinguished scholars cited no evidence for their assertions, and did not feel it necessary to provide any.

> The emotionalism of this document strikes us as keenly as its ingenuousness. It is signed by men who are out of their wits with excitement. They are banging the

[18] Angell, *The Great Illusion* (1914), p. x.
[19] In fairness we must note some of the names that are not there: Otto Hintze, Hans Delbrück, Friedrich Meinecke, Hermann Oncken.

doors and throwing the books about. And these are the greatest minds in Germany.[20]

More interesting for our purposes, these scholars and artists emphatically denied 'that the combat against our so-called militarism is not a combat against our civilization, as our enemies hypocritically pretend it is. Were it not for German militarism, German civilization would long since have been extirpated'. And to drive the lesson home, a few days later 3,200 teachers in 53 German universities subscribed to a document complaining at the attempt of their enemies

> to make a distinction between the spirit of German science and that thing they name Prussian Militarism. ... Our belief is that the salvation of the whole *Kultur* of Europe hangs upon the victory which German Militarism will win, and win through the manly discipline, through the truth, through the spirit of sacrifice of the united free German people.[21]

No doubt many of these three thousand signed the document rather to safeguard their tenure than because they entirely endorsed its contents, but there can be little doubt that it expressed the general mood of public opinion in Germany at that time, elite as well as popular. Six months later nothing had changed. In June 1915 Heinrich Class collected a total of 1,347 signatures for his famous 'Petition of the Intellectuals', including 352 professors, 252 artists and writers, and 158 clergy and schoolteachers. This warned the Imperial Chancellor that

> A statesman who returns without Belgium – soaked with German blood, without strong extension of the frontier in east and west, without a substantial indemnity, and before all, without the most ruthless humiliation of England, such a statesman will have to expect not only the worst discontent from the lower and middle classes about the increased burden of taxation; he will also find much bitterness among leading circles, which will endanger new peace and may even affect the foundations of the monarchy.[22]

Clearly Bernhardi's views were far from atypical.

How did all this affect poor Norman Angell? Naturally his enemies used these German statements as evidence to prove how misled and misleading he had been all along. Angell, on the contrary, saw it as justifying everything

---

[20] The Appeal is printed, with these comments, by J.J. Chapman, *Deutschland über Alles* (New York 1914).

[21] Chapman, *Deutschland üben Alles*, p. 99.

[22] Hans Gatzke, *Germany's Drive to the West* (Johns Hopkins University Press, Baltimore 1950), p. 117ff.

he had written. This 'Prussianism', as he called it, was exactly what he had been attacking: 'the belief that the things of greatest value in life ... are best promoted by adding to the political and military power of the State, by making it dominant over others, by extending its rule and by expanding its territories'. But this doctrine, he insisted, was not specifically German: 'It is world wide. In all powerful nations it lurks avowed or unavowed in some degree'.[23] The war had come about because this doctrine had become dominant in Germany. It was, he wrote, 'the work of half a dozen professors and a few writers and theorists ... (who) have radically transformed the nature and character of a nation of some 70 million souls. ... This miracle of transformation, the work of a few professors, has been accomplished within a period of half a century or less'.[24]

As an analysis of Germany's tragic *Sonderweg* this was of course quite comically inadequate. The militaristic culture of pre-war Germany could not be explained, or explained away, as the result of an academic doctrine; nor was that doctrine identical all over the world. Even if it were, even if the teaching of Treitschke and the Berlin historical school had not been rooted quite consciously in a unique historical culture, it still had to be explained why Treitschke had been so much more influential in Germany than Professor Cramb had been in England, and why the writings of even such influential imperialist historians as J.A. Seeley did not create in England a similarly militaristic cast of mind.[25] It would not be difficult to find, in Edwardian England, half a dozen militaristic academics and theorists whose writings paralleled those of Treitschke and Bernhardi, but why had they not effected a comparable transformation of the philosophy of the British people? Above all, as G.G. Coulton sardonically asked, why had Angell, in any of his prolific pre-war writings, failed even to mention the militarization of German society as a possible obstacle to his programme of achieving world peace?

Nevertheless, however shallow Angell may have been in his analysis and optimistic in his prescriptions, his views still commanded widespread agreement among British liberal thinkers in 1914. He was able to quote in his support H.G. Wells, who wrote on 29 August 1914, 'This is a conflict of cultures and nothing else in the world. ... Our business is to kill ideas. ...

[23] Angell, *Prussianism*, pp. xiii, xvi.

[24] *Ibid.*, pp. 2, 5.

[25] British intellectuals were certainly affected by a powerful war psychosis once the war began but it was based on the anger of betrayed Liberalism than on any positively militaristic philosophy. See Stuart Wallace, *War and the Image of Germany: British Academics 1914–1918* (John Donald, Edinburgh 1988).

The ultimate purpose of this war is propaganda'. The liberal journalist A.G. Gardiner wrote a month later, 'We are fighting not against a nation so much as an evil spirit that has taken possession of that nation, and we must destroy that spirit if Europe is to be habitable to us'; and above all, Asquith himself, who declared on 15 September, 'The Allies will go to Berlin to settle accounts. ... Not until the capital is reached, and not until they see the conquerors in their midst will the Germans turn from Treitschke and Nietzsche to Luther and Goethe once more'.[26] The work of this handful of professors had to be undone, and the German people re-educated.

Like his former associates of the Northcliffe Press, Angell therefore believed in total victory. 'It is essential', he wrote, 'to the best interests of Europe and mankind that the Allies should win, and that Prussian military autocracy should realise its helplessness as against its united neighbours'. 'But', he went on perceptively, ' ... unless victory is accompanied by political wisdom on our part, the crushing of Germany may leave us in a worse condition than before the war'.[27] Even if the Prussian state is destroyed, Angell warned,

> the problem of Prussianism will remain almost as great a problem as though this war had never been fought. There will be the material fact of the existence in Central Europe of a hundred millions of Germans, bred and trained in the ideas of Prussianism, with all sorts of opportunities ... for some military renaissance in the not very distant future.[28]

The only hope for the defeat of 'Prussianism', he concluded, 'resides in the triumph of a new and better doctrine, the realisation that the struggle for military ascendancy must be abandoned, not by one party alone, but by all alike'.[29]

So the work of spreading 'Norman Angellism' must continue, and did continue, once the war was over; among the elites with the foundation of bodies such as Chatham House and the New York Council on Foreign Relations; among the general public with the establishment of the League of Nations Union; not least in universities with the establishment of Chairs and Departments of International Relations, with the explicit or implicit assumption that war was a futile and counter-productive instrument for attaining national objectives and that reasoned analysis could discover means to avoid and ultimately abolish it.

[26] Angell, *Prussianism*, pp. 6, 7.
[27] *Ibid.*, p. 41.
[28] *Ibid.*, p. xviii.
[29] *Ibid.*, p. 69.

Unfortunately 'Prussianism' survived as well, in the far more virulent form of Fascism and National Socialism, and proved no more vulnerable to reasoned debate after the war than before it. Bernhardi did not live to see how successfully another generation of German leaders would work, as he had urged them, to rouse in their people 'the unanimous wish for power ... together with the determination to sacrifice on the altar of patriotism, not only life and property, but also private views and preferences in the interests of the common welfare [so as to] stamp a great part of humanity with the impress of the German spirit'; but shortly after his death Dr Goebbels and the ideologues of the Nazi Party set out to do just that. But Norman Angell did live to see, and to give timely warning about, it.

Ultimately Angell's critics were proved right. 'The Great Illusion' was itself an illusion. In the long run, nations do not fight simply about business and profits; but they do fight about power and ideology. Those Germans who wished to attack England before 1914 – or who at least wished to acquire the capacity to attack England – did so not because they believed that such an attack would increase their wealth but because they hoped it would increase their power and diminish, if not destroy that of Britain. The British went to war not to preserve their profits but because they believed that war necessary to preserve their power, and with it a society in which Angell's ideas, whether one agreed with them or not, could continue to flourish – although, inevitably, they did not flourish very well in wartime. The First World War was for the British no less an ideological conflict than the Second: for liberals, even more than for conservatives, it was total war.

Eventually it did prove necessary, as Asquith had foretold, for the Allies to 'go to Berlin to settle accounts'. Re-education proved to be, in the end, the only means of eradicating so formidable a cultural tradition as that embodied in Wilhelmine, or even more in Nazi Germany. But re-education involved more than defeating the arguments of half a dozen professors and theorists. It required power; and in Europe in the first half of the twentieth century no less than in Mao Ze Dong's China, power, alas, still grew out of the barrel of a gun.

6

Gallipoli Memorial
Lecture 1997

War and the Making of Nations

It is a truism to say that national self-consciousness, a sense of national identity, has almost invariably been moulded by memories of past wars and sustained by celebrating them. In France the wars of the Revolution and Napoleon are commemorated by that most splendid of all war memorials, the Arc de Triomphe, where all the glories of France are celebrated every 14 July by spectacular military parades. For Britain national identity became defined during the century of naval and military victories over France after 1689, culminating at Waterloo in 1815; although these British triumphs did not entirely blot out the Scottish sense of national identity forged in their own earlier wars against the English. For the Germans, it was the victories over the French in 1813–14 and again in 1870–71 that forged a nation out of a dozen separate states – a nation that it was to take two terrible wars to destroy. For the United States it took seven years of war against the British to create among the thirteen original colonies a sense of national identity, which is refreshed every 4 July and reaffirmed on every possible occasion with the singing of *The Star Spangled Banner* – a rather redundant reminder of yet another war against the British. Imperial Russia constantly harked back to the victory of 1812, while for the former Soviet Union victory over the Germans in the Second World War stirred a sense of communal pride that might have created a great nation had it not been so disastrously squandered by the follies of Stalin and his successors. Other, less happy nations are equally sustained by memories of defeats – the Hungarians by Mohács, the Serbs by Kosovo, the Poles less by defeat in the field than by memories of constant betrayals. In the Far East, Japan came of age as a modern nation with her victory over China in 1895 and, more spectacularly, over Russia ten years later. For China, it was her victory over Japan between 1937 and 1945 and the subsequent eviction of the United States from her soil that provided the foundation for that sense of national renewal on which Mao Ze Dong was to build. And for Australia and New Zealand there is, of course, Gallipoli.

Why should it be Gallipoli? After all, the campaign was a minor episode in a far greater conflict in which Anzac forces were to gain greater laurels and endure far worse sacrifices on other fronts. Strategically it was a disaster. Most historians now agree that even if the campaign had succeeded in its objective, it would have made little difference to the outcome of a war that could be won only by the defeat of the main German armies on the Western Front. Tactically all that the Allied forces succeeded in doing was to ward off total catastrophe and escape with whole skins – apart, that is, from the 33,000 Anzacs, 120,000 British and 27,000 French troops who were killed, wounded, or invalided out during the course of the campaign. It was a horrible experience; but if one wanted to celebrate horrible experiences that of Pozières in the Battle of the Somme was perhaps even worse; and if one wanted to do the natural thing and celebrate a victory, it would be hard to beat Villers-Bretoneaux. The whole Dardanelles campaign was a shambles. Why not forget it, and leave the military historians to pick over its bones?

There are two reasons why Gallipoli has remained so fixed in the Australian (and New Zealand) national consciousness; both perhaps fortuitous. The first was the decision of the Australian government to celebrate the anniversary of the Gallipoli landings on 25 April 1916 as 'Anzac Day', before Australian forces had gone on to their further achievements on the Western Front. Celebrations were held not only throughout Australia but in London, where a service of commemoration was held at Westminster Abbey in the presence of the King and Queen and Lord Kitchener. In these ceremonies there were constant references to Australia and New Zealand having 'endured their baptism of fire', 'proved themselves as Nations' and 'come of age'; war being seen, in those Social-Darwinian days, as a rite of passage through which all peoples had to pass in order to prove their fitness for Nationhood. Whatever adolescent uncertainties the Australians and New Zealanders may have felt about their identity before 1914 – and there were many – the experience of Gallipoli had resolved them. Whatever happened thereafter, the pattern of celebration had been established and was not subsequently to be changed. April 25th was to be the equivalent of July 14th in France or July 4th in the United States; the day on which subsequent generations were to celebrate the Birth of a Nation.

The second reason why the memory of Gallipoli was to become so deeply embedded in the national consciousness was the work of that dedicated and remarkable man, Charles Bean, who set himself quite deliberately to create what became known as 'The Gallipoli Legend'. Charles Bean was quite the finest military correspondent and arguably one of the great military historians of the twentieth century. He landed with the Anzac forces and remained with them until the end of the campaign, meticulously recording everything that happened to them. He was to go on to do the same for two years on the Western Front, but it was Gallipoli that stuck in his mind and that he was determined to commemorate in a fashion worthy of the men who lived and died there. While the campaign was still in progress he collected the material for 'The Anzac Book', a popular compilation that was rushed out with government backing and by September 1916 had already sold 100,000 copies. The success of this volume may in itself have done much to persuade the Australian government to institute Anzac Day when they did.

For Bean the Gallipoli campaign embodied what, as a journalist, he had already identified as all the peculiar Australian virtues; self-reliance, scepticism towards authority, a sardonic and deprecatory sense of humour, and above all, 'mateship' – the comradeship of equals, especially male equals. He saw in Australia an egalitarian society sharply different from the British class-hierarchy embodied in the British armed forces and which he increasingly despised as archaic, humiliating, and above all *inefficient*. The Anzac contribution at Gallipoli *was* distinct and distinctive. It was possible to describe and celebrate their achievements with little or no reference to the contribution of the far larger British contingent – to say nothing of the French – which was also present and whose sufferings and achievements were at least as considerable. In the background there was certainly the Royal Navy, but in the background it stayed. In the background was also the British High Command and General Staff, whose performance was universally damned by the troops in the front line and whose staunchest defenders find it hard to say emerged from the campaign with any great credit. Behind them again were the British politicians who had blithely set on foot an enterprise whose difficulties they had barely begun to assess, and whose utility was, to put it mildly, very questionable indeed. The men in Anzac cove lived in an apparently isolated and self-contained world, one ruled by unpredictable and capricious gods; much as the Homeric Greeks had seen themselves living when they landed slightly further south to besiege Troy a few thousand years earlier. But this time there was no expectation that the right kind of sacrifice to the right kind of god or goddess would make things any better.

The reaction of the Anzac forces to their predicament was not to display 'heroism' of the classic kind, still admired by the classically educated British officers with whom Bean had been educated at Clifton College. They rapidly found that heroism in modern war was not only selfish but suicidal: a machine-gun bullet rapidly put an end to it, if dysentery enabled them to display it at all. Courage – yes: there was no lack of courage, especially in the early days of hand-to-hand fighting and such later encounters as Lone Pine. But on the whole the courage needed was of a different kind; the courage that enabled people just to 'stick it'; to be loyal to their mates, to do what they were told by officers whom they respected because they were their own sort and shared all their hardships, and to make the intolerable tolerable by a mixture of grumbling, humour, and ingenuity in 'making do'. In fact British troops on the Western Front were developing exactly the same defence-mechanisms, which were to prove equally effective in the Second World War: the stoical anthem 'We're here because we're here because we're here because we're here' was sung with equal relish by both armies in both wars. The virtues that Bean identified as being peculiarly Australian were more widespread than he was prepared to admit. But they were virtues none the less, and, combined with such identifiable Antipodean characteristics as self-reliance, skill at improvisation and a contempt for such superficialities as saluting or wearing clean or even recognizable uniforms, they were to be found in a state of high concentration in Anzac Bay in 1915.

Another peculiarity about the Anzac campaign was this. There was no 'generalship' of a traditional kind; or at least, none that anyone could observe. The generals were certainly there and highly visible; Birdwood, Bridges, Walker, Godley, Monash, White; and because they *were* there and highly visible they earned the respect, if not always the affection of the troops they commanded. But the scope for exercising their talents was little more than that normally enjoyed by battalion commanders; planning small-scale actions and keeping up the morale of their men. They did as well as could be expected under the circumstances, and Bean gave them due credit. But the Anzac campaign consisted not of skilfully planned operations but of soldiers' battles, each of which was to be meticulously chronicled by Bean, for which credit must be shared almost equally among the hundreds – thousands – of officers and men who took part. The names that survive are those after whom, almost at random, physical features were named: Quinn, Russell, Courtney, Owen, Steele; together with a handful of quite exceptional commanders such as Leane and Malone. And this suited the Australian character as well. The British on the whole rather like generals, if they are any good; the Australian instinct is to cut them down to size. It was an egalitarian campaign, fought by an egalitarian army: history has not distributed credit for its achievements in proportion to rank.

A third and appropriate peculiarity was the *indecisiveness* of the campaign. Not that the Australians are indecisive; far from it. But imagine two alternative scenarios. One is a catastrophe – the landings being decisively repulsed at the outset, or the Anzacs being later swept into the sea by a successful counter-attack. Neither was at all impossible. Gallipoli would then have been a disaster best forgotten, not even redeemed by the successful evacuation that enabled the British to forget the humiliation of Dunkirk and remember it as a miracle of deliverance. There would then have been no celebrations of April 25th; the effect on Australia's self-image, and indeed on the cohesion of the British Empire, would have been as disastrous as the capitulation of Singapore a generation later.

Alternatively, what if it had been a success? The Dardanelles would have been cleared in short order; Constantinople (perhaps) captured; but whatever happened thereafter, the actual landings that opened the campaign would have been remembered as a mere incident preliminary to wider operations in which the Anzacs would have played their part as a sub-ordinate corps on a British-led army – as they went on to do on the Western Front. Something equally memorable might have happened to provide an appropriate occasion for national celebration, but it is hard to visualize anything having the distinctive quality of Gallipoli. In that campaign the courage and endurance of those who took part cannot be considered simply as contributions to a final success that overshadowed all that had gone before. They were their own justification. Disaster might have made them tragic, while in triumph they might have been almost forgotten. As it was, the Anzacs could leave the Gallipoli peninsula ten months after landing there knowing that they had done all that they could. They had much to be proud, and nothing to be ashamed about. If there was fault to be found, it was not with them. And it was in that mood that they would celebrate the first Anzac day four months later.

There is one final aspect of the campaign that gives us cause to be grateful. It was not a triumph, and provided no incentive for triumphalism. It is remembered, not as a victory over the Turks – which it certainly was not – but as a victory over circumstances; something that Anzacs and Turks could celebrate together, as they do. That has been the trouble about commemorating other wars as the 'birth of nations': what were, for some, memorable triumphs were for others equally memorable humiliations. The victories the French celebrate at the Arc de Triomphe were largely won at the expense of the Germans. The victory sealed by the proclamation of the German Empire at Versailles in January 1871 was not to be easily forgotten by the French. Anglo-French relations were not improved by the laying out of Trafalgar Square or the naming of Waterloo Station. And it is only thanks to the abysmally low level of history-teaching in British schools that few Englishmen understand what the Americans are on about when they sing *The Star Spangled Banner* – though it is some consolation that probably very few Americans do either. Australia and New Zealand were born as nations without triumphing over anyone else in the process. That in itself may have done something to shape their self-image.

But it has to be admitted that few memorials of twentieth-century warfare are 'triumphalist'; I certainly know none commemorating the campaigns of the First World War. Victory came at too high a price, and it was the price that people remembered rather than the victory that it achieved. In London the Cenotaph and the tomb of the Unknown Soldier in Westminster Abbey – memorials to be imitated all over the world – were symbols of mourning, not of triumph, and the emotion annually renewed in remembrance ceremonials is still one of grief rather than of pride. This is as it should be. We have learned the hard way that war is not to be glorified, even if we still very properly wish to commemorate, with pride and gratitude, those who died in it. But it can be taken too far. In mourning the dead of the First World War the victorious democracies tended to forget what they had actually died for, and the possibility that they might have to fight for it again. 'Never Again' became the watchword, and it was very nearly a fatal one.

This was not the message of Gallipoli. 'Never again get involved in such a Godalmighty cock-up', perhaps; but the overriding sentiment of the celebrations – as it is of the Australian War Memorial – was pride in what Anzacs had accomplished, and at belonging to a nation – two nations – that could produce such men. And quite right too.

Charles Bean concludes his great work *The Story of Anzac* with the words: 'In no unreal sense it was on the 25th of April 1915 that the consciousness of Australian nationhood was born',[1] and the same of course can be said of New Zealand. But it was consciousness not only in the minds of Australians and New Zealanders, but those of everyone else as well; those of their British and French allies, of their Turkish and German adversaries, and of all those, all over the world, who followed the press accounts of the campaign during those months when the Western Front was deadlocked and the Germans were winning huge victories on the Eastern Front at unpronounceable places of which nobody had ever heard. The men who fought at Anzac showed that they were no mere colonial levies, but the representatives of proud and independent peoples who had to be taken into account both in the waging of war and in the making of peace. Of course it suited the political book of that master-politician, David Lloyd George, that they should be represented in the Imperial War Cabinet that he created in 1917, and even more that they should appear as independent nations at the Paris Peace Conference in 1919; but it was universally admitted that they took their seats as of right – a right earned by the men who had suffered and died at Gallipoli four years earlier. The failure of the campaign was unimportant: it was the sacrifices made there that mattered. They have borne lasting fruit.

[1] C.E.W. Bean, *The Story of Anzac*, Vol.2 (University of Queensland Press, Canberra 1944), p. 910.

7

A Thirty Years' War? The Two World Wars in Historical Perspective

The great Helmuth von Moltke, addressing the German Reichstag in May 1890 in the last year of his very long life, gave a sombre warning of wars to come:

> Gentlemen, if the war which has hung over our heads for more than ten years like a sword of Damocles – if this war were to break out, no one could foresee how long it would last nor how it would end. The greatest powers in Europe, armed as never before, would confront each other in battle. None of them could be so completely overthrown in one or two campaigns that they would have to admit defeat, accept peace on harsh terms, and not be able to revive again after a years-long interval to renew the struggle. Gentlemen, it could be a Seven Years' War; it could be a Thirty Years' War; and woe to the man who sets Europe ablaze, who first throws the match into the powder barrel![1]

We now tend to think of the two World Wars as discrete and separate, rather than as a Thirty Years' War divided by an interval for recovery, such as von Moltke so darkly foresaw. The image and the experience of the two wars, at least for the British, could hardly have been more different. In the twenty years that separated them, technology had transformed military techniques. The deadlock of trench warfare had been broken; mechanization, air power and radio-communications had restored mobility to the battlefield. Air power had extended destruction to the cities of the belligerents, so that the horrors of the Somme and Passchendaele were to be eclipsed by those of Coventry and Dresden. Above all, the extension of hostilities to the Pacific set on foot a new, complex and terrible conflict in that region whose battles bore almost as little resemblance to those of the First World War as they did to the Battle of Waterloo.

But were the two World Wars really one war, two acts, as it were in a single drama? This is of course a deeply controversial issue in Germany. For the Germans, the suggestion that both wars resulted from a continuous

[1] Reichsarchiv, *Der Weltkrieg 1914 bis 1918: Kriegsrustung und Kriegswirtschaft, Anlagen zum ersten band* (E.S. Mittler & Sohn, Berlin 1930), p. 43.

national policy pursued by both the Second and the Third Reich calls in question their entire structure of national values;[2] whether through the thesis advanced by Fritz Fischer that the Second Reich, so far from fighting a defensive war, had hegemonic intentions as grandiose as those of the Third, or, conversely, the suggestion that Hitler's ambitions were simply a continuation of German traditional statesmanship; that impish Taylorian thesis which, however often it is crushed by argument and scholarship, refuses, like those other imps Petruschka or Till Eulenspiegel, to lie down and die. In a more recent *Historikerstreit* we have seen how sensitive German historians have been both to the suggestion, put forward by Ernst Nolte, that Hitler's policy should be seen as part of some historical continuum, and to the plea from Michael Stürmer that not only the Second but perhaps even the Third Reich embodied values that should not be totally jettisoned by a Germany seeking a new identity.[3]

British historians can sympathize with the sensitivities of our German colleagues and would not wish to exacerbate their problems. None the less, from the point of view of Germany's adversaries and victims in those wars, the continuity is more apparent than the differences; however much military methods may have been transformed in the interval between them. So far as Britain and France were concerned, 1939 simply brought a renewal of war against a Germany who presented the same kind of threat as she had in 1914, and over a very similar issue. Neither went to war simply to preserve Polish independence, any more than Britain went to war in 1914 simply to preserve Belgian independence. Both fought to check what they saw as a renewed German bid for continental if not world hegemony. In 1939, as in 1914, British participation turned what might have been a purely European into a World War; and as was the case in the First World War, support for British resistance ultimately drew in the United States, thus decisively weighting the balance against a Germany who, against a purely European coalition, would almost certainly have prevailed. The crushing of Germany in 1945 was seen by Britain and her allies, at least by the generation which had experienced the First World War (and this, we must remember, included virtually all their military and political leaders), as the completion of business left unfinished in 1918. An interesting symptom of this attitude was the continuing identification during the Second World War of 'Prussia' as the continuing focus of German militarism, in spite of the negligible part

[2] See e.g. sources cited by Karl Dietrich Erdman in H.W. Koch (ed.) *the Origins of the First World War: Great Power Rivalry and German War Aims* (2nd edn; Macmillan, London 1984), p. 345.

[3] For a summary of the *Historikerstreit*, see *German History* Vol. 6 (1988), pp. 63–78.

played by Prussia, and indeed by Prussians, in the promotion of the Nazi revolution and the formulation of National Socialist ideology.[4]

For Britain indeed, as for her continental allies, both wars were really about a single issue – what might be called 'the German Question'; and the German Question had been defined so well by Sir Eyre Crowe in the famous memorandum he wrote in January 1907 in the aftermath of the Tangier crisis, that it merits the constant quotation that it has received.[5]

No one, argued Crowe, could doubt that 'the mere existence and healthy activity of a powerful Germany is an undoubted blessing to the world' or that Germany had every right to compete for 'intellectual and moral leadership': but

> If Germany believes that greater relative preponderance of material power, wider extent of territory, inviolable frontiers and supremacy at sea are necessary and preliminary possessions without which any aspirations to such leadership must end in failure, then England must expect that Germany will surely seek to diminish the power of any rivals, to enhance her own by extending her dominion, to hinder the co-operation of other States, and ultimately to break up and supplant the British Empire.

And he posed the question, which was to be of startling relevance in 1938 for Czechoslovakia and in 1939 for Poland,

> Whether it should be right, or even prudent, for England to incur any sacrifice or see other, friendly, nations sacrificed merely in order to assist Germany in building up step by step the fabric of a universal preponderance, in the blind confidence that in the exercise of such a preponderance Germany will confer unmixed blessings on the world at large, and promote the welfare and happiness of all other peoples without doing injury to any one.

When he wrote those words in 1907, Eyre Crowe was doing no more than summarizing the *Weltpolitische* ambitions being expressed at the time in Germany by public figures from the Kaiser downward; ambitions arising from a consciousness of capabilities denied opportunities, of huge power denied outlet – and denied outlet, it was believed, specifically by Britain. I will not weary you with the familiar quotations: Max Weber's Inaugural Lecture at Freiburg in 1895, with its declaration 'that the unification of Germany was a youthful folly ... if it should be the conclusion and not the starting point for a German *Weltpolitik*'; Hans Delbrück's statement in the

---

[4] See Michael Howard, 'Prussia in German History', in *Lessons of History* (Clarendon Press, Oxford 1991), p. 49.

[5] In G.P. Gooch and Harold Temperley (eds) *British Documents on the Origins of the War 1898–1914*, Vol. 3 (HMSO, London 1928), pp. 397–420.

Preussische Jahrbücher of November 1899, that, 'We want to be a World Power and pursue colonial policy in the grand manner ... the entire future of our people among the great nations depends on it'; to choose only the most moderate and respectable of the academics, and ignore the outpourings of the Pan-German League.[6] These advocates of *Weltpolitik* threw down an explicit challenge to Britain. 'We can pursue this policy with England or against England', Delbrück had continued. 'With England means peace; against England means – through war'. For Admiral von Tirpitz and his followers in the Navy League, peaceful accommodation with England was to be obtained through pressures and threats of a kind indistinguishable, in the British view, from expressions of hostile intentions; and to make those pressures credible German leaders found it politic to stir up among their public opinion an *England-hass* that was almost without precedent in the history of international politics. It was to find expression when war broke out in Lissauer's notorious 'Hymn of Hate'.[7]

So in 1914 there was for Britain quite certainly a German Problem – a problem of great capabilities compounded by very evident hostile intentions. The full measure of those capabilities became clear only when war broke out, with the spectacular victories of the German armies on every front. Probably not even the Germans had appreciated the formidable extent of their military power until they saw it in action, much less realized the opportunities that their victories would present. Fritz Fischer has documented very thoroughly the full range of German ambitions that was maturing before 1914, even if he failed – as in my opinion he did fail – to prove that Germany deliberately began the war in order to fulfil them. Most of them were to find a place in the famous 'September Memorandum' of 1914, and Chancellor Bethmann-Hollweg defined their overall object as being to provide   —> PTO

[6] Quoted by Immanuel Geiss in Koch, *Origins of the First World War* pp. 50–2. See also Woodruff D. Smith, *The Ideological Origins of Nazi Imperialism* (Oxford University Press, Oxford 1986) and Paul Kennedy, *The Rise of the Anglo-German Antagonism* (Allen and Unwin, London 1980).

[7] Ernst Lissauer, *Germany's Hymn of Hate* first appeared in the Munich journal *Jugend* and was published in an English translation by Barbara Henderson in 1914 by the Central Committee for Political Organisations, Leaflet No. 112. Its refrain ran:

We shall never forego our hate
We have all but a single hate
We love as one, we hate as one
We have one foe and one alone
ENGLAND!

security for the German Reich in west and east for all imaginable time. For this purpose France must be so weakened as to make her revival as a great power impossible for all time. Russia must be thrust back as far as possible from Germany's eastern frontier and her domination over the non-Russian peoples broken.[8]

To this others add their glosses: the virtual annexation of Belgium and the mineral resources of France; a great African empire; a powerful *Mitteleuropa* as the basis for an expanded German economy; a vassal Poland; perhaps some German settlements to provide security in the East.

But extensive as they were, these were war aims of a traditional kind, a quest for absolute security through extension of territorial control; an objective not unusual among continental powers. But absolute security for Germany was absolute insecurity for everyone else – not least the British. Hence the conclusion of the British government in 1914 that the German problem could be solved only by the destruction, not so much of German power, as of the regime and the philosophy, generally stigmatized at the time as 'Prussianism', wielding that power.[9]

That was easier said than done. German military power and military skills proved immense, and the uninterrupted course of her military victories only strengthened the determination of her military and most of her political leaders to secure objectives commensurate with those victories and the sacrifices involved in gaining them. Although the Social Democrats remained true to their objective of peace without annexations and indemnities, the growth and influence of the Fatherland Front showed that expansionist war aims were not a monopoly of the military elites – certainly not the 'Prussian' elites targeted by British propaganda.

Nor could 'Prussianism' be destroyed after the war simply through the overthrow of the monarchy that embodied it; any more than Germany's power could be destroyed by the dissolution of her armed forces and the limited occupation of her territories. Whatever the peaceful intentions of the Weimar Republic, the basis of that power remained intact in the size of Germany's population, in her industrial strength, in the excellence of her technology, and in a military expertise too deep-rooted to be destroyed by the abolition of her General Staff. The essence of that power remained intact, and available for any government willing to develop and make use of it.

There were few illusions about this at the Paris Peace Conference in 1919.

[8] Fritz Fischer, *Germany's Aims in the First World War* (Chatto & Windus, London 1967), pp. 103ff.

[9] See e.g. Norman Angell, *Prussianism and its Destruction* (Heinemann, London 1914).

But short of the kind of total conquest, occupation, division and debellation imposed on Germany in 1945, which probably lay beyond the capacity if not the ambitions of the victorious allies in 1918, what could be done about it?

The French had the clearest idea: cripple German economic power by annexing the Rhineland, by giving the industries of Silesia to the Poles, and by imposing massive reparations on Germany; the latter, admittedly, not so much in order to weaken German economy as to justify long-term occupation of the Left Bank of the Rhine. But how practicable was such a policy in the long run – and how much sense did it make for the economy of Europe as a whole? In any case it was a programme unacceptable to the British; both to British conservatives who did not want to see a German domination of Europe replaced by a French or, worse, a Bolshevist one, and to British liberals whose temperamental inclination to conciliation was strengthened by the arguments of Maynard Keynes.

Once that programme proved impossible, France turned to another course of action; accepting the inevitability of German revival but trying to create a balance against it, by building alliances in Eastern Europe. But these new, weak East European states could provide no serious substitute for France's traditional ally, Russia; and Russia's revolutionary intentions now alarmed many people even more than did the spectre of a revitalized Germany. In any case the French political leadership was incapable of providing an army that could implement the projects of their diplomats. Meanwhile the British were indifferent, and both the United States and the Soviet Union had ruled themselves *hors de combat*. It had taken, we must remember, the combined efforts of all these powers to defeat Germany in 1918.

It is thus not surprising that within six years of the war's ending we find all Germany's former adversaries abandoning the attempt to destroy her power, and instead pursuing the path of conciliation, whether via Rapallo or via Locarno. Within twenty years the verdict of Versailles had been effectively reversed without a shot being fired. By November 1938 the reparations question had been settled and the German economy was booming. All servitudes imposed on Germany with respect to her western borders had been lifted. The German rump of the old Habsburg Monarchy had been peacefully absorbed into the Third Reich. The principle of national self-determination was being applied in the multi-ethnic conglomerate of Czechoslovakia. German economic power dominated Central Europe. There was left only the question of Germany's borders with Poland; and given the acquiescent posture of both the British and the French governments there is no reason to suppose that a tough, skilful, and above all patient German government could not have settled those in its favour as well. By 1938 Germany had regained a dominance in Europe at least comparable to that of Bismarck; and like that of Bismarck, it was exercised with the willing consent of the British government and the glum acquiescence of the French. Why, therefore, did a Second World War break out in September 1939?

*   *   *   *   *

The short answer is that Britain decided that it should. War takes place, as Clausewitz pointed out, mainly for the defender: 'the conqueror would like to make his entry into our country unopposed'.[10] If Britain had so decided, war would have broken out a year earlier over the Sudetenland, or indeed three years earlier in 1936, when Germany re-occupied the Rhineland. As it was, by guaranteeing the independence of Poland in March 1939, the British government quite deliberately created a risk of war, and did so with overwhelming public support. It did not want war: not even Neville Chamberlain's bitterest adversaries can accuse him of war-mongering; but on the assumption that Hitler did not want war either, the creation of such a risk was the only deterrent at Britain's disposal against an extension of German power far transcending the acceptable continental dominance established by 1938.

The assumption was of course false. Hitler *did* want war, if not that particular war at that particular time; and even if he had not wanted war, he wanted objectives which, whether achieved peacefully or by violence, would have established Germany in a hegemonic position undreamed of by even the most ambitious statesmen of the Wilhelmine Reich. As was becoming increasingly clear, his adversaries were faced with the stark alternatives of resistance or surrender.

Eyre Crowe's analysis, in fact, was still valid after thirty years. A powerful Germany in itself posed no threat to British interests or international stability: after all, Bismarck had provided stability in Europe for a quarter of a century. Indeed in the 1930s a powerful Germany – especially a powerful right-wing Germany – was widely believed to provide a further advantage by acting as a bulwark against Bolshevism; and for that the possessing classes in both France and Britain were prepared to forgive Hitler a very great deal. For many of them, indeed, Hitler's Germany provided not so much a threat as a reassurance, if not indeed a model. To a Germany, however powerful, offering real stability, Britain and France would have yielded much – certainly not excluding the Polish Corridor.

[10] Karl von Clausewitz, *On War*, Book VI (Princeton University Press, Princeton 1976), Chapter 5.

But in the latter half of the 1930s Eyre Crowe's rhetorical question became more relevant with almost every day that passed:

> whether it could be right, or even prudent, for England to incur any sacrifice or see other, friendly nations sacrificed merely in order to assist Germany in building up step by step the fabric of a universal preponderance, in the blind confidence that in the exercise of such a preponderance Germany will confer unmixed blessings on the world at large.[11]

By 1939 the answer to that question had become clear. German power and intentions were once again threatening the structure of a world-system on whose stability British power precariously depended. Hitler was no Bismarck; he was not even William II; he was Hitler.

*   *   *   *   *

Even in 1939 few people in Britain appreciated who Hitler was, and what he intended to do. Neville Chamberlain, broadcasting to the nation on the outbreak of war, rightly told his listeners that 'it is evil things we shall be fighting against', and he went on to define them: 'brute force, bad faith, injustice, oppression and persecution'.[12] It was an accurate enough description of Hitler's methods but hardly an adequate account of his objectives. Nor did it really explain why the British people found themselves at war. Hitler might be guilty of all these crimes and still pose no threat to British interests. But Chamberlain can hardly be blamed for his lack of understanding if, twenty years later, a British historian so expert in the history of Germany and Central Europe as A.J.P. Taylor could, like Mr Chamberlain, stigmatize Hitler as being 'wicked', but doubt whether he had any long-term objectives at all.[13]

In their baffled and insular incomprehension of Hitler's ultimate objectives, both Neville Chamberlain and A.J.P. Taylor were probably typical of the bulk of their fellow countrymen. But the British were concerned less with the details of the Nazi programme than with the revival of the power and ambition of the German State, however horrific that programme might be. Britain did not go to war in 1939 to destroy Fascism, or to defend democracy, much less to rescue the Jews. Even the destruction of Poland – another far-away people, like the Czechs, of whom the British knew nothing – would hardly have constituted a *casus belli* if it had not been seen to add

[11] See n. 5 above.
[12] Keith Feiling, *Neville Chamberlain* (Macmillan, London 1970), p. 416.
[13] A.J.P. Taylor, *The Origins of the Second World War* (Hamish Hamilton, London 1961), pp. 69–71.

an intolerable accretion to the menace of German power. Britain went to war in 1939, thus ultimately turning a Central European border-dispute into a world holocaust, for the oldest, the least reputable, but the most basic of all motives – power politics; to resolve Humpty Dumpty's question 'Who will be master – that's all'. But power-politics, as a rather repentant pacifist Norman Angell had found himself forced to confess in the 1930s, is sometimes the politics of not being overpowered.[14]

The British decision left Hitler baffled and angry. He did not want war with England and did not see the need for it. His long-term aims are now clearer to us than they were to Neville Chamberlain and even to A.J.P. Taylor, but they had been set out in *Mein Kampf* for all to see. His policy was amazingly consistent as to ends, however flexible it may have been as to means. His object, set out in *Mein Kampf* and constantly reiterated thereafter in speech after speech, was the recreation of a new German Nation, cleansed of all the cultural and racial imperfections that had resulted from the process of modernization, and above all from the termite-like activities of those enemies of culture and of cleanliness, the Jews; microbes in the body-politic that had to be eliminated, if necessary exterminated, if the Germans were ever to be restored to sanity and health.[15] Further, the industrialization and urbanization of Germany which had done so much to rot good, healthy German stock was to be balanced and counteracted by the preservation and extension of the German peasantry, rooted in good, healthy German soil. But since there was not enough suitable territory within the existing frontiers of Germany to provide adequate living space for such an extension, more must be acquired: much as the British, Hitler pointed out, another over-industrialized people, had acquired colonies of settlement all over the world.

But such overseas settlements, Hitler realized, were likely to break away and create new states of their own. Even if they did not, links with them had to be defended by an expensive navy, the creation of which had proved so disastrous before 1914. Germany had therefore to find its *Lebensraum* in the contiguous territories to the East; territories not only temperate and fertile, but providentially left in a state of chaos by the collapse of a Russian Empire that had in any case only been kept going by its German elites. As a superior *Kulturvolk*, the Germans had as much right, and indeed duty, to take possession of and rule these territories as the Anglo-Saxons had to extend

[14] Norman Angell, *After All* (Hamish Hamilton, London 1951), p. 137.
[15] Adolf Hitler, *Mein Kampf*, trans. Karl Mannheim (Hutchinson, London 1969), *passim*, esp. pp. 126–37. On the Jews, see *Hitler's Table Talk 1941–44* (2nd edn; Weidenfeld & Nicholson, London 1973), p. 332.

their rule throughout the extra-European world. The inferior peoples who inhabited them were to be either subordinated, as the British had subordinated the native inhabitants of their African and Asian colonies, or eliminated, as the Americans had eliminated the 'Redskins'.[16]

Hitler recognized that in order to achieve these objectives it would certainly be necessary to have a final settlement of accounts with France;[17] but why should Britain object to them? One of the principal grounds for Hitler's objections to German *Weltpolitik* before 1914 was that it had brought Germany into an entirely unnecessary conflict with England. Unlike so many *Weltpolitiker* of the Wilhelmine era, Hitler did not consider the humiliation of Britain as a necessary step in the fulfillment of Germany's destiny as a World Power. Indeed, Hitler seems to have been far less concerned with Germany's world status than he was with her cultural integrity: unlike the imperialists of the Wilhelmine era, he wanted colonies and expansion for reasons of domestic stability and racial health rather than for global prestige, or even national security. There was much to be lost by antagonizing Britain – Hitler's experiences on the Western Front had given him a healthy respect for her as an adversary[18] – and everything to be gained by befriending her; so long as she did not block his ambitions to the East. If the worst came to the worst he would have to fight, and, if need be, invade her; but he could never quite believe that, ultimately, good sense would not prevail and that the right-minded people in whose influence he stubbornly believed would not at the last moment mount a *coup* to overthrow the Jewish warmongers and their leader Churchill. There is indeed an interesting parallel to be drawn between the hopes he placed on such a development, and those that British optimists placed on a comparable coup against Hitler.

We know that such 'right-minded people' did exist; but the remarkable thing is not that they should have existed, but that there should have been so few of them, and that their influence should have been so slight. There was after all little affection among the British for the French, and even less for the small nations of Eastern Europe. There was, at least on the right wing, endemic fear of communism and some respect for the measures Hitler had taken to eradicate it. There was, to put it mildly, less sympathy for the Jews than one would wish, although anti-Semitism had not penetrated so deeply into British society as it had into French. There was an overriding concern for the security of the Empire and much suspicion of any

[16] Norman Rich, *Hitler's War Aims: Ideology, the Nazi State and the Course of Expansion* (Andre Deutsch, London 1973), pp. 212–49.
[17] Hitler, *Mein Kampf*, pp. 609, 616.
[18] *Ibid.*, p. 133.

continental commitment; and among the population as a whole, there was a deep disinclination to go to war.

Yet none of these considerations could override the fundamental perception that, confronting a powerful and dynamic Germany dominating the Continent – and, now, commanding considerable air power – Britain was not safe; or that at best her security would depend on the whim of an unpredictable ruler in Berlin. The distinction between *Weltpolitik* and *Lebensraum* as German objectives was, for the British people, academic: what mattered was the huge accumulation of German power and the evident determination of Germany's leaders to use it to extend their dominion. Even those who most sympathized with Hitler's objectives disliked the prospect of Britain becoming a tributary kingdom within the German Reich, even if their own suzerainty still embraced half of the extra-European world. So with immense reluctance, and in full realization of the unfavourable odds, the British government decided once again to confront German power with armed force as they had in 1914, and to overthrow the regime wielding it.

But the odds were now not only unfavourable; they were impossible. The balance of power had radically shifted since 1914. After the interval foreseen by von Moltke, Germany had remobilized her resources and the will to use them. Of her former adversaries, Russia and the United States had dropped out of the contest, France was exhausted and Britain had barely begun the remobilization of military strength needed to turn her once more into an effective continental power. Within less than a year German domination of the Continent had been converted by military conquest into a hegemony that Britain was no longer in any position to contest. Even if the subjugation of Britain herself was not immediately practicable, the British could hope to do no more than stave off defeat unless, improbably, the United States emerged from its isolation and once again came to their rescue. The ambitions listed in the September Memorandum of 1914 could now be realized. France was debellated. A protectorate was established over the Low Countries. German naval control was extended from Norway to the Pyrenees. German dominance in *Mitteleuropa* was unchallengeable. Certain aspirations in the Baltic remained unfulfilled, but if a limited war with the Soviet Union proved necessary to 'liberate' the Baltic Republics, there was no doubt who would have been the victor. *Weltpolitik*, the acquisition of an overseas Empire, still awaited the defeat of England, but few people in Germany were any longer interested; Hitler least of all. The war for the mastery of Europe that had begun in 1914 was over, and the Germans had won it.

*　*　*　*　*

With that victory the overwhelming majority of the German people would no doubt have been content, and sooner or later Britain would have had to accept it. Had the German military victories of 1939–40 led to the creation of a politically and economically stable Greater Germany at the centre of an acquiescent Europe, they might have been regarded as the logical continuation and fulfillment of those of 1866–70. Hitler would have established his place as the rightful successor of Bismarck and of Frederick the Great. But that was not the role in which he had cast himself. The dynamic of the Nazi revolution had not been exhausted; the objectives outlined in *Mein Kampf*, never lost to sight, had not yet been achieved. So a year later, to the astonishment of the world and not least of the Germans themselves, Hitler launched a new and apparently quite unnecessary war against the Soviet Union, in pursuit of objectives that would have amazed the German policy-makers of 1914.

To the British, of course, it did not look like a new war. They saw the German invasion of the Soviet Union as a necessary preliminary to the defeat of Britain. It fitted comfortably within their historical experience of the Napoleonic wars from which, under the tutelage of Sir Arthur Bryant, they had been deriving much-needed comfort.[19] But German historians who claim that Hitler represented a divergence from rather than a continuation of the mainstream of German history argue that this truly was a different war, one fought for different objectives and using radically different methods from the war for European hegemony that had been fought and won in the West. In my view they are correct.

There were certainly strategic arguments for attacking and defeating the Soviet Union even before the defeat of England. There was the erroneous belief that the British were sustained by expectation of Soviet help; together with the quite correct view that since Roosevelt's America would not easily permit Britain to be destroyed, the war might be a long one. There was the realization that the Soviet Union would continue to be a tough rival both in the Baltic and in the Balkans.[20] But none of these arguments were compelling. Stalin showed no signs of abandoning his complaisant neutrality or interrupting his substantial deliveries of war material to the Third Reich; while the lamentable performance of the Red Army in the 'Winter War' against Finland makes highly implausible the argument sometimes advanced that the Soviet Union was itself planning a surprise attack. There

[19] See Arthur Bryant, *The Years of Endurance* and *The Years of Victory* (Collins, London 1942, 1944).
[20] Andreas Hillgruber, *Hitlers Strategie: Politik und Kriegsfuhrung 1940–41* (Bernard und Graefe Verlung, Frankfurt am Main 1965).

was no strategic compulsion for Hitler to attack the Soviet Union when he did. No: the only convincing explanation of his decision is that he was anxious to proceed as quickly as possible to the next and final stage of the programme he had outlined in *Mein Kampf*, for which his victories in the West had been no more than a necessary preliminary. The Soviet Union was to be destroyed; the frontiers of Slavdom were to be pushed back to the furthest possible extent; the newly conquered territories were to be settled with good German peasant stock, and the native inhabitants either sub-jugated or exterminated. Poland had already provided a testing bed for this programme. A few months later, at the Wannsee conference in January 1942, the decision was taken to use the extermination techniques being developed on the Eastern Front to provide a final solution to the Jewish problem in Europe as a whole.[21]

Was this programme a mere extension of the German war aims of 1914? I find it hard to believe so. In 1914 the German people went enthusiastically to war for vague and splendid causes; to assert and extend the greatness of their country, to destroy encircling enemies, to show that the spirit of 1870 was not dead. Would they have marched eastward with equal enthusiasm in 1941 if they had known what Hitler's very precise war aims were? It must be said that if they did not know, it was hardly Hitler's fault; after all, he had presented a copy of *Mein Kampf* to every newly wedded couple, and the work is by no means so turgid and unreadable as is so often depicted. But Hitler himself had repeatedly expressed his doubts as to the will and the capacity of the German people to carry out his intentions unless they had been carefully indoctrinated, and indeed bred, to do so.[22] Many of them were so indoc-trinated in the short time available, and carried out Hitler's gruesome pro-gramme with enthusiasm. But it is only fair to note that it was not only the Germans who did this: Balts, Poles, Austrians and Ukrainians all assisted in the extermination process. Even in the 'liberal' societies of Western Europe the police made no difficulties when called on to round up the Jews. In France and the Netherlands they did so with exemplary efficiency.[23]

---

[21] Norman Rich, *Hitler's War Aims, Vol. II: the Establishment of the New Order* (Andre Deutsch, London 1974), p. 7.

[22] Hitler, *Mein Kampf*, pp. 31, 307. See also Esme Robertson, *The Origins of the Second World War* (Macmillan, London 1971), p. 13.

[23] See Omer Bartov, *The Eastern Front 1914–45: German Troops & the Barbarisation of Warfare* (Macmillan, London 1985). For European support for Hitler's policies see John Lukacs, *The Last European War* (Routledge, London 1976) and Rich, *Hitler's War Aims, Vol. II, passim.*

Further, Hitler's ideas were not specifically German.[24] Many of them he had absorbed in pre-war Vienna from the Austrians Karl Lüger and Georg von Schönerer. If one had to name the major focus of anti-Semitism in pre-1914 Europe, one would probably cite France, or possibly Russia, before even considering Germany. The concept of *Lebensraum*, a healthy balance between population and soil, was implicit in much British Imperialist literature in the 1880s and 1890s, and one of the earliest expositors was a Scandinavian scholar, Rudolph Kjellen. Hitler learned his racism from a Frenchman, Gobineau, and an Englishman, Houston Stewart Chamberlain; while the idea of compulsory sterilization of the unfit was sufficiently respectable to have been taken up, enthusiastically, if briefly, by the British Home Secretary in 1910; Mr Winston Churchill.[25]

None of these ideas were, in fact, peculiar to Germany. Before 1914 they were as marginal there as they were in the rest of Europe. Although they may have been germinating in the minds of a few German right-wing thinkers at the time, they certainly did not figure in the war aims of the Wilhelmine Reich. It required Hitler's malign genius, first to crystallize them into a coherent programme, and then to play on the hopes, the fears, and the resentments of the German people to gain an ascendancy over them so absolute as to make them his willing accomplices in carrying it out. Hitler was the product of a European, not specifically a German culture; certainly not that of the Germany of 1914.

Nevertheless it was only Germany's victory in the long European war foreseen by von Moltke – a twenty-five, rather than a thirty years' war – that made it possible for Hitler to implement his programme. Germany had to win the interrupted First World War before he was able to embark so disastrously on the Second.

---

[24] Hitler, *Mein Kampf*, p. 91, 109, 111.
[25] Paul Addison, *Churchill on the Home Front 1900–55* (Jonathan Cape, London 1992), pp. 124–6.

A Missed Opportunity? Britain and the German Resistance, 1938–1944

The historiography of most wars passes through three stages. First, there is the crude triumphalism of the victors, accompanied by sullen acquiescence or shrill complaints of betrayal from the vanquished. Then, a decade or so later, come the revisionists, who focus on the mistakes made, the opportunities missed, and sometimes the crimes committed by the victorious powers. Eventually the whole episode becomes viewed in the perspective of its era, and the writing of the history passes from the participants and their protagonists to academics, who see their task as being neither to condemn nor to justify but to explain, and who in consequence write books of little interest to anybody except one another.

But the wars of the twentieth century have stirred such strong feelings that it is still difficult to view even the First World War with academic equanimity, much less the Second. Indeed, attempts to 'historicize' the Third Reich, to try to set it in historical perspective, have set off a *Historikerstreit*, a historians' brawl in Germany which shows little signs of dying down. In our own country such controversies as those over the rights and wrongs of the Strategic Bombardment of Germany, or the policy of 'Unconditional Surrender', or the wisdom of General Montgomery's strategy, or the acceptance of Soviet domination in Eastern Europe allegedly under the Yalta agreement, all these have eventually died down; only to be succeeded by bitter arguments about the wisdom of having supported Tito rather than Mihailovich in Yugoslavia, and the even more ferocious attacks on those allegedly responsible for the repatriation of Soviet prisoners on German hands to the Gulags or execution squads of the Soviet Union. As for the arguments over Appeasement, I doubt whether we shall ever see the end of them.

Among these massive controversies there is a rather quieter one that has never been entirely laid at rest, and was recently revived in at least three works: *The Ghosts of Peace*, by Richard Lamb; *The Unnecessary War*, by Patricia Meehan; and *German Resistance against Hitler: The Search for Allies*

Abroad, by Klemens von Klemperer.[1] The authors of these books, working from newly available documents in the Public Record Office, chart what they see as the opportunities missed by British statesmen for avoiding or preventing the Second World War, or shortening its course. They are melancholy chronicles, full of the wisdom of hindsight, which go to prove the truth of Oxenstierna's observation about the paucity of wisdom with which the affairs of the world are carried on.

One of the central issues with which these authors deal is the negative reaction by the British government to overtures from oppositional elements within the Third Reich, both before and during the war. In this story there were two crucial episodes. One was Neville Chamberlain's 'surrender' at Munich in September 1938, which pre-empted a plot by members of the German High Command to seize Hitler and overthrow the Nazi regime. The other was Churchill's rejection of the overtures of the conspirators who requested British support, through guarantees of a 'reasonable' peace, for the coup that failed so disastrously in July 1944. But for the first, the critics believe, the war might have been avoided altogether; but for the second, it might have been shortened by ten months, thousands of lives might have been saved, and the wholesale destruction of Germany from the air might have been avoided.

The literature about the Resistance in Germany is now vast, and I have not even begun to try to master it. But let us first survey briefly what happened from the British viewpoint, and then consider who the conspirators were. We then have to ask four questions. First, what were their objectives? Second, were their plans practicable? Thirdly, would their terms have been acceptable to the Allies? And finally, would Allied support have made any difference to their success or failure?

During the course of summer 1938, shortly after the German annexation of Austria, dissident elements in the German Foreign Office and High Command made contact with the British government to warn them that Hitler was determined on a course of settled aggression to the East, from which he could be deterred only by a show of strength by Britain and France. These sources also indicated that if war broke out over German claims to the Sudeten regions of Czechoslovakia, the High Command had plans to arrest Hitler and take over control in Germany. This information was ignored. Chamberlain compared the emissaries to the Jacobites at the

---

[1] Richard Lamb, *The Ghosts of Peace* (Michael Russell, London 1987). Patricia Meehan, *The Unnecessary War: Whitehall and the German Resistance to Hitler* (Sinclair Stevenson, London 1992). Klemens von Klemperer, *German Resistance against Hitler: The Search for Allies Abroad* (Oxford University Press, Oxford 1992).

French court in the reign of William and Mary. The Munich agreement followed. The German High Command abandoned such plans as they had for the overthrow of the regime, and thereafter dutifully did Hitler's bidding.

Over the next twelve months, as Hitler swallowed what was left of Czechoslovakia and cast a predatory eye on the rest of Eastern Europe, messengers from Germany flocked to London with proposals for a peaceful settlement. Not all were opponents of the regime. Indeed, it was not always easy to distinguish the source of some of the overtures: Goering and other members of the Nazi establishment were equally alarmed at the prospect of a war they considered to be premature. But all had one feature in common: it was a requirement of any settlement that Germany should not only retain Austria and the Sudetenland, but regain the Polish Corridor that divided East Prussia from the rest of the Reich. Although there were elements in the British government that found such proposals attractive, Hitler's seizure of Prague in March 1938 made them clearly unacceptable to the electorate as a whole.

These overtures continued even after the war had begun. Indeed, as one British historian has nicely put it, 'There were so many amateur and professional contacts between the protagonists in the various neutral countries that one is left with the impression that it must have been hard to get to the bar in any Swiss cafe during the Phoney War for all the spies discussing peace with one another.'[2] All these proposals, however, were also based on the assumption that Germany should retain her eastern frontiers of 1914, together with the territories she had acquired in 1938. It was a settlement that the British might have gladly accepted if they had lost the war. As it was, they had only just begun to fight it.

Then came the catastrophic summer of 1940 when Britain very nearly did lose the war, and Hitler himself put forward peace terms little less reasonable than those that had been on offer from the Opposition. But by now it was clear to everyone concerned that the problem was not so much the terms of settlement, as Hitler's own ambitions. Winston Churchill, with massive public support, made it clear that Britain would accept no overtures even from a victorious Nazi regime: Hitler had to be destroyed before any peace could be made. But in the summer of 1940 Hitler was at the peak of his power. The German people supported him as never before, and the High Command, stunned by their own successes, had fallen docilely into line. The

[2] Andrew Roberts, 'The Holy Fox': A Life of Lord Halifax (Macmillan, London 1991), p. 182.

few courageous spirits within Germany who were plotting his downfall could do nothing for another two years.

Then, with the beginning of the disasters on the Eastern Front at the end of 1941, Hitler's opponents began to recover their strength. Resistance revived within the German Army itself, one or two of whose members made heroic but abortive attempts to assassinate him. Messages were passed to the Western Allies (communications with the Soviet government still remain obscure) alerting them to the existence of a shadow government inside Germany preparing to seize power. In June 1942 a specific request was conveyed to the British government, through the good offices of the Bishop of Chichester, asking whether the Allies would be prepared to negotiate terms with a new German government that intended to establish a regime of 'law and social justice' within Germany, and of international co-operation within Europe; and whether they would make a public declaration to that effect.[3] To this request, the British refused to respond. Churchill had already determined on a policy of 'absolute silence' in response to any further soundings from the German Opposition. The British government had understandable doubts as to how far the movement was genuine, and others, better founded, as to how far it was effective. In any case the British were no longer free agents; the views of their American and Soviet allies had to be taken into account.

Further, militarily speaking, the summer of 1942 was not a good moment to consider negotiating with anybody. The British themselves, their forces in the Far East humiliated where they had not been destroyed, were fighting to stave off defeat in North Africa. The Soviet Union was facing a new major offensive, and the Americans were fighting one of the bloodiest battles of the war in Guadalcanal. In any case, the German proposals remained evasive about the frontier issue: reference was made to 'a free Polish and a free Czech nation', but that was as far as they went. It is hardly surprising that at such a moment the overture should have been regarded as ambiguous and irrelevant and have been firmly rebuffed. The attitude of those in the British government who knew about it is probably best summed up by then Permanent Undersecretary at the Foreign Office, Alexander Cadogan: 'What would be interesting would be to see what any group of this kind can *do*.'[4] Some evidence of effectiveness was necessary before anyone could take these offers seriously.

---

[3] The text of their communication is reprinted in the collection of translated documents, *Germans against Hitler*, ed. E. Zimmerman and H.A. Jacobsen (Berto Verlag, Bonn 1960).

[4] Lamb, *Ghosts of Peace*, p. 254.

Two more years were to pass before the 'group' could provide such evidence. Then on 20 July Colonel von Stauffenberg mounted his famous and disastrous assassination attempt. Although the Allies had received indications of the plot as recently as May 1944[5] the event itself took them by surprise. Their immediate reaction was to dismiss it as an *attentat* by a militaristic clique whose peace aims would be no more acceptable than those of Hitler himself. Churchill informed the House of Commons on 2 August that 'the highest personalities in the German Reich are murdering one another, or trying to', and reminded the House that 'it was largely the military caste that put Hitler where he is today. ... It would be a fatal mistake if we were to present any better terms to the militarists of Germany than we have done to the discredited Nazis'.[6] British experts in the Foreign Office actually welcomed the failure of the coup. John Wheeler-Bennett, whose knowledge of the German military was unrivalled, wrote: 'If it is true that a number of the more distinguished generals, together with such civilians as Schacht, Neurath and Schulenberg, have been eliminated, the Gestapo and the SS have done us an appreciable service in removing a selection of those who would undoubtedly have posed as "good" Germans after the war, while preparing for a Third World War. It is to our advantage therefore that the purge should continue, since the killing of Germans by Germans will save us from further embarrassments of many kinds'.[7] The British government thus washed their hands of the conspirators, who went in solitude to their terrible deaths.

*   *   *   *   *

Before expressing any opinion about the British government's action, or lack of it, we should now turn to the next question: of what, or whom, did the German Opposition consist?

First, we must take account of the warning given by one of the few survivors of the conspiracy, Hans Gisevius, who wrote in his memoirs:

> Any attempt to classify the German Opposition must necessarily fail. Basically, there were only oppositionists. Each of these more or less strong personalities had a group of friends who agreed with him. Each of them sought to extend his influence and therefore tried to establish contact with other groups and circles. This resulted in those many intersecting and tangential lines which so confused the picture.[8]

[5] *Ibid.*, p. 275.
[6] *Ibid.*, p. 300.
[7] Quoted in *Ibid.*, p. 297–300.
[8] Hans Gisevius, *To the Bitter End* (Jonathan Cape, London 1948), p. 415.

We should also make the obvious point that the overwhelming majority of these 'oppositionists' consisted of people, both civil and military, who had compromised with the Nazi regime sufficiently to retain their jobs, or if not their jobs then at least their status as (to use a term from a later and no less grisly epoch) 'untorturables'. Apart from one or two former trade-union leaders such as Wihelm Leuschner and Julius Leber, they contained no one from the Left, let alone any communists. The leaders of these groups had been swept up into concentration camps at an early stage in the Nazi Revolution, and if they survived at all it was in impotent cells which had to struggle even to survive. The active Opposition thus consisted of people from the upper and professional classes, whose expertise was useful to the regime and who had preserved their status and livelihood by accepting the Nazi Revolution, however much they may have privately deplored its excesses. It is easy enough to condemn them for that; they were to purge their guilt, if guilt there was, in a truly terrible fashion; but it was only people of that kind who, five years after the Nazi Revolution, were in any position, or rather who felt themselves to be in a position, to act effectively against the regime.

Bearing Gisevius's warning in mind, we can identify three foci of the Opposition. There were the conservatives of the professional classes, officials or former officials, who congregated around the former Mayor of Leipzig, Carl Goerdeler: Paul Lejeune-Jung, Hans von Dohnanyi, Johannes Popitz, and Gisevius himself, together with the Foreign Office officials Ulrich von Hassell, Ernst von Weizsaecker, and the brothers Erich and Theodore Kordt. Then there were the senior officers of the Wehrmacht, centring around Generals Beck and von Witzleben, with their associates in the Abwehr, Admiral Canaris and Hans Oster; a group whose size fluctuated according to the progress of the war. Finally, there was the so-called 'Kreisau Circle' formed by Helmuth von Moltke, an eclectic group consisting partly of high-minded aristocrats like Moltke himself – Peter Yorck von Wartenburg, Adam von Trott zu Solz – but drawing in labour leaders like Leuschner and Leber as well as business-men, economists, and clerics like Dietrich Bon-hoeffer and Alfred Delp.

Of these it was the group around Goerdeler that had the greatest continuity and was, through Goerdeler himself, most explicit about their objectives. Their intentions so far as foreign policy was concerned appeared little different from those which Hitler himself appeared to be pursuing in the 1930s; that is, to restore the German Reich within its frontiers of 1914, together with the Germanic elements of the Habsburg Monarchy; but in their case these involved not only Austria and the Sudetenland, but also South Tyrol. Such a Germany could, they believed, peacefully co-exist with its neighbours within a new European order of free co-operation and movement in which customs barriers had been eliminated; so that (to quote from a statement of Goerdeler's from 1941) 'If the peace is truly just, by the time ten years have elapsed the new boundaries will hardly be regarded as onerous any more, since by that time the European peoples will of themselves strive to merge and have learned to co-operate.'[9] As for constitutional arrangements, Goerdeler and his colleagues wished to undo the work of the Nazi Revolution to the extent of creating once again a *Rechtsstaat*, a constitutional State in which the rule of law would prevail; but they had no desire to return to the pluralistic party democracy of the Weimar Republic. The constitution they proposed was one heavily weighted to ensure the maintenance of social order and traditional values, preferably under a hereditary monarchy.[10] The Reichstag would be elected only by the soberer elements in the population, and its role would be very much as it had been under the Second Reich: primarily advisory to a government with full initiatory and executive powers.

No doubt few of Goerdeler's colleagues would have accepted his ideas in every detail, but the outlines were clear. These conservatives were reactionary in the literal sense of the word: Neville Chamberlain's analogy with the Jacobites was very perceptive. They wished to put the clock back, not to 1933, nor even to 1918, but to 1914; that Wilhelmine era which was, for people like themselves, a golden age. But in doing so, as Ralf Dahrendorf has reminded us, they were wishing to restore (as indeed the Jacobites were wishing to restore) not simply a political but an entire social order, and one that the Nazis had swept away with massive popular support.[11] The old hierarchies, the dominance of the upper-middle and professional classes, the values rooted in local, predominantly agrarian communities, were no longer seen as relevant to the age of industrial mass society, whose needs and aspirations the Nazis had known very well how to exploit. For most Germans in the 1940s Goerdeler and his colleagues would have been voices from a past to which few of them wished to return.

The military elements in the opposition did not formulate their objectives with equal precision, but it is reasonable to suppose that these would have differed little from Goerdeler's proposals. They were concerned with more immediate objectives. In September 1938 they wanted to prevent Hitler from

---

[9] Quoted in von Klemperer, *Germans against Hitler*, p. 50.
[10] Goerdeler memorandum of September 1944, 'Thoughts of a Person Sentenced to Death', in von Klemperer, *Germans against Hitler*, p. 27.
[11] Ralf Dahrendorf, *Gesellschaft und Demokratie in Deutschland* (Piper, Munich 1965).

initiating a large-scale war which they were not yet ready to fight and anyhow believed that they would ultimately lose. In the autumn of 1939 they wanted to stop him from initiating an offensive in the West for which they still thought themselves unprepared; and in 1944 they simply wanted to get rid of him. The Kreisau Circle did indeed have their own objectives, but they were far less precise and more far-reaching than those of Goerdeler. Most of them professed some form of Christian Socialism, and some were prepared to abandon the concept of the German State altogether. Von Moltke himself wished to see it replaced by smaller, more viable self-governing communities, existing within the framework of a European federation. He was not, indeed, proposing any specific terms to the allies: indeed he told his American contacts in 1943 that he considered 'an unequivocal military defeat of Germany and her subsequent occupation to be absolutely essential on moral and political grounds'.[12] Whereas the conservative and military elements in the Opposition had at least foreign-policy objectives that would probably have been acceptable to the German people as a whole, von Moltke demanded of them a change of heart that could only be brought about by total defeat and unconditional surrender.

The Kreisau Circle can thus not, by the most generous stretch of the imagination, be depicted as voicing the deepest aspirations of the German people. Nor can any of the other elements in the opposition. They were not, as they claimed to be, 'the other Germany': at best, they were *another* Germany. The German people as a whole showed no signs of wishing either to go back to the days before 1914 or forward to the reign of virtue promised by von Moltke. Even if their coup had succeeded, any attempt by the new regime to impose its ideas would have had to be forced through against profound popular opposition. Until at least 1942 the mass of the German people were very comfortable with a regime that had restored prosperity at home, status abroad, and introduced an unprecedented degree of social mobility from which everybody (excepting always the Jews) stood to benefit. Even the greatest admirers of the German Opposition agree that they commanded little support among the workers, none whatever among the lower-middle classes, and precious little even among the business classes and upper ranks of the bourgeoisie. Most important of all, apart from tiny, heroic groups like the White Rose, the younger generation, indoctrinated into the Nazi regime since early childhood, remained solidly loyal to Hitler. Unlike the Resistance elsewhere in Europe, whose activities commanded the tacit if not the active support of large elements of the population,

[12] Quoted in Hermann Graml and others, *The German Resistance to Hitler* (Batsford, London 1970), p. 52.

the German Opposition consisted of isolated individuals working against the social and political grain. They had to contend not so much with the ruthlessness of the Nazi regime, as with its popularity.[13]

Conscious of their isolation and mistrustful of the trend of public opinion, the plotters thus did not aim to spark off and canalize any popular revolt. They planned only to seize the machinery of government, and hoped that that would be enough. In 1938, it is true, General Halder and his military colleagues hoped that the general fear of war would swing the population to their support once they made public the course which Hitler was set on pursuing; but that was to assume a remarkable degree of rationality in a people who had already been subjected to five years of successful indoctrination and who had been able to track in Hitler's record nothing but continuous success. In 1944 the conspirators no doubt predicated a high degree of war-weariness that would make the people at least submissive to change; but all the evidence suggests that the German people, no less than the British, had settled into a mood of stubborn endurance, fortified by well-founded fears as to what would happen to them if they were to lose the war – especially on the Eastern Front. If either coup had led, as they almost certainly would, to a struggle between the party *apparat* spearheaded by the SS on the one side, and the Opposition led by the dissident military on the other, there is no reason to suppose that the latter would have enjoyed any great degree of popular support.

More important, there is no reason to suppose that it would have enjoyed any greater degree of *military* support either. Even in 1938 the junior ranks of the Wehrmacht were filling up with *führertreu* young officers who had little time for the superannuated brass-hats of the old Reichswehr and who looked forward with enthusiasm to the promised war. If we add to their number the SS and the party organizations in general, and consider the degree of social control which those had established over the population during the previous five years, it is hard to avoid the conclusion that the coup planned by Generals Halder and von Witzleben in 1939 – if indeed they had had the nerve to launch it at all – would have lasted about as long as that of Herr Kapp in 1919, and have been about as equally effective.

What can one say of the *coup manqué* of 20 July 1944? Certainly the odds would have been more favourable if Hitler had been killed as planned. But even then the SS and the party organisations would not have simply rolled

---

[13] See e.g. the contributions of K.D. Bracher and Martin Broszat in Hedley Bull (ed.) *The Challenge of the Third Reich* (Oxford University Press, Oxford 1986), and Hans Mommsen, 'German Society and its Resistance to Hitler', in his *From Weimar to Auschwitz: Essays in German History* (The Polity Press, Cambridge 1991).

over and let the conspirators have their way; and it remains highly questionable how much of the Wehrmacht – especially on the Eastern Front –
would have rallied to the support of a group that was undermining the
defence of the homeland at such a crucial moment of the war. Whatever
their differences, Goering, Goebbels, Himmler and Bormann would have
united to restore party control and probably have achieved it in a matter of
days. What would have happened then is anyone's guess. They might indeed
have made peace overtures, but to such a leadership the Allies would have
been no more inclined to mitigate their demand for unconditional surrender than they would have been to Hitler. Without the ferocious will-
power of the Fuehrer to keep it going, German resistance might have collapsed very much sooner than it did, but few of the conspirators would have
survived to reap the benefit.

*　*　*　*　*

That brings us back to the Allies; and by 1944 it is the *Allies* of whom we are
speaking, and not just the British. Should they, or could they, have supported the conspirators; and would their support have made any difference?

We now know that their suspicions of the bona fides of the German
Opposition were unfounded. But such suspicions were entirely understandable at the time. After all, two leading members of MI6 had been
kidnapped when responding to a highly plausible overture made through
the Abwehr. Well-placed members of the British Establishment might vouch
for the bona fides of that tragic and attractive figure, Adam von Trott zu
Solz, but it remained mysterious why so open a critic of the regime should
have been allowed to travel so freely outside Germany at all. Further, the
proposals they put forward were not particularly appealing. The internal
regime they proposed to establish in Germany was their own affair, and
almost anything would have been preferable to that of the Nazis. But there
was little point in negotiating with them if they were aiming at recreating
the German Empire of 1914 – indeed, by embodying so much of the old
Habsburg territories, going even beyond that. This, after all, was all that
Hitler seemed to be asking. As a German historian has rather unkindly
observed, 'Goerdeler's criticism of Britain's appeasement policy was not
directed at its underlying concept, but at the fact that London was negotiating with the wrong partner'.[14] It is hardly surprising that William Strang
of the Foreign Office observed in 1938, of Goerdeler's proposals, 'It is not

---

[14] Graml and others, *German Resistance to Hitler*, p. 10.

easy to see what we should gain – except a year or two's uneasy quiet – by putting people like Goerdeler and the Army into Hitler's place'.[15]

When a few years later the war turned against Germany, the Opposition softened their terms. In March 1944 von Trott asked only for a cessation of the bombing and 'reasonable terms' 'even if it reduces Germany to a smaller state than the Versailles frontiers'.[16] But it is doubtful how far his colleagues would have gone along with this: in a memorandum of May 1944 von Stauffenberg still made clear his intentions of demanding the Reich borders of 1914, together with Austria, the Sudetenland, South Tyrol and 'autonomy for Alsace-Lorraine'.[17]

More significantly, Gisevius promised Allen Dulles in Switzerland that the conspirators, if successful, would cease all resistance in the West, but continue to hold fast in the East; a suggestion that hopelessly overestimated the divisions within the allied leadership. Alec Cadogan deduced that the sole object of the conspirators was now 'to preserve Europe from Bolshevism, i.e. to help Germany against Russia, which is unthinkable'. The judgement of his colleague Ivone Kirkpatrick was brutally dismissive: 'The opposition are unlikely to be able to do anything to shorten the war. They are not powerful enough, the terror is too efficient, and moreover they would not act unless we gave them assurances that would gravely embarrass us later. At the worst, to give them a glimpse into our minds might drive them into the Nazi camp!'[18] Such a glimpse would have revealed the continuing determination of the Allies to fight on to the unconditional surrender and total occupation of Germany, and it is an open question how many of the conspirators, even within the Kreisau Circle, were prepared to accept this, and collaborate with their former enemies – necessarily including the Soviet Union – in enforcing it upon the German people.

Critics of Allied policy have suggested first, that the demand for unconditional surrender was in itself a mistake; and second, that the Western allies should have been prepared to conduct a *renversement des alliances*, accept the now chastened Germans as their allies, and join them in defending European civilization against the looming threat of Soviet communism; to put into effect the policy that they were in fact to carry out only five years later.

With these criticisms I cannot myself agree. The demand for unconditional surrender was primarily a declaration of Allied solidarity, a mutual

---

[15] Quoted by Peter Ludlow in Bull, *Challenge of the Third Reich*, p. 146.
[16] Lamb, *Ghost of Peace*, p. 273.
[17] Von Klemperer, *Germans against Hitler*, p. 85.
[18] Lamb, *Ghost of Peace* 283.

assurance that none of them would detach themselves from the Alliance to make a bilateral compromise peace, either with Germany or Japan. Goebbels certainly used the declaration to fortify the resolution of the German people, but he was quite skilful enough to use any different material that came to hand. And the question must be asked: what terms *could* the Allies have accepted that any German government, whose armies had not yet been defeated in the field, would have been willing to offer? The very minimum that they could have demanded would have been a with-drawal of Germany to her frontiers of 1937; something, as we have seen, that not even the German Opposition was prepared to yield. The Allies were in effect fighting to reimpose, at the very least, the constraints imposed on Germany by the Versailles settlement, having seen what happened when those restraints were removed; and although the German Opposition might sincerely claim that the newly enlarged Germany would in their hands be a trustworthy partner, the Allied governments were understandably sceptical. Even if, *per impossibile*, the Allies made peace on Goerdeler's terms – which until 1944 were the only terms on offer – for how long would a Goerdeler government survive in Germany, and what would be the policy of its suc-cessors? At root what was at issue in the Second, as in the First World War, was not just the way in which Germany used her power: it was German power in itself.

What about the anti-Soviet card, which the conspirators played, albeit rather half-heartedly, in July 1944? All one can say is that they could not have chosen a more unfortunate moment to play it. The Soviet Union was at the peak of its popularity in the West, particularly in Britain. The British had seen themselves saved from invasion and probable conquest by the Russian absorption and eventual defeat of German military power. They were uneasily conscious that they had, through no fault of their own, been able to make only peripheral contributions while the issue of the war was being determined on the Eastern Front, and sympathy for their Russian allies had plumbed the depths of *Schwärmerei* with the presentation of the Sword of Stalingrad, so properly ridiculed by Evelyn Waugh.[19] The uglier side of Soviet military success had yet to be revealed with the Warsaw Rising of August 1944 and the confirmation of the atrocities at Katyn. Allied military leaders were always apprehensive that Stalin might make a separate peace, and their political colleagues saw no prospect for creating a peaceful post-war settlement of Europe except in close co-operation with the Soviet Union. A conflict with the Soviet Union at such a moment was a nightmare

[19] See Evelyn Waugh, *Unconditional Surrender*, Chapter 1, pp. 17–61 (Chapman and Hall, London 1961).

that nobody would willingly contemplate. When Cadogan termed any support for the Germans against the Soviet Union as 'unthinkable' he was not exaggerating.

Further there was the influence of public opinion in Britain, to say nothing of that in the United States and, for what it was worth, the Soviet Union. The demand for unconditional surrender had originally been made in response to a storm of public protest at the accommodation that General Eisenhower had negotiated with Admiral Darlan to ensure a peaceful Allied occupation of French North Africa, and nothing had occurred in the meantime to change the mind of the public in either of the Western democracies. Even if the Allied governments had thought it desirable to negotiate with the German Opposition, it would have been impossible to sell any agreement to their respective nations. The stock of the peacemakers (not to use the loaded term 'appeasers') was at an all-time low. It would have been hard to explain to the public that, whereas it had been proper for Britain to have rejected terms recognizing German conquests in 1940, when she was on the verge of defeat, it was proper to accept them now that she was on the verge of victory.

Finally, even if the British government had given the conspirators their covert or open support, what difference would such support have made to their success? The kind of open declaration requested through the Bishop of Chichester in 1942 would only have identified the Opposition as internal supporters of the external enemies of the Reich, and we can imagine the field-day that Goebbels would have had over that. A private undertaking would have been no better; the conspirators could hardly have made any such undertaking public, and if they had, it would hardly have won them much support. If they could not get rid of Hitler on their own, there was nothing that the Allies could do to help them.

*   *   *   *   *

My conclusion is the bleak one, that the German Opposition to Hitler could not have succeeded in their objectives, and that the British government was right not to have encouraged them. Neither in 1938 nor in 1944 was a great opportunity missed, either to avoid war altogether or to shorten it. But where the British government was entirely at fault was in questioning the bona fides and the motivation of the conspirators. Churchill himself was to acknowledge shortly after the war:

> In Germany there lived an opposition which was weakened by their losses and an enervating international policy, but which belongs to the noblest and greatest that the political history of any nation has ever produced. These men fought without

help from within or abroad – driven forward only by the restlessness of their own conscience. As long as they lived, they were invisible and unrecognisable to us, because they had to camouflage themselves. But their death made the resistance visible.'[20]

Their activity has been well described as 'resistance as witness'.[21] It was the activity itself that mattered, rather than its success. The situation was well summed up by one of the conspirators, General von Tresckow, in July 1944:

> Even if it should fail, the coup d'état nevertheless should be attempted. For it is no longer a matter of the practical purpose, but rather that the German resistance has dared, before world opinion and before history, to make the decisive attempt at risk of life. Compared with that, everything else is unimportant.[22]

Indeed it is almost better that they should *not* have succeeded. They would then have had to demean themselves by innumerable compromises and deals in order to stay in power, and then face an unpopularity little less than that of their Weimar predecessors when they tried to broker the Allied peace terms. As it is, their reputation is unsullied, and it is better so. They did provide a model for 'another Germany', and one that has triumphed over the memory of the evil regime against which they so courageously fought.

[20] Lamb, *Ghosts of Peace*, p. 301.
[21] Charles Maier in David C. Large (ed.) *Contending with Hitler: Varieties of Resistance in the Third Reich* (Cambridge University Press, Cambridge 1991), p. 150.
[22] Von Klemperer, *Germans against Hitler*, p. 249.

III

The Cold War

The Cold War: A Personal Retrospect

The fifty years of my active adult life, from 1945 until 1995, coincided almost exactly with the onset, course, and immediate aftermath of 'The Cold War', and I shall try to chart its impact on me through a series of 'snapshots' from a notional photograph album. The camera has been of European, more specifically of British make, for which I make little apology. It is also that of a historian rather than a political scientist, more concerned with events and personalities than abstractions and models, and for that I make no apology whatever. It may be intensely egotistical; but as any economist will tell you, private vices can sometimes become public virtues.

The first snapshot is of a young officer in a snowbound village in the Italian mountains south of Bologna in January 1945, lecturing his platoon with a large map of Europe provided weekly by the information services to show the progress of the war. The map showed deadlock on our own front and in France, but huge red arrows indicated the continuing advances of the Red Army across Poland, into the Balkans, and beginning to penetrate into Germany itself. We all cheered when we saw those arrows. First, they meant that there would be less fighting left for us to do, with a consequently increased prospect of our personal survival; a prospect that at times had seemed unpleasantly remote. Secondly it meant that the Russians would take a larger slice of Germany off our hands and treat the Germans as, we believed, they thoroughly deserved. Letters from my family in London showed that these sentiments were widely shared at home. Admiration for the Red Army was universal – admiration and gratitude. It became tinged with slight apprehension when we encountered them in Austria six months later, but it took a long time to fade.

It was my own fate to meet, not the Red Army, but Tito's partisans north of Trieste, when my unit was rushed into Venezia Giulia to hold the line of the Isonzo against Yugoslav penetration. Here my snapshot is of a bridge over the Isonzo, guarded at one end by a magnificent Sikh sentry, turbaned and bearded, his equipment gleaming white, his bayonet fixed; the very embodiment of the British Raj. At the other was a little old lady in grey skirt and jacket, red partisan star in her cap, a belt of ammunition over her shoulder and a sub-machine-gun tucked under her arm. In the event of conflict my money would have been on the little old lady – and I am not sure that my sympathies would not have been with her as well. But she clearly loathed us and all we stood for. For her, we were not liberators but enemies.

So here were two hostile worlds locked in confrontation, and it seemed touch and go whether that confrontation would remain 'cold'. When a few weeks later I was demobilized and returned to complete my degree at Oxford, I could not help wondering how soon it would be before I had to put on uniform again and go back to what I now regarded as the 'normalcy' of war.

This apprehension, I must emphasize, was not due specifically to anything that the Russians were doing or seemed likely to do. As a student of European history I am afraid that I regarded their behaviour in Eastern Europe and East Germany, brutal though it was, as natural, predictable, and not particularly threatening to anyone else. I felt deeply sorry for the Poles, having seem something of that heroic but tragic people in Italy, but reckoned that the Germans deserved all that they got. What was more directly alarming was the sheer *mess* that the war had left in Europe; the chaos and misery with some nine million 'displaced persons' (as we then called refugees) needing to be housed and fed, epidemic disease prevented, cities reconstructed, and entire civil societies rebuilt that had disintegrated under occupation and war.

For the next ten years I was occupied with getting my own life in order and played no part, however humble, in great events. There are no snapshots; only a flickering newsfilm in black-and-white. Living in London I was colder and sometimes hungrier than I had ever been during the war. Exchange controls restricted foreign travel to a few weeks a year, but Europe was no place for tourists. I have one memory of being marooned in 1947 in a small Paris hotel by a train-strike, while in the street outside the police broke up a riot with a brutality that appalled me; and another, the following year, of a holiday in North Italy, where in every city that I visited huge communist demonstrations dominated the streets. That was a particularly bad moment. The Berlin blockade had begun. Italy was in flames following the attempted assassination of the communist leader Togliatti. I clutched the return half of my rail ticket and prayed that I would be able to get home in time. This was the Europe that George Marshall had seen when he travelled through it in the winter of 1946–47 to Moscow, and had resolved on the great blood-transfusion of Marshall Aid. It was a Europe concerned not about a Soviet invasion as such, but about a social disintegration that would make such an invasion unnecessary.

The results of Marshall Aid took some time to appear; while as for

NATO, the newspapers reported the difficulties of its gestation rather than the triumph of its achievement. All one knew about either were endless meetings of diplomats in Paris, Brussels and London. Life remained *couleur de merde* for the rest of the decade. I was teaching in the University of London, where sympathy with communism remained powerful among the student body; combined with a rather mean-minded anti-Americanism fed by the contrast between the abundant wealth of the United States and our own threadbare poverty.

Then came the Korean invasion, and suddenly all was changed. Our perspective was transformed. Until then, Europe and its problems were still the centre of our world, with the United States on the periphery. Important decisions were still made in Paris or London, even if the Americans dictated what they should be. Now the conflict appeared global. Suddenly we became aware of the Pacific – a region hitherto the concern of specialists. In a political Copernican revolution, the centre of the world shifted almost overnight to Washington, the imperial capital to which European statesmen had now to go cap in hand; even British statesmen, even eventually an ailing and almost senile Winston Churchill. It was a development equally unacceptable to the Left and the Right in British politics, but the illusions of both were to be destroyed in November 1956. The left-wing belief in an essentially benign Soviet Union was shattered by the Soviet invasion of Hungary, while right-wing confidence in a still powerful and independent British Empire did not survive the fiasco at Suez.

The second result of the Korean War was the militarization of NATO. George Kennan and others look back on this as a terrible and unnecessary error, but at the time it came to many of us as a relief. Now we knew where we were – back in the wartime world that had shaped my generation and where, in a perverse kind of way, we felt at home. It was so much easier to go back to a familiar confrontation than forward into an unknown chaos. We felt heroic again. Generals emerged from obscurity and reassembled their staffs; armourers throve, even if the economy as a whole did not; and the apparatus of 'civil defence', protection against air raids that had served us so well during the last war, gallantly faced the almost unimaginable challenges of the next. I do not think that historians or military analysts have ever fully appreciated this recidivist element in the formation of NATO. I suspect that the situation was very much the same in the Soviet Union.

I suppose that it was as part of this social re-mobilization that the University of London decided, in 1953, to invent a subject called 'War Studies' and put me in charge of it. But with that appointment, what had previously been just a troubled background to my life became the foreground, and with the simultaneous emergence of thermonuclear weapons my new topic took on an urgency and a complexity such as the sponsors of my subject in the university could never have foreseen. The death of Stalin and the emergence of a more conciliatory Soviet government created a further complicating dimension, and I found myself one of the small group of people in my country outside official circles discussing the problems that were to fill most of our lives for the next forty years: how to avoid nuclear war but at the same time credibly to threaten it; how to maintain effective armed forces on ever-decreasing defence budgets; how to preserve the credibility of the American nuclear guarantee to Western Europe; how to develop a mean-ingful dialogue with the Soviet Union over the control or reduction of nuclear weapons; and, assuming that what Winston Churchill termed a 'balance of terror' could be preserved, how to manage the affairs of the world so that the former colonies of European Empires did not gravitate naturally, as Khrushchev hoped and believed that they would, into the Soviet camp.

It was out of these initial discussions that the Institute for Strategic Studies was born, and it was on behalf of, and as a missionary for the Institute that I paid my first visit to the United States in the spring of 1960. Here comes another snapshot; this time in full colour. It was of a Washington that was now a *military* capital. There were almost more uniforms on the streets than I remembered in wartime London. The mood was defiantly militaristic. On my first night in the dining-room of my hotel a male-voice choir gave a spirited rendering of the Battle-Hymn of the Republic; and when they belted out the lines

As He died to make men holy
Let us live to make men free

there was an electric excitement in the air that I found terrifying. This, I thought, was what Europe must have been like before 1914. Even so must Englishmen have belted out 'Land of Hope and Glory', and Germans 'The Watch on the Rhine'. This seemed a people who, in spite of the Second World War and Korea, had not really experienced war, and who found the prospect an invigorating challenge. It was in just such an atmosphere, I thought, that wars began.

I was even more alarmed when a few days later I went to California. At the Stanford Research Institute I sat in on a seminar on 'Soviet Intentions' in which the speaker gave an expert analysis first, of the tenets of Marxist-Leninism and then of nuclear weapon technology. From these premises he derived the apparently incontrovertible conclusion that Soviet nuclear surprise-attack was inevitable within the next few months, if not indeed the next few weeks. When I suggested that some knowledge of Russian history might also be relevant, not least of their experiences during the past forty years, I was wondered at like a man from the moon. Next day at RAND I attended a talk by the ineffable Hermann Kahn about nuclear war-fighting which froze the marrow in my bones. Driving me back to my hotel afterwards, my companion gestured towards the conurbation of Los Angeles and said in an off-hand way, 'I suppose that after a nuclear strike it would only take about ten years to rebuild this'. No doubt, I said to myself, if you really wanted to rebuild it; but you would never, ever, be able to rebuild or recreate everything that I knew and valued in my own country and my own continent. I began to wonder who was actually in charge of the engine to which we in Western Europe had coupled our train.

It is important to recall quite how worrying those years were; the years, roughly between the launching of Sputnik in 1957 and the Cuba Missile crisis of 1962. Behind the technological hubris of California, behind all the gung-ho bravado of Washington, there was evident in the United States a deep visceral fear. Not only did the Soviets seem to have drawn level with thermonuclear weapons, but the launching of the Sputnik space satellite, followed by the achievement of Yuri Gagarin, suggested that they were ahead with space technology as well. Albert Wohlstetter and his colleagues at RAND were demonstrating the technical feasibility of a crippling Soviet 'first-strike', and what was technically feasible seemed politically probable. Khrushchev was testing Western nerves over West Berlin. The 'wars of national liberation' that were erupting all over the world seemed easy meat for Soviet penetration and propaganda – especially in Latin America, where Fidel Castro was defiantly thumbing his nose at the power of the United States. Works were appearing with such portentious titles as 'Can the West Survive?' It was in this atmosphere that John F. Kennedy was running for the presidency, and his campaign literature did little to discourage such fears.

What about the Russians – or rather, what did *I* know and think about the Russians? (As an old-fashioned historian I still thought of them as Russians rather than Soviets.) Here I have only one snapshot, and that is of the Pugwash conferences – in particular, the first that I attended, at Stowe, Vermont, in 1961. No doubt with Kennedy's encouragement, the West fielded a strong team: from the States George Kistiakowski, Hans Bethe, Leo Szilard, Henry Kissinger, Robert Bowie; from Britain John Cockcroft, William Penney, Solly Zuckerman and Patrick Blackett. The Soviet team were no doubt equally eminent, but for the most part seemed defensive and bewildered, out of their depth and their element. Understanding only their own language, they huddled round their interpreters. When they spoke at all, it was clearly to previously prepared briefs, which did nothing to advance the dialogue. The running was made by a small group of obvious apparatchiks whose academic credentials were obscure but whose objective was clear: to ensure that the final communique of the conference should advance a world-orchestrated Soviet 'Peace Offensive'. This group included some of the nastiest, most ruthless and intellectually dishonest men that I have ever met, and the encounter did me a world of good. I realized for the first time what we were up against. What alarmed me was not so much their intentions, which I was still prepared to believe, perhaps rather naively, were fundamentally defensive: it was the patent impossibility of doing business with them. Their minds seemed as hermetically sealed as their country. That was what made them so dangerous.

But I have another snapshot relevant to the East–West confrontation of those years, and that is of the Berlin that I visited in 1959 and 1960. The Wall was not yet built, and one passed easily from West Berlin to the East. The contrast between them was one not so much between freedom and oppression as between wealth and desperate poverty. West Berlin, sustained by Western capital, was booming, with the Kurfürstendamm bustling like the Champs-Elysées, and exciting new buildings rising on every side. In the East, behind the garish façade of the Stalinallee, the bomb-damage had barely been cleared. Rebuilding, where it had occurred at all, was shoddy and already deteriorating. Surviving ruins were camouflaged with huge red banners bearing political slogans. If Berlin was like this, I thought, what must be the state of the other cities in the DDR – and of the economy in general? No wonder the flow of refugees from the East through Berlin was becoming a flood. To us, West Berlin might appear a vulnerable hostage, but to the Russians it must feel like a stiletto in the heart of their most vulnerable possession. This also, I thought, was the way in which wars start.

Behind Khrushchev's bluster, therefore, perhaps the Russians felt as vulnerable as the Americans, and there seemed no easy way out of the dilemma they faced over Berlin. In fact there was one; so easy as to be quite shocking. It was to build a wall; and this they did in August 1961. I suspect that all Western political leaders realized that the purpose of the wall was purely defensive, but none of them dared say so out loud. As a result it was seen throughout the West as a humiliating defeat. At a conference in Bonn a few months later I found my hitherto docile and co-operative German colleagues raging at what they saw as American betrayal. In New York a sophisticated journalist took me out to dinner, drew a highly dubious comparison with the Danzig crisis of 1939, and assured me that this time the United States would not let us down. Then came the Cuba Missile crisis, when for the first and only time, like many other people, I felt for a few hours a sense of pure dread.

Enough has been written about the Cuba Missile crisis, which seems to grow in significance the more we know about it. I would make only two points. One, I doubt whether it could have been so peacefully resolved if the building of the Wall had not effectively removed Berlin from the Soviet agenda. Second, its resolution reassured both the protagonists – and, I would add, their allies – that in spite of appearances sensible people were in charge on both sides; and, on our side, I would add, people with some sense of history. I have some professional doubts about Barbara Tuchman's interpretation of the 1914 crisis in *The Guns of August*, but it was exactly the book that I would wish President Kennedy to have been reading during the summer of 1962. A salutary flood of realism cooled the fevers of the past five years, and the Superpowers gradually settled down to a *modus vivendi* that would last for another fifteen.

During those years – say 1963 to 1978 – academics like myself were engaged in endless conferences about arms control and extended deterrence that kept us out of mischief but had no evident effect on events in the real world. In the United States, serious decision-makers were increasingly concerned with the tragic adventure of Vietnam, which destroyed the American hubris that had so worried me in 1960, as effectively as the First World War had destroyed that of Europe in 1914. It was a tragedy from which we Europeans kept a prudent distance. That experience, and its appalling domestic consequences, made American foreign policy conservative and cautious; qualities matched, fortunately, by that of the Soviet Union. There the rise of an antagonistic communist China; the failure of their intervention in the Third World to pay the hoped-for dividends; the ageing of the *apparat* and the growing difficulties of managing their economy; all this made the Soviet leadership apparently willing partners in Henry Kissinger's plans essentially to maintain the status quo. So it was that, almost unnoticed by the Superpowers, the Europeans were able to take the initiative for the first time since the 1940s.

By 'the Europeans' I mean of course the Germans. About the marginalization of my own country during those years, partly because of its too close – indeed almost supine – identification with the United States, partly because of its hesitant wooing of the European Community, I could give another long, sad lecture; watching, as I did, the action shifting irrevocably from London to Brussels, Paris and Bonn. It was from the Bonn of Chancellor Willi Brandt that the initiative came for *Ostpolitik*, the reconciliation of the two halves of Germany and the two halves of Europe on the basis of the recognition of a territorial status quo that had remained stable for twenty-five years and that no one any longer had the capacity, even if they had the will, to change. There seemed little enthusiasm in the State

Department for the treaties whose recognition of the DDR, and affirmation of the frontiers of Central Europe effectively concluded the unfinished business of the Second World War; nor for the Conference on Security and Co-operation in Europe and the 'Helsinki Process' that it set on foot. It was widely seen in Washington as a victory for the Soviets and accepted only with grudging acquiescence. In any case during those years American attention was occupied elsewhere; with the final agonies in Vietnam, with the Arab–Israeli conflict, above all with the domestic turmoil of the Watergate scandal. As for the Russians, they naturally welcomed a territoral settlement that apparently gave them all that they had fought for; while of course they had no intention of observing the conditions of free political, economic and social intercourse that were stipulated in 'Basket Three'.

None the less, Helsinki began a process that, by easing communication between the two halves of Europe, was gradually to undermine, first Soviet control of its satellites, and then the legitimacy of the Soviet regime itself. In spite of all that their governments could do to prevent it, the peoples of Eastern Germany and the other Warsaw Pact powers became increasingly open to Western influence and resentful of the regimes that were denying them the consumer satisfactions of the West; consumer satisfactions that probably bulked larger in their eyes than political liberties. My chief memory of these years is of the increasing number of students and professors coming to our own universities from Eastern Europe, with whom we were developing close personal and professional links. Dissidence in Poland and Hungary became almost respectable, while even the imprisoned Czechs heroically flourished their Charter 77. At the same time in Western Europe communist parties had either become insignificant or, as in Italy, were being peacefully reconciled to the democratic process. The only remaining Marxists, it was said with only a little exaggeration, were to be found in American universities. But perhaps my most significant recollection is of a seminar at Oxford at the end of the 1970s at which our economists analysed, to our growing amazement, the appalling and apparently irredeemable morass into which the economy of the Soviet Union appeared to be sinking. From the point of view of many if not most Europeans, things seemed to be going remarkably well.

From the United States, however, the view was significantly different. I was astounded when I visited this country in 1979 to find an atmosphere of almost apocalyptic gloom. This arose from much the same visceral fears as had been prevalent twenty years earlier, but this time they were unrelieved by the gung-ho bravado that had so struck me on my first visit to Washington.

There were clearly multiple reasons for this. The humiliations of Vietnam and Watergate still cast long shadows. The leadership provided by President Carter appeared uncertain and incoherent. Abroad, not only had the whole structure of security that the Americans had erected in the Persian Gulf been demolished by the Iranian revolution, but the United States itself had been humiliated by the imprisonment of its diplomatic staff and, even worse, by the failure of the attempt to rescue them. And then, finally, the Russians invaded Afghanistan. In Europe, this was seen as a sign of failure – a desperate attempt to keep a rebellious satellite in order. In Britain, where we had our own experiences of trying to subdue the Afghanistanis, we rather gloated. But the apprehensive geopoliticians in Washington saw it as the first stage of a plot to dominate if not overrun the whole of the Middle East and establish a 'warm water port' on the Indian Ocean. 'Do you know what the Russians are doing in Afghanistan?' one of them asked us at a Ditchley Conference. 'They are *building roads!*' We were not so impressed as he would have wished.

The Russians, it must be said, had not been behaving well. It became increasingly clear that they regarded *détente* with the United States – or as they preferred to call it, 'peaceful co-existence' – not, as did Henry Kissinger, as a Metternichian structure for the maintenance of the status quo, but as a continuation of the ideological struggle by other means. They did not cease their intervention, whether directly or by proxy, in the Third World, particularly in Africa. They had proved highly unreliable partners in the management of. the Arab–Israeli crisis of 1973; and above all, they showed themselves entirely unresponsive to American attempts to achieve a balance in nuclear weapons, let alone to reduce them. To all appearances they were still implacably bent on changing the global 'correlation of forces', and American weakness seemed to be making it easier for them to do so.

Thus there developed what has been called 'The Second Cold War', and it is a period on which I still look back with rueful amazement. The difference in perceptions was not a simple transatlantic one. There were powerful voices in the United States – that of George Kennan notable among them – who contested the views of the Committee on the Present Danger. In Europe the dangers of the growth of the Soviet nuclear arsenal was fully appreciated in governing circles, but their apprehensions were not widely shared. The gap between popular and official perceptions in Europe was revealed during the INF controversy which raged throughout the first half of the 1980s. In this I found myself fighting a war on two fronts. To my deep regret I found myself on the opposite side to those of my friends in the United States whose views I most deeply respected, in particular Paul Nitze and Albert Wohlstetter. Their analysis of Soviet military strength and the likelihood that they might use it, if not to attack, then to 'blackmail' the

United States and its European allies seemed to me to hark back to the worst fantasies of the early 1960s. In Britain, on the other hand, I found myself locked in combat with the Campaign for Nuclear Disarmament, which had risen with renewed strength, captured the political opposition in Britain and Germany, and virtually dominated opinion in the Netherlands. The fact that cruise- missiles were installed at Greenham Common, just over the hill from where I live in Berkshire, lent for me a certain piquancy to the situation.

In the United States the strength of European opposition to the installation of cruise-missiles, and the increasing hostility to the unilateralism of the Reagan administration, was seen as evidence of 'Finlandization', of a weakened Europe submitting to Soviet dictation, and I found it extraordinarily difficult to persuade people that exactly the opposite was the case. It was because so many of us in Europe no longer saw the Soviet Union as a threat that we saw no point in the installation of cruise-missiles. The rigorous analysis of the nuclear balance that justified their introduction was well above the head of the average voter. It was in any case no longer easy to persuade the electorate to accept an American leadership that had been solicited and welcomed a generation earlier when we really had been alarmed by Soviet power. This time indeed the threat seemed to come from the United States.

And then, suddenly, it all ended.

What is there to say about the conclusion of the Cold War? In one way at least it was highly satisfactory: we can all claim credit for it. American 'hawks' can maintain that President Reagan had a hidden agenda: his arms build-up and the Strategic Defense Initiative was deliberately designed to persuade the Soviet leadership that they could never maintain strategic equality, let alone achieve strategic dominance. European 'doves' respond that it was the exposure of the Soviet Empire to Western influence and Western models – an exposure greatly assisted, if not initiated, by the Helsinki Process – that made the failure of the Soviet system so blatantly clear that its implosion was only a matter of time. Generations of historians will probably be occupied debating this; but what is beyond debate is the achievement of President Reagan in restoring American self-confidence. This, admittedly, was partly done by a huge investment in military strength from which the American economy has yet to recover; but even more it was through the force of a warm, confident, and attractive personality. In this respect a valuable analogy can be drawn with the achievement of Franklin Delano Roosevelt in the 1930s, but when I do so it is not clear whether I make more enemies among the Republicans or the Democrats. I must admit that I met Reagan only once, when he came to London and delivered a speech in the Guildhall. What he said was largely balderdash – indeed, total balderdash; but he moved us all to happy tears – all of us, including me.

So all credit to Reagan for his part in ending the Cold War. But for the confidence he had built up among the American people, he could never have persuaded them to accept the bona fides of Mikhail Gorbachev and the honourable surrender that he offered. As for that even more remarkable man Gorbachev, I met him when he came to London in 1984 and persuaded my own Prime Minister – no mean feat – that she could do business with him. Like everyone else, I marvelled that such an intelligent, dynamic and independently minded individual could have not only survived but prospered in the world of the grey apparatchiks I had met at Pugwash. That two such remarkable men should have appeared simultaneously on the world scene seemed better luck than we altogether deserved.

I have one final snapshot in my album. In February 1996 I visited Singapore, where the university authorities briefed me there about the courses that they were initiating with the University of Hanoi: *Management Studies*. In Hanoi!

I then knew that we really had won the Cold War.

1945–1995: *Fifty Years of European Peace*

It seems fitting that we should today be celebrating not the end of a war, but the beginning of a peace; the longest period of unbroken peace that Europe has ever known, and one that looks set to continue for many years yet. It would seem equally appropriate that, while we are celebrating the skill of the generals, the courage of the armies, the resolution of the peoples and the wisdom of the political leadership that gave us the victory, we should not forget the diplomats whose professional expertise ensured that that victory should establish the foundation for two generations of peace, rather than, like that of 1918, laying a powder trail for yet a third destructive war. After all, we venerate the wisdom of Metternich, Castlereagh and Talleyrand, the architects of a European concert that played in harmony of a kind for forty years. We applaud the skill and restraint through which Bismarck gave Europe a further generation of peace after the Wars of German Unification. Diplomatic historians (now about the only people who remember it) admire the solidity of the structure erected by the Congress of Berlin in 1878 that kept the peace in Eastern Europe for a further thirty years; while the architects of the Versailles and associated treaties of 1919 are quite reasonably reviled for the mess that they made of the peace settlement after the First World War. Should we not therefore give credit where credit is due – to the statesmen and their professional advisers who crafted the peace settlement of 1945, which has lasted until the present day?

The trouble is that there *was* no peace settlement in 1945. Arguably no peace settlement was made until November 1990 forty-five years later, when, during that brief window of opportunity between the reunification of Germany and the disintegration of the Soviet Union, the representatives of the former belligerent powers again assembled in Paris to confirm a settlement of the frontier disputes in Eastern and Central Europe that had been the immediate cause of the Second World War. Tidy-minded historians – and almost all historians are tidy-minded – can be grateful that one turbulent chapter in European history was thus concluded before another, far more complex, opened before them. In the perspective of that chapter the year 1945 seems only a suspension of activity, a chord awaiting resolution for a further half-century. It did not bring a settlement; but it did, mercifully, bring peace that made a settlement ultimately possible. The diplomats of the time should therefore be given the credit, if not for building a new peace, then at least for averting another war.

It is this unique situation that makes any attempt to compare the events of 1945 with those of 1918, or 1814, or indeed any previous war-termination in modern history, rather a waste of time. I can think of no previous major European conflict that was not concluded by a formal peace settlement within a year or so of termination of hostilities; settlements regarded as convenient milestones in the unfolding history of the continent. Certainly in 1945 the diplomats saw it as their job to fashion such another peace settlement, and studied previous examples to see how, or how not, to do it. 1919, of course, was seen as an example to avoid: this time an unreconciled enemy must not be left with the capacity to recover. Germany should be, if not split up again as many of her enemies desired, at least thoroughly debellated. Further, whatever their differences, the victorious allies had to remain united. The leaders of the United States realized that their country could not afford once again to turn its back on the outside world, but had to create a mechanism for the preservation of world order in which America would this time play a leading role.

For the British at least, 1814 seemed a desirable model. The arguments of its later detractors, that the architects of the Vienna settlement had unwisely attempted to repress the growing forces of nationalism rather than accommodate them, seemed rather less convincing once people had experienced the conflicts which those forces had unleashed. What did seem admirable about the settlement was the clear-sightedness with which its makers had recognized the danger which the dynamic power of revolutionary France had posed to the peace of Europe and redrawn the map to ensure that this should not happen again, without attempting the impossible task of eliminating France as a major power. If this model were followed the United States would have to play the part that Britain had in 1814, of the off-shore power whose wealth had made victory possible and whose support would be needed to ensure the stability of the settlement. The Russian role was unchanged: once again, Russia was the nation principally responsible for the defeat of the aggressor's armies, but one whose power and possible ambitions still needed to be guarded against in the creation of any new balance. Britain would now play the role of Austria, with Anthony Eden as her Metternich. The only trouble was the defeated adversary. There were no tame Bourbons in Germany to restore to their throne, and no Talleyrand to negotiate on their behalf. The German State had ceased to exist, and there were fundamental disagreements among the victorious allies as to the form in which it should be recreated.

The conditions for a stable settlement based on a new balance of power were in many ways more favourable in 1945 than they had been in 1918. Then, inevitable conflicts of interest had been compounded and made irreconcilable by the pressures of angry public opinion. The French would be satisfied with nothing less than a Carthaginian peace, but one which they did not have the power to enforce without the support of Britain and the United States. In the United States, Congress rejected all the responsibilities that President Wilson had assumed on behalf of the American people and showed themselves concerned only to recover their war debts. In Britain a fickle public opinion veered rapidly from blind hostility to all things German to a sentimental desire for reconciliation, combined with a total indifference to an Eastern Europe where the newly created nation-states were a natural prey to a revived Germany and Russia unless they received explicit support from the West. As for Germany, an irreconcilable section of public opinion refused to accept that they had been defeated at all, and never forgave the messengers who told them that they had. With the partial exception of England, the statesmen of 1814 had been able to pursue balance-of-power politics without too much concern for domestic opinion. When the Germans showed signs of making trouble, Metternich slapped down on them the Carlsbad Decrees. But it is hard to know what Metternich, Castlereagh and Talleyrand could have done in 1919, at the head of ships that would not answer the helm and whose crews were on the verge of mutiny.

In 1945 public opinion was far more biddable. The Germans were in no position to object to any settlement imposed on them. Soviet public opinion is a matter of guess-work, but it is unlikely that there was much objection to the Carthaginian peace that Stalin showed himself anxious to impose on the people who had caused so much suffering to the Soviet Union. The Americans, although they wanted to get their boys back home as fast as possible, accepted their inevitable involvement in and responsibility for a settlement in Europe, while in Britain political leaders were given a very free hand by an electorate primarily concerned with domestic affairs, and whose main interest in foreign policy was that the German menace should be scotched for good and all. So the difficulties that confronted the diplomats in 1945 were not, as in 1918, largely home-grown, and their failures were not the result of their own ineptitude. They arose from the intractability of the situation with which they were confronted.

The main problem of course – give or take a generation of revisionism and counter-revisionism – was the attitude of the Soviet Union. There had never been any illusion that Stalin would be an easy partner. The 'Uncle Joe' image current in public opinion, and encouraged for wartime purposes, had not percolated into Whitehall, whose officials observed with some concern how Stalin seemed to be charming Winston Churchill as effectively as Hitler had charmed Neville Chamberlain. Stalin had always been quite frank about his war aims. In November 1941, with the Germans literally at the gates of Moscow, he had made it clear to Anthony Eden that a victorious Soviet Union would be content with nothing less than the East-European frontiers of the former Tsarist Empire. Three years later in October 1944 he had negotiated with Churchill a very specific agreement as to how far Soviet influence should extend westward beyond those frontiers. The Yalta Conference the following spring did little more than recognize a *fait accompli*, accomplished by the Soviet armed forces that already stood along Germany's frontiers, and by the prior agreement reached by the European Advisory Commission on occupation zones within Germany itself. A well-merited sense of deep obligation to the Poles made Churchill do his best to elicit promises of fair treatment for them from Stalin, but they were promises that the West could do nothing to enforce. The British government realized very clearly that they could influence events in Eastern Europe, in so far as they could influence them at all, only through maintaining good relations with Moscow, and this was one reason among others why such good relations had if possible to be preserved.

If there was an illusion about Stalin in diplomatic quarters in 1945, it was that he could be dealt with on a simple basis of *Realpolitik*, on the assumption that he would define and defend his own interests but in his turn respect those of the other actors on the international scene; that he was a statesman in the mould of Metternich rather than of Lenin – certainly not of Trotsky. Up to a point this was true. His invitation to the British to establish bases on the mainland of Western Europe, even if not seriously meant, indicated an awareness of the value in retaining British co-operation in the containment of German power. But if his tactics and strategy were those of a *Realpolitiker*, his ultimate objectives were those of all Marxist-Leninists – the destruction of the capitalist world-order and the triumph of the workers of the world under the leadership of the Soviet Union. For him and his associates, the Soviet Union had been in a state of war with the West ever since the 1917 Revolution. Fascism was for him only a particularly menacing form of capitalism, and he had found it necessary to ally with the class enemy in order to destroy it. Its destruction none the less left the main body of enemy forces intact: sooner or later he believed that they would resume their hostile activities against the Soviet Union, if only to stave off the inevitability of their own collapse. Britain and the United States had been temporary if necessary allies – and highly unsatisfactory allies at that – but they were permanent enemies. With the end of the war, and the final elimination of Germany, there was no reason why they should not now be treated as such.

It is possible that the Foreign Office – not an environment in which ideology is encouraged to flourish – did not take these long-term objectives seriously enough, whereas in the United States they were perhaps taken too seriously. But the *Realpolitiker* in Stalin did make it possible to do a limited amount of business with him. His short-term objective in 1945 was almost certainly compatible with that of the West – a period of stability, to enable the Soviet Union to recover from her enormous losses. The instructions received by the Communist parties in Western Europe, somewhat to their consternation, was to co-operate with the bourgeois parties and not cause undue trouble, while in Eastern Europe at least a simulacrum of a multi-party system was allowed to camouflage the reality of tight and brutal communist party control. With half of Germany occupied by Soviet troops, the rest of Western Europe economically shattered and the United States once more abandoning, to all appearances, her involvement in Europe, there was no longer any immediate threat from the West. Perhaps a truce might have been preserved, at least for a few years longer, even if it did not lead to permanent *détente*, had it not been for the second intractible factor; the problem of Germany.

As we have seen, the fundamental difference between 1814 and 1945 – indeed, between the end of every major war in the history of Europe and 1945 – is that there was no enemy left to negotiate with. There was no Talleyrand to play so skilfully upon the rivalries of his former enemies that a chastened Germany could be peacefully re-incorporated into the European political system, and even if there had been such an aspiring figure there was no Germany left for him to represent. This is not the place to discuss whether the allies were indeed wise to prosecute the war to the point of unconditional surrender, and to refuse their support to those resistance-leaders who offered themselves as an alternative regime. For the moment, I would say only that I find entirely legitimate the scepticism general in the Foreign Office at the time, as to how far those leaders, however heroic, did offer a serious alternative to the Nazi regime; how far that alternative – overwhelmingly right-wing in its personnel – would have been acceptable to the Soviet Union; and what conditions they would have demanded, not least in respect of Germany's eastern frontiers. Their supporters often visualize – as many of them did themselves – that they would have concluded a peace with the Western allies alone, to enable them to fight more stubbornly on the Eastern Front; but anyone who seriously believes in such a possibility has no conception of what public opinion in this country, to say nothing of that in occupied Europe, would have been prepared to tolerate in 1944–45.

Rightly or wrongly, such a *renversement des alliances* in 1945 was politically inconceivable. It was to take five years, and a very different Germany, before it was possible even to contemplate it.

So the war ended without even a puppet German government to do the conquerors' bidding, and the conquerors had to do the job themselves. Even if Stalin had been far more willing to co-operate than he actually was, it is hard to see how the problem of Germany could have been solved by any means other than virtual partition. In the first place, Stalin was implacable in his determination to extract every scrap of economic retribution that he could from his defeated enemy; not only to replenish his own exhausted economy, but permanently to weaken an adversary whose capacity for rapid economic recovery was a matter of very recent record. The West, however – or at any rate the British – had learned rather a different lesson from the experience of the 1920s; that the prosperity of Western Europe was indivisible, and their own economy could not flourish if their neighbour was bankrupt. If the shattered West-European economies were ever to recover, the economy of Germany had to recover with them – a lesson not lost on General Marshall when he travelled through the devastated continent in the spring of 1947 and saw with his own eyes the need for a massive transfusion of American resources if society in Western Europe was to avoid total collapse. Between the objective of keeping Germany permanently weak and the desire to build her up as a necessary economic partner, it is hard to see how any compromise would have been possible.

Beyond this, there was a geopolitical zero-sum game. Germany's central position in Europe and her huge economic potential – to say nothing of her all-too-well-proven military capacity – made her an asset that neither side could afford to lose. For Stalin the restoration of a capitalist, Western-oriented Germany would simply recreate the threat of the 1930s. After all, it was out of the bowels of just such a society that militaristic Fascism had emerged, and it might well do so again. He could trust only a Germany that he controlled, and that meant one where, as in Eastern Europe, power was effectively in the hands of the Communist Party. But for the Western powers, communism was frighteningly strong in Western Europe already. Soviet control over Germany would effectively mean that Stalin would dominate the entire continent without the Soviet armed forces having to move a single man or a single tank. As for an independent, 'neutral' Germany of the kind after which German Social Democrats hankered for a full decade – that aspiration for 'disengagement in Europe' over which so much ink was spilled in the 1950s – that would be a recipe either for continuing covert intervention by both sides which might well lead to a re-run, on a far larger and more dangerous scale, of the Spanish Civil War; or an opportunity for Germany to re-establish herself as a Great Power by playing off each side against the other. It was a dilemma of which European statesmen in 1945 were well aware, but they had no idea how to solve it.

It was ultimately far simpler to leave matters as they were, and I suspect that most policy-makers in London knew it, even if they did not say so or write it down. There was no enthusiasm in either Western or Eastern Europe for the recreation of a United Germany and there was no will whatever for an armed confrontation with the Soviet Union in order to create one. For both Stalin and the West, the continued division of Germany was so obviously the best practicable solution to the problem, that subsequent generations may well wonder why it could not have been agreed with very much less fuss, let alone armed confrontation. Indeed it might well have been agreed, had it not been for the anomalous situation in Berlin, and the brinkmanship adopted by Stalin to compel the Western allies to abandon their rights in the city. That event, more than any other, was responsible for transforming the Soviet Union, in the eyes of the West, from a difficult but necessary partner into a potential enemy, and the Germans from former enemies into potential and necessary allies. It also did more than anything else to transform the United States from a sympathetic and generous, though still somewhat detached, former ally into a partner whose zeal for confrontation was to prove almost an embarrassment even to those who had most urgently solicited it.

Even if, as revisionist historians claim, Soviet intransigence should be interpreted as a purely defensive mechanism against the invasive forces of American capitalism, and even if the West had been more sympathetic to Soviet interest than they actually were – and it is hard to see, reading the documents of those sterile conferences of 1946, how we *could* have been any more sympathetic – it is now difficult to visualize any different outcome other than the division of Germany and with it the division of Europe; or one that could have provided a more stable basis for peace.

Let us remember what the two World Wars had been fought about – or at least, what this country and our European neighbours had gone to war about. In both cases we went to war to contain the power of Germany, as we had fought in previous generations to contain the power of France. Certainly in the First World War there was also much talk about defending the rights of small nations, and indeed we did our best to establish them at the end of it. In the Second we spoke about the destruction of Fascism and the restoration of democracy, and, again, we did our best after the war to live up to our promises. But ultimately in both wars Britain fought, and the British people were mobilized to fight, for the destruction of German power. The rights of small nations could not have been established after the

First, and democracy could not have been restored after the Second, until that had been achieved. There was much concern among intellectual elites in both wars, not least in the Foreign Office itself, about Britain's war aims, though it must be admitted that much of it arose from a desire to enlist the support of the United States. But the mass of the people in this country in both wars were fighting simply to beat the Germans, and that was war-aim enough. Churchill struck exactly the right note when he informed the House of Commons, when he addressed it for the first time as Prime Minister, that his administration had only one war aim – Victory.

For the destruction of German power was the necessary basis for any peace in Europe – at least any peace that would be in the least compatible with British traditions, sentiments, ideals and interests. A new, sardonic generation of historians is suggesting that we would have been far wiser to have accepted in 1940 a *Pax Germanica* that would have relinquished control of the Continent to the Third Reich in return for being allowed to keep our Empire. It is a scenario that I see little point in exploring, except to wonder for how long, if Germany had controlled the Continent, we would have been allowed to keep our Empire – or indeed have been left effectively to govern ourselves at all. If Germany had been governed by a bourgeois democratic regime that shared our values, such as that which rules it today, it is conceivable that we might have yielded parity, indeed primacy, to it as equably as we did to the United States; but this was not the case even in the First World War, let alone the Second. In the First World War the dominant elements in the German government were not interested in a 'peaceful settlement' in any sense in which we understood it: for many of them war and conquest was an end in itself. In Hitler this philosophy was overt, and only blind wishful thinking prevented us from seeing this from the very beginning. And Hitler would not have achieved the success that he did had he not reflected a mood and a philosophy in German society as a whole to an extent that it has long been rather unfashionable for us to admit.

So one necessary element in the fifty-year peace that we have enjoyed has been the destruction of German power; much as the long peace that succeeded the Napoleonic wars rested at least in part on the destruction of French power. Those who now fear that a reunited Germany will once more threaten Europe are making much the same mistake as those who believed that Napoleon III of France would prove a reincarnation of his formidable uncle. Even if he had the will to do so, French society would no longer provide the armies and the ideology to attempt a reconquest of Europe, and German society is even less likely to do so today.

Secondly, the destruction of German power made possible the solution of the problem that had been the immediate occasion of the Second World

War; that of Germany's eastern borders. Even if a democratic regime had survived in Germany between the wars, and even if one had been effectively recreated after 1945, the stubborn dilemma would have remained, how to reconcile the claims of the Germans to territories which they had learned to regard as their historic heartlands with the ethnic distribution of populations in those regions, and the need for Poland to have access to the sea. The problem of the Germans in the Sudetenland was also one that would not go away. These problems were settled – perhaps finally – by the application by the Soviet Union, with the tacit approval of the Western allies, of Bismarckian blood and iron. Poles were evicted from the regions of the Ukraine, Ruthenia and Belorussia that they had occupied after 1921, while Germans were evicted, not only from the Sudetenland and the regions of West Prussia and Silesia conquered for them by Frederick the Great and his successors, but from the purely German lands of East Prussia. It was certainly *Realpolitik* at its most outrageous. It would not have worked had not the Soviet Union possessed the power and the will not only to enforce such a solution, but to maintain it over two generations until the wounds inflicted by this brutal surgery had healed. The presence of millions of these 'expellees' with votes in a democratic West Germany made it impossible for any West-German government to accept this settlement for a full generation, and the existence of this irredentism was a very significant factor in making Soviet domination more acceptable to both Poles and Czechs. It was only twenty-five years later that a German government came to power that was able, with sufficient public support, to move towards acceptance of this settlement and sign treaties effectively recognizing the status quo.

So the peace rested upon the destruction of German power and the settlement of the issues about which she was most likely to exercise that power. That in its turn depended on the continuing Soviet occupation of Eastern Europe. It is unpleasant to have to recognize it, but that occupation, with all the injustices and oppression it involved, was none the less a major factor in preserving post-war stability. If the West had successfully rolled back Soviet power, as some considered so desirable in the 1950s, it would only have uncovered all these traditional problems of the extension of German power again to the Baltic, and the revival of the historic antagonisms of Poles against Germans, Germans against Czechs. Recognition of this may have made British policy more acquiescent in the status quo than advocates of democratic values and human rights would have wished. Neville Chamberlain has been understandably criticized for his tactless reference, during the Munich crisis, to quarrels between 'far away people of whom we know nothing'; there was, and remains, resentment that we should have fought allegedly to preserve the independence of Poland against

Germany only to acquiesce in her subordination by an equally evil regime; but the sad fact was that after 1945 there was no desire whatever in this country to go to war to redress injustices in Eastern Europe even if there had been the capacity. And the British government knew this very well.

Can it be said therefore that, in spite of appearances, Soviet power was really a factor of stability in post-war Europe and that we should now recognize it? The answer must be, at best, only up to a point. The jury is still out, but a good case can be made that Stalin was quite prepared to acquiesce in the division of Europe and would have lived happily with this solution. The trouble arose less from Soviet strength than from West-European weakness. Unless the United States could be persuaded to become part of the European balance, the ugly geopolitical fact of Soviet power was bound to evoke constant alarm and apprehension among the weakened and divided nations of Western Europe, and would have done so even if it had been in the hands of a far more friendly and co-operative regime. As it was, the regime was neither friendly nor co-operative. It was the patron of powerful communist parties in the West that were instantly responsive to Soviet political directions, and who profited immensely from the post-war political confusion and economic weakness in their countries. It was in Stalin's interest to keep Western Europe weak and divided, and he had the capacity to do so. It rapidly became clear that the nations of Western Europe could protect their interests only by an unprecedented degree of mutual co-operation, economic and military; and that such co-operation would be insufficient, indeed impossible, without the committed support of the United States. With their instant acceptance of the offer of Marshall Aid, and the patient ground-work that went to the creation of NATO, the British statesmen and diplomats really earned their keep in creating the foundations for a stable peace.

With the establishment of NATO, even though no formal settlement had been reached, a balance of power was established that provided both sides with a framework for the peaceful development of their own societies. When the balance was threatened, it was to be in consequence not of Western but of Soviet fears. The presence of Allied forces and a democratic regime in West Berlin was a constantly destabilizing factor for the Soviet control of East Germany until it was sealed off with the building of the Berlin Wall in 1961. Fears for the solidity of the Warsaw Pact led to the bloody Soviet invasion of Hungary in 1956, and the crushing of Czechoslovakia in 1968. But neither event provoked the West to intervene. With nuclear weapons now in the armouries of both sides, the stakes were too high. The balance of power had become a balance of terror. In any event, the destinies of the former Great Powers of Europe had now been to a large extent taken out of their own hands. They were now either protectorates of the United States or satellites of the Soviet Union, and their fate depended on decisions taken in Washington and Moscow. The task of Western diplomats was now not so much to handle a hostile and suspicious Soviet Union as to cement good relations among themselves and to influence the policies of their friendly Superpower – a Superpower for whom Europe, however important, was only one region to be considered in a global confrontation.

The long peace was thus bought at a price, and one that some critics have thought excessive. Some on the one hand have lamented the militarization of our societies, the development of a 'cold war mentality', and above all the risk of nuclear war that we had to accept in consequence; believing that all this endangered rather than stabilized peace. Others, at a different end of the political spectrum, have complained of our cold-blooded abandonment of Eastern Europe to a regime little better than that from which we had tried to rescue it. Both groups had good cases. But the policies advocated by such critics, however well intentioned, carried with them the risk of destabilizing the structure on which the entire post-war system had been erected – the first by weakening the West's capacity and will to defend itself, the second by provoking a violent reaction from an adversary whose minimal good-will was a condition of maintaining any kind of effective intercourse at all. Between these unacceptable alternatives our leaders have had to navigate, without really having any objective other than to avoid them and to keep the ship afloat. When suddenly the mists lifted and there appeared in sight a destination in whose very existence they had hardly dared to hope, they were as surprised as anyone else. None the less they knew exactly what to do.

If there is a parallel with the events of 1814–15, it is to be sought, not in 1945–46, but in 1989–90, when the statesmen of East and West at last came together to make a settlement on a basis of genuine understanding and justice: restoring a united but chastened Germany to the community of powers, defining the now accepted frontiers of Eastern Europe, and including a now co-operative Russia as a guarantor of the new settlement. In the entire annals of diplomatic history it is hard to find so signal an example of rapid and sensible settlement of disputes that had torn the continent apart for the best part of a century. But could so rapid and just a settlement have been achieved if the ground had not been prepared by so long, and so unjust, a peace?

11

The Ditcheley lecture
1993

Cold War, Chill Peace

Four years ago, as the Berlin Wall crumbled and the Cold War came so miraculously to an end, I was rash enough to conclude an essay with the words: 'As one whose conscious political experience now extends over fifty years I can say that I would rather be living in 1989 than in 1939 – or indeed any date between the two'.[1]

Should I now regret or retract that statement? Do I still feel so confident about the world today as I, and I think most of us, did then?

I am not inclined, at present, either to regret or to retract them. It was a view that would probably have been shared at the time by the overwhelming majority of Europeans, East and West. During the previous half-century we had, most of us, been under dire physical threat. For much of the time during the Second World War a lot of people – very clever, highly motivated people – had been trying very hard to kill me, and I did not like it. Then, after a very brief interval, came the long era of 'nuclear deterrence', when it was impossible for any reasonably well-informed observer to contemplate the risks inherent in the situation without a spasm of visceral terror. These were years in which we worked out our salvation almost literally 'in fear and trembling'. Nobody in their right mind could wish to live through them again.

It would be legitimate, indeed, to extend that nightmare period back for a generation, to 1914, for the two World Wars had a basic continuity. So far as Europe was concerned the two World Wars were really a single Thirty Years' War. In broader historical perspective the years between 1914 and 1989 may come to be seen as ones of continuous major international conflict broken by periods of uneasy truce, not unlike the wars of the French Revolution and Napoleonic conquest between 1793 and 1815; except that in our own time we had to endure not one but two prolonged conflicts with two different major adversaries. Those conflicts shaped the minds, not of one generation, but of three.

Now, like the statesmen gathered at Vienna at the conclusion of the Napoleonic wars, we have to adjust ourselves to an entirely new situation.

[1] Michael Howard, *The Lessons of History* (Clarendon Press, Oxford 1991), p. 5.

An era dominated by major military confrontations has ended. The huge armed forces made necessary by that confrontation are being disbanded, with all the consequent economic disruption and social stress. The political attitudes and social structures shaped by nearly a century of warfare no longer appear to be relevant. The problems we now face arise not from the threat of foreign conquest or hegemony, but from social dislocation on a vast, indeed a global scale; dislocation arising in part from the social and economic results of the wars themselves, but partly from long-term secular trends that we cannot control and to which we can only adjust as best we can.

If we take that analogy seriously, the good news is that after 1815 nearly half a century was to pass before Europe saw another international war, and a century before there was a conflict on anything like so considerable a scale. The bad news is that during those years developments were under way that made the European system increasingly unstable: unstable internally, as industrialization transformed the economies of Western Europe, bringing in its wake growing class-conflict and fear of revolution; externally, as the growth of railways (in particular) created a new major power in the centre of Europe which was to shatter the international system with a new series of wars – wars that began with the Prussian challenge to the Austrian Empire in 1866 and did not really conclude until the defeat and destruction of Nazi Germany in 1945. It would be rash to assert that similar economic and technological changes will not sooner or later transform the underlying power-structure of the world in a way that may have to be tested – as has always been the case in the past – by military conflict. This is a long-term possibility that cannot be lost to sight. But there are shorter-term probabilities that must quite rightly receive our prior attention.

*   *   *   *   *

Before looking at those shorter-term problems, let us consider for a moment the huge conflicts, fought or unfought, that have wracked the world for most of our troubled century. What were they really about? What were the causes for which millions of young men were required to die and as many civilians were required to suffer? The simple answer might be that given to Alice by Humpty-Dumpty: 'Who's to be Master; that's all'. For some – perhaps for most – of the belligerents, the two World Wars were fought simply to prevent Germany achieving a hegemony over Europe, as earlier wars had been fought against France and Spain. Similarly the Cold War was 'fought' to contain Soviet power; not just in Europe but throughout the world. For many of those who fought, or were prepared to fight them, that was probably reason enough, especially during the First

World War. Soldiers fought loyally for their countries, and civilians unquestioningly supported them. For that perhaps rather naive generation, 'King and Country' was in itself a quite sufficient cause for which to fight and if need be die.

We may now look back and condemn, or pity, the frenetic nationalism of the First World War, which saw in the enemy the embodiment of absolute evil and claimed for its own side a monopoly of virtue. But even then the national cause was equated, rightly or wrongly, with a higher morality and could command the loyalty of rational as well as honourable men and women. The young men who then fought and died 'for England' did so because they believed that 'England' embodied certain ideals of liberty and justice and individual freedom; ideals threatened, so they thought, by the jackboot of 'Prussian militarism'. For the Americans of course, the war was ideological from the very beginning. The United States entered the war, after long hesitation, to make the world 'safe for democracy', since only if there was universal democracy could there be universal peace. The Germans for their part were told that a combination of Western decadence and Eastern barbarism threatened their unique culture; a culture rooted in deep historic instincts and finding expression in a State whose leadership demanded from its people total individual subordination and heroic self-sacrifice. It was only after defeat and humiliation in a war that most of them regarded as entirely defensive and 'just', that the Germans came to acquiesce in a regime whose philosophy was an evil caricature of their traditional patriotism; one which denied all individual rights against a State that claimed to embody the general will, whose power was its own justification, and which claimed a mandate to cleanse its own society of those groups it regarded as alien, and to subordinate others it stigmatized as inferior.

It is worth taking a moment to consider the creed of National-Socialism, or as it is more generically known, Fascism, for it is beginning to have uncomfortable resonances for our own times. It was a philosophy that quite consciously rejected the whole tradition of the liberal Enlightenment that had been developing in the West over the past two centuries and for which the liberal democracies of the West continued, however inadequately, to stand. For the rights of the individual, Fascism substituted the authority of the group, and of the Leader who embodied it. For the brotherhood of man it substituted the right of the strong to enslave the weak. For the rule of reason it substituted the primacy of visceral prejudice; and for the vision of peace among nations, it substituted that of perpetual war.

This was not a purely German phenomenon. It was a creed that, appealing as it did to primitive emotions of the nastiest kind, struck a chord in all societies, developed or undeveloped. Unfortunately it still does. There are, and I am afraid always will be, those who are born Fascists. Perhaps most of us are, and have to be educated out of it. But there are those – and the Germans were an example – who have had Fascism thrust upon them through the catastrophic failure of the liberal political and economic ideals derived from the Enlightenment to solve the basic social problems which they brought in their train. Reason might decree that all men should be free to work out their own political and economic salvation, emancipated from traditional religious or hierarchical authority. But what happens when such freedom results, as it did in post-war Germany, in ten million unemployed? Communism might appeal to the proletariat for whom it was designed, but society consists of many more groups than the proletariat. For self-employed business-men; petty-bourgeois employees; small farmers; dispossessed or threatened members of the old ruling classes; for all these people a creed that seemed to defend traditional values in an age of chaotic change; that provided employment and restored their self-respect; that promised the young a life of adventure and excitement, and that clearly identified alien groups, internal or external, as the cause of all their miseries; such a creed had much to recommend it. The price was abdication of independent judgement to an authority that would take all decisions for them; but it was an authority that understood their prejudices and skifully played on them to maintain itself in power. That was Fascism, and it still is. It is a creed that always appeals to misfits; and when a large proportion of society feels itself to be misfits it becomes really dangerous.

But there was another and parallel reaction against the philosophy of freedom. Representative democracy was only one child of the Enlightenment. It had a sibling which, appearing first in the latter days of the French Revolution, was to grow to maturity, after a hefty dose of Hegelian dialectic, as Marxism, and ultimately to achieve power in the Soviet Union and elsewhere as Marxist-Leninism. If Reason enabled man to understand and ultimately to control the processes of Nature, so the argument went, it should no less enable him to understand and control the development of his own society. A combination of historical understanding and scientific analysis showed that the capitalistic system was only a harsh if necessary stage on mankind's road to a communist resolution of all social and political conflicts, and one to be traversed as quickly as possible. Those truly enlightened spirits whose superior insight enabled them to understand the inward meaning of History had not only the right but the duty to take charge of society, and to transform it in accordance with the intrinsic laws of social development which they alone understood. For those who suffered most from the misery and alienation brought about by the early years of industrialization – not just the unemployed but the far larger number of those employed on starvation wages – the promise of communism looked seductive; not so much because it promised Utopia, but because it offered to industrial workers a measure of security that they could never enjoy in a world ruled by market forces. Further – and perhaps even more important – it offered to intellectuals the promise of a world that they believed that they would be able to control.

Thus the Second World War was a war, not simply of nations, but of ideologies, in which the victor would shape the world in his own image. The two branches of the Enlightenment family temporarily sank their differences and united to destroy a creed that threatened them both. Then, as Hitler had always hoped, they turned against one another, and the Cold War began. Because both creeds were international, or rather supranational, each had its adherents in the other's camp. If the Soviets had played their cards more skilfully, they might have had many more. In the immediate aftermath of the Second World War communism offered to many in the West an attractive alternative to the failures of pre-war capitalism – and to many in the rest of the world an even more attractive alternative to pre-war colonialism. As it was, confronted by a regime that had more in common with the worst kind of Czarist oppression than with the Brave New World depicted in Marxist propaganda, the Old Believers in the West, those hapless and hopeful Sorbonne and Oxbridge intellectuals of the 1930s, died out and were not replaced. The new countries of the Third World eventually came to recognize that the Soviet Union was a Great Power like any other, to be exploited for what it was worth, but unable to provide help on a scale even remotely approaching that of the West. And eventually the Old Believers in the Soviet Union itself lost confidence in a regime so patently incapable of living up to the promises of its founders and justifying the terrible sacrifices it had imposed on its peoples by producing effective results.

So Fascism had failed: it had appealed to the sword and had perished by the sword. Marxist-Leninism had equally failed: it had appealed to historical processes that History, in due course, had discredited. Western democracy emerged apparantly triumphant, and at least one American publicist claimed that history had now come to an end.

*   *   *   *   *

Fortunately perhaps for historians, but unfortunately for everyone else, this obituary was premature. The Gibbonian chronicle of the crimes, follies and wickednesses of mankind is continuing uninterrupted, and those who believed that with the defeat of communism these would disappear and that we would see the dawn of yet another New World Order are sadly disillusioned. The failure of rival creeds does not mean that our own is bound to succeed; only that it has been given another chance. Both Fascism and communism emerged in Europe because liberal democracy failed to live up to its expectations. If we fail again, we may expect new and similar challenges, both in our own continent and throughout the world.

But such challenges are bound to recur, if only because the process of change that brought our own Western societies into existence will continue, unendingly, to operate, creating new problems to which we may prove fatally slow to adapt. The fundamental cause, both of the triumphs and of the failures of liberal democracy, has been the continuing impact of the Enlightenment itself. It was this that set on foot the whole process of modernization and industrialization two centuries ago, which continues with unslackening momentum. The Enlightenment taught us that we are free agents, endowed by reason with the capacity to understand the world around us and with the right to shape it in accordance with that under-standing. Over the past two centuries, political and ecclesiastical authorities, social structures, and economic practices that had endured for a thousand years have been called in question, and, as often as not, overthrown; sometimes by violence, more often through a gradual erosion of their credibility. Their place has been taken by societies that have transformed the world; beginning in Europe and North America in the nineteenth century, spreading throughout the globe in the twentieth. They have spanned it with railways and steamships and, ultimately, aircraft. They have created world systems of instant aural and visual communication which have created a single global economy. They have conquered most of the diseases that since the beginning of recorded history have ravaged mankind, and vastly increased the world population as a result. They have created huge cities, providing markets whose demand transformed traditional methods of agriculture, destroying entire rural communities in the process and sending their inhabitants further to swell the populations of the cities. Mankind has struck his tents, in Jan Christian Smuts's wonderful phrase, and is on the march. We have not yet found a resting place.

It is true that in the twentieth century Western societies have overcome many of the problems we had created for ourselves in the nineteenth, and the dire prophecies of Karl Marx and his followers did not come true. Indeed it may well be that posterity will look back on the half-century between 1939 and 1989 as the golden age of capitalism. The war itself solved the problem of unemployment, and the need to maintain social solidarity during that war nurtured a welfare system that underwrote security from the cradle to the grave. Called into being in order to defeat Fascism, the same solidarity had to be maintained to repel Communism. Underwritten by the huge wealth and defended by the military power of the United States, the pluralistic democracies of Western Europe and the Pacific Rim were able to provide their entire populations with a standard of living beyond the wildest imaginings of the most optimistic prophets of the nineteenth century; a model with which the Soviet Union could not begin to compete, and which was the envy – and, increasingly, the despair – of the rest of the world. Apart from the ever-present danger of nuclear war – and not very many people thought about this for very much of the time – it was easy to believe that we had 'got it made'. Politics was simply concerned with the creation and distribution of an unending abundance of goods, both internally within our own societies and globally between North and South. All that seemed necessary for the achievement of global peace and prosperity was the maintenance of full production, and the elimination of a communist threat which as time went on seemed increasingly threadbare. When that happened, surely history was bound to come to an end as the benefits of liberal democracy extended themselves throughout the world?

But it was possible to believe this only for those who lacked any sense of historical perspective. The Enlightenment has from the very beginning brought not stability, but processes that have been the motors of revolutionary change. Communist regimes, whatever their revolutionary professions, have in fact always attempted to restrain the process of change, excluding disruptive Western influence, destroying entrepreneurial talent within their own borders and imposing an artificial stability through totalitarian rule. The process of 'modernization' unleashed and encouraged by the West, on the other hand, is unending and ineluctable. We have seen how in Europe it has destroyed traditional structures – the dominance of an authoritarian Roman Catholic Church, the rule of imperial dynasties and a privileged feudal aristocracy – beyond hope of recall, and brought into being, after many travails, a new mass, egalitarian society which is still far from stable. Throughout the rest of the world, modernization is certainly improving living standards for many; but this is often being achieved at much the same cost in disruption, misery and alienation that characterized our own experiences in Europe a century and a half ago.

These problems are complicated, in what one must still call for lack of any better term the 'Third World', by the difficulty of applying Western-generated political and economic models to non-Western societies. The fact that the communist model has failed is no guarantee that that of the West will necessarily succeed any better; that free-market economies can produce full employment, or that 'human rights' as defined by Western jurists will be compatible with the cohesion developed in other cultures through generations of tribal or familial loyalties. In Asia and Africa today, as in Europe a century ago, improvements in science, medicine and hygiene have produced an increase in population far larger than modern methods of agricultural production can absorb, or the land itself can sustain. The surplus flock to cities whose industries do not need them, and emigrate to wealthier countries who do not want them. But whereas their European counterparts of a hundred years ago could find in the United States an effective safety valve, these new unfortunate 'huddled masses' cannot. Like their European counterparts they are vulnerable to dreams of revolutionary Utopianism; but they are even more vulnerable to the kind of xenophobic nationalism or religious fundamentalism whose leaders identify – and not without reason – the source of their discontents in the secular Western ideas that destroyed the old order, and who in consequence assert traditional values in novel and extreme forms.

Nor do our own societies show any greater degree of stability. I am not an economist or a sociologist but a very naive historian, but it seems to me that we face, in Europe and the United States, a two-fold problem. First, there are the technological advances that enable us to produce an ever greater quantity of goods with an ever less input of manpower, with such manpower as is needed requiring pretty high technical qualifications. The Marxist prophesy has been almost reversed: so far from development in means of production enabling the proletariat to destroy the bourgeoisie, they have enabled the bourgeoisie very effectively to destroy the proletariat. As a result we see, in most Western societies, a large measure of systemic and apparently irreducible unemployment; and this unemployment is exacerbated by a global mobility of capital and expertise that can leave whole regions desolate almost overnight. This can cause social dislocation and misery almost as drastic as that which resulted from the transition from agrarian to industrial production in the early nineteenth century. Today, thanks to the acceptance by the State of an ethic of social responsibility then confined to the private sector, unemployment no longer means the kind of penury and desperation that it did in the 1840s, but its social and psychological consequences hardly need to be spelled out. The resulting situation does in fact bear a disquieting resemblance to the Two Nations then depicted by Disraeli. One of those nations is doing very nicely. The other is an increasingly alienated underclass, unemployed and perhaps increasingly unemployable, uninterested in contributing and indeed unable to contribute to the society that supports it, and kept quiet by a diet of mass-produced sport and entertainment; if not indeed by more dangerous drugs.

To the second set of problems I have already briefly referred. They are those resulting from the erosion of traditional values and social norms; values that may have been developed under different and now anachronistic social conditions, but which did provide a measure of social cohesion, and show no sign of being replaced by new ones more appropriate to the conditions of our own times. This sense of anomie may be more intense in Britain than elsewhere, because traditional values and standards have survived for longer in this country than elsewhere, and we are having to make adjustments that the Germans made fifty, the French and the Americans two hundred years ago. But the impact of the sexual revolution consequent on the development of reliable means of birth-control is universal and, one of the most fundamental that has occurred in the history of mankind. The entire relationship between men and women has to be rethought. New generations are left to work out their own morality, with little if any guidance from the past. The result may be liberating, but it is also bewildering, and can occasionally be disastrous. It is not surprising if visitors from the Third World, however enamoured they may be of our technology, see in the society which it has produced not a model to be imitated but one to be shunned.

These problems, the domestic and international, are interconnected. The impact of Western science and technology has loosened the cohesion of non-Western societies where it has not destroyed it altogether, and the same technology has made it possible for their peoples to come in large numbers to our own shores. Their presence is seen as an additional threat by those in our own societies who already feel insecure. The introduction of their cultures has sometimes had a salutary effect, inducing in our own people a spirit of wider comprehension and tolerance; but often, as all of us know, it has had the opposite effect, producing intolerance and reactive dogmatism of the nastiest kind. If the social dislocation created by modernization has led to a fundamentalist backlash in developing societies, it has also evoked in Western societies the kind of xenophobic racism that Hitler and his imitators found it so easy to exploit a couple of generations ago.

As if that were not enough, we face a third category of problems; those caused by the disintegration of former communist societies. We can now see how effectively the communist regime destroyed the basis of civil society in the regions that it dominated, and how shallow and artificial was the social order it imposed in its place. Our instinct, that we should do all that we can to draw our neighbours in the East into our own political and economic system, must be right. But we can do no more than provide the facilities to enable them to solve those problems themselves, whether those facilities are technical, economic or political.

*   *   *   *   *

What then is to be done? Out of this unpromising material, what hope is there of a new world order? My survey has been depressing, but after all, we have been here before. After every great war, whether hot or cold, there has been a chill peace. There was a decade of disruption and social misery after 1815, when Europe was kept in order only by the police powers of the Habsburg and the Russian Empires, and the spectre of communism was stalking the continent a good twenty years after that. There was a similar period of wretchedness and confusion in Europe after 1918, interrupted only by the false dawn of the Locarno era. As for the aftermath of the Second World War, many of us will remember the sense almost of despair with which we contemplated the ruins of Europe and wondered how, if ever, the continent could be restored to anything like a peaceful and democratic order. War, even Cold War, concentrates the mind wonderfully: too wonderfully. Too many problems have to put on the back burner; too many debts are incurred that eventually have to be paid. Enjoy the war, we said to each other presciently, the peace will be terrible; but somehow we survived both the war and the peace.

We shall survive this peace, if we do not set our sights too high and try to do too much too fast. We cannot solve the problems of the world, even if television brings them every night into our sitting rooms. Nor, I believe, should we try to impose our own standards on the world; different cultures have to solve the problems of modernization in their own way. For the foreseeable future a global order must be inevitably multicultural, and its enforcement minimalist. We should therefore approach world problems not with the universalism of the lawyer, but with the pragmatic *triage* of the surgeon on the battlefield who divides his patients into those who do not need help, those he cannot help, and those he can and must help. But the limits of our capacity to help anyone will be set by our ability to solve, or at least to control, the problems of our own no longer very rich, and no longer unadulteratedly white world.

12

Foreign Affairs magazine
1999

NATO: *An Unhappy but Successful Marriage*

NATO was always intended to be both more and less than a military alliance. The original idea was the brain-child of Britain's Foreign Secretary Ernest Bevin. In January 1948, confronted by a Western Europe still in ruins and a Soviet Union triumphantly consolidating her own conquests, Bevin suggested to Washington that it would be possible to stem the further encroachment of the Soviet tide only 'by organising and consolidating the ethical and spiritual forces of Western civilisation.'[1] Peace and safety, he maintained, 'could only be preserved by the mobilisation of such moral and material force as would create confidence and energy on the one side and inspire respect and caution on the other. The alternative was to acquiesce in continued Russian infiltration and watch the piecemeal collapse of one Western bastion after another.'[2] Cynics may allege that this downplaying of material and emphasis upon ethical force was deliberately tailored to the susceptibilities of isolationist Congressmen, but at that time the threat from the Soviet Union was not perceived primarily in military terms. The real danger seemed to lie in the moral and material exhaustion of a Western Europe that, in spite of Marshall Aid, still looked like a push-over for communist infiltration and propaganda. A purely military alliance did not seem the appropriate answer, but what did?

States are cold monsters who mate for convenience and self-protection, not love, and this became very clear during the negotiations for the creation of the Alliance that dragged on throughout 1948. The State Department, both conscious of a Congress still hostile to any further 'entangling alliances' and anxious not to accept the division of Germany and Europe as final, was at first prepared to act as no more than benevolent godfather to a Western European alliance. The French on the other hand, remembering the desertion by their former allies in the aftermath of the First World War, were demanding immediate military aid, to protect them as much against a German revival as against any Soviet threat. Canada, whose peoples were as

[1] Nicholas Henderson, *The Birth of NATO* (Weidenfeld & Nicolson, London 1982), p. 3.
[2] *Ibid.*, p. 4.

reluctant as their neighbours to the south to become involved in any more foreign quarrels, constantly emphasized the economic and social purposes of the treaty. Given the reluctance both of Canada and of the United States to enter into any specific military obligations, the final text might have lacked any military core at all if the Soviets had not helped matters along, first by mounting the communist coup in Prague in April 1948 and then by imposing the Berlin blockade. The impact of these events on public opinion on both sides of the Atlantic was enough to ensure the inclusion in the final text of the treaty of the famous Article 5; whereby the signatories agreed 'that an armed attack against one or more of them in Europe or North America [should] be considered an attack against them all; and [that they would] assist the Party or Parties so attacked by taking forthwith ... such action as it deems necessary, including the use of armed force, to restore and maintain international security'.

Imprecise though it was, this clause provided the reassurance the Europeans wanted; but in Washington and Ottawa it was Article 2 that had the greater resonance, whereby the signatories pledged themselves to 'contribute towards the further development of peaceful and friendly international relations by strengthening their free institutions, by bringing about a better understanding of the principles upon which these institutions are founded, and by promoting conditions of stability and well-being. They [undertook to] seek to eliminate conflict in their international economic policies and [to] encourage economic collaboration between any and all of them.' With this bland assurance of mutual goodwill matters might have rested but for the outbreak of the Korean War a year later; an event that was seen in Washington as the first shot in an overt Soviet bid for global expansion.

At once the aspirations expressed in Article 2 were eclipsed by the demands of Article 5; the mobilization of military forces, and the creation of a military infrastructure, to make possible a credible defence of Western Europe against an adversary who already enjoyed a crushing superiority in conventional weaponry and was already showing an alarming capacity to compete in the nuclear field. This involved the recreation of the wartime 'Grand Alliance', this time without the Soviet Union. The British were delighted. Although the expenditure involved was to wreck their barely convalescent economy, they found themselves back where they felt they belonged; if not quite the equals of the United States, then their adjutants and mentors; certainly in a different class to the continental neighbours they had either conquered or liberated. The French had more mixed feelings. While they welcomed the immediate influx of military aid from the United States, they resented the reassertion of a *de facto* Anglo-American hegemony, and – like their Benelux and Scandinavian partners – strongly objected to the price the Americans now exacted for their protection; the integration into the Alliance of a Western Germany without whose territory, resources and man-power Europe would be indefensible, but whose occupation of French soil was fresh in their memories. But the price they in their turn exacted – American support for their attempt to reconquer Indo-China – was to prove in the long run disastrous. As for the Germans, although the lure of American protection and the rewards that went with it was irresistible, there was understandable support for the attempt by Kurt Schumacher and the Social Democrats to find a non-aligned solution that would preserve the unity of their country and preserve them from a nuclear war being fought over their own territory. A popular cartoon at the time showed Germany as a battered little boy in a nursery where his older companions were happily re-equipping themselves with toy guns and swords, plaintively asking '*Bitte, darf ich diesmal nicht mitspielen* (please, do you mind if I don't play this time?)'.

But how *was* Europe to be defended, with or without nuclear weapons? At first the solution appeared simple: the Europeans, with substantial American stiffening and under overall American command, would provide a conventional 'shield', while the nuclear 'sword' of US Strategic Air Command struck devastating blows deep inside the Soviet Union. When it became clear that the European allies, even with the addition of the West Germans, would be quite incapable of meeting the force-levels demanded of them if their economies were ever to recover, the emphasis shifted. 'Conventional' defence was downgraded to the status of a 'trip-wire', a burglar alarm that would still trigger an instant and overwhelming nuclear response. This, it was hoped, would 'deter' a Soviet attack. But would it? During the 1950s the Soviets not only caught up with the United States in the production of thermonuclear weapons, but developed the capacity, albeit one hugely overestimated by the West, to deliver them across the Atlantic. Under these circumstances was the American 'nuclear guarantee' still credible, and if it was not, what could be done to make it so? For the next thirty years strategic thinkers on both sides of the Atlantic wracked their brains in search of an answer. They never really found one.

Throughout the 1950s this nuclear dilemma was increasingly complicated by political tensions. First, whatever doubts strategic analysts may have felt about the credibility of the American military guarantee, the peoples of Western Europe felt sufficiently secure to develop thriving economies, laying the foundations for an economic community that bade fair to rival that of the United States. To some Americans this seemed, as it still seems, to be a solution rather than a problem. For President Kennedy, in one of those ill-fated 'Grand Designs' that geopolitical architects in Washington were hopefully to churn out over the next four decades, European unity should be encouraged so as to provide a 'second pillar' of an 'Atlantic Community'. But the Europeans proved unco-operative. The Germans under Chancellor Adenauer were helpful enough, so long as their allies pledged themselves to a reunification of Germany in which none of them believed and most of them dreaded; but the British still kept their distance from their continental neighbours and insisted on preserving their nuclear autonomy. As for the French, their resentment at the Anglo-Americans was brought to boiling point by the Suez crisis and by what they saw as betrayal by their allies over their attempts to retain control in Indo-China and Algeria. Under de Gaulle they began to chart their own agenda: nuclear independence, an arms-length relationship with the Alliance, a 'special relationship' with the Germans, and transformation of the European Economic Community into a close political consortium dominated by Paris. To make matters worse, as the Europeans became more prosperous so their defence industries began to revive and they no longer went shopping for arms in the United States. Grumbling tensions began over 'burden sharing' that would not go away.

Secondly, the death of Stalin in 1953, and the more amenable attitude of his successors, was to provide another source of division within the Alliance. In the view of Washington the softer winds now blowing from Moscow were the result of the staunch attitude adopted by the West, which should not in consequence be relaxed: the Soviets had simply changed their tactics in a conflict that was global, continuing and ineluctable. The Europeans saw things differently. There political forces on the left, which everywhere remained influential even where they did not actually hold power, were always inclined to give the Soviets the benefit of any doubt, even though the brutal suppression of the Hungarian uprising in 1956 shattered the unity of all European communist parties. Domestic pressure for '*détente*' became a permanent feature of the European scene. This was particularly the case in West Germany, where demands grew for an accommodation with the Soviet Union that would make possible the re-establishment of human contacts with fellow-countrymen – in many cases close relations – behind the Iron Curtain. But even such right-wing governments as those of Harold Macmillan in Britain and Charles de Gaulle in France tended to take a traditional view of the Soviet Union, seeing her not as a permanent and implacable foe but as a Great Power with whom they had had their difficulties in the past but with whom they had been allied in two great wars; one who had interests that should be respected, but with whom an accommodation was both desirable and possible. It was an attitude that Washington found very difficult to assimilate until Henry Kissinger himself adopted it a decade or so later. Increasingly European governments had to explain to their electorates that defence existed primarily to serve the purposes of *détente*. After a decade of increasing acrimony this was made official policy for the Alliance by the Harmel Report of 1968.

Finally, divisions were growing between the allies over the geographical scope of the alliance. Ironically, it was the United States who had been most insistent on limiting it to the territory of Europe and the Atlantic approaches. She had no intention of underwriting European colonial rule elsewhere in the world, and consented only with deep reluctance to include even 'the Algerian departments of France' within its scope. A decade later she was having second thoughts. The abandonment of European colonial rule throughout the world seemed to leave 'a vacuum of power' into which the United States feared that the Soviet Union would feel herself free to expand, and which Nikita Khrushchev's explicit support for 'Wars of National Liberation' suggested that she intended to do so. Blocked in Europe, Soviet power appeared to be extending dangerously everywhere else. What, Washington demanded, did the Europeans intend to do about it?

The answer was, not very much. The British felt that they were discharging their obligations by doing their best to ensure a peaceful transition to independence within their own imperial possessions, especially Malaysia. The French, having painfully extricated themselves from Algeria, imposed an effective control over the rest of the *Union Française*, and felt that they had no reason to help out the Americans who had been so reluctant to assist them in their own hour of need. In any case, both British and French were sceptical of the capacity of the Soviet Union to affect the course of events in what was now called 'the Third World' for good or ill, and feared that American attempts to counter it, whether in Latin America or South-East Asia, were likely only to make matters worse. As for the Germans, they were mainly concerned lest the United States would become distracted from the only issue which to them really mattered, the deterrence of Soviet aggression in Europe; a view shared by all the smaller European powers. So the United States had to soldier on alone in Vietnam, and did not like it.

Deterrence, *détente*, burden-sharing, and 'out of area'; these four issues surfaced again and again throughout the troubled history of the alliance, and would not go away. Hardly a year was to pass in which one or more of them did not cause acrimony at meetings of the NATO Council – sometimes indeed, all four. But there were two periods when these simmering tensions seemed to reach boiling point: 1958–63, and again twenty years later, 1979–83.

In both cases the cause was the same; a sudden upsurge of doubt on the part of the United States as to whether her military deterrent posture was still credible. In 1958 this was set off by the realization that the Soviets possessed not only thermonuclear weapons, but a capacity to deliver them onto American soil. The flight of the manned satellite Sputnik in 1957 indicated indeed that Soviet space technology might be even more advanced than that of the United States, where fears of a 'missile gap' grew almost to panic proportions. In 1958 Khrushchev exploited this in an attempt to heal his own chief source of vulnerability, the haemorrhage of East Germans fleeing from communist rule through Berlin; first by demanding the termination of four-power rights over the city, then in 1961 by consenting to the erection of the Berlin Wall. The peoples of Europe suddenly saw themselves confronted by the alternatives of a bloodless Soviet victory and a suicidal nuclear war, and a cry went up for nuclear disarmament and disengagement from the United States. The crisis came to a head over Cuba in 1962 and was weathered by a firm American leadership that did much to restore European confidence. The Americans themselves were reassured by the discovery that their original fears had been largely groundless, but they initiated a major armament programme to ensure that no such perceptions of vulnerability should occur again.

The Europeans remained deeply unsettled by the experience. Both the British and the French were reinforced in their determination to retain their own nuclear reinsurance systems. Fears that the Germans might wish to follow their example led the United States to propose the construction of a Multilateral Nuclear Force – a project that merely evoked universal mockery and was deservedly rejected. In fact the Germans were far more seriously concerned by Washington's attempt to create a more credible deterrent posture with the doctrine of 'flexible response'. Whose territory, asked the Germans with good reason, did the Americans intend to be flexible with? In general the crisis left both sides badly bruised. The Europeans resented the *de haut en bas* didacticism of Washington's brilliant young strategic analysts, while the Americans were exasperated by the constant European demands for reassurance from their protectors without doing anything to make that reassurance realistic. Henry Kissinger was to voice American frustrations, but again to reawaken European fears, when in 1979, under very similar strategic circumstances, he told a conference celebrating NATO's twentieth anniversary that 'our European allies should not keep asking us to multiply strategic assurances that we cannot possibly mean, or if we did mean, we should not want to execute because if we execute, we risk the destruction of civilization'.

The tensions within the alliance relaxed somewhat over the next fifteen years. The United States entered into arms-control negotiations that did something to draw the sting of the European Left. Washington's attention was diverted to 'out of area' problems, first Vietnam, then the Middle East, in the resolution of which Kissinger tended to treat the Soviet Union almost as a colleague rather than an adversary. But these distractions created their own difficulties. Bilateral negotiations over arms-control were complicated by the fears and interests of the European allies, who voiced alternately complaints about their lack of progress and fears that the Superpowers were reaching agreements that ignored their own security interests. Over Vietnam, as we have seen, the Americans intensely resented the lack of European support, while the Europeans observed with alarm the apparent degradation of United States forces in Europe and the growing demands in Congress for yet further American troop withdrawals. As for the Middle East and the crisis that arose there in 1973 over the Yom Kippur War, Americans with their pro-Israeli sympathies and Europeans dependent on Arab-controlled oil, found themselves virtually on opposing sides. The fact that in Britain, for the first time since the war, an administration was in power under Edward Heath that rated good relations with its European neighbours more highly than the 'special relationship' with the United States, and that in Germany a Social-Democratic government had come into office pursuing an independent *Ostpolitik*, did nothing to help; while the French remained predictably unhelpful under de Gaulle's designated successor President Pompidou. Kissinger's ill-judged and patronizing attempt to soothe European susceptibilities by declaring 1973 to be 'the Year of Europe' only made matters worse.

After that relations improved, though ill-tempered arguments about burden-sharing and support-costs grumbled on at lower levels of the alliance bureaucracy. In 1974 an emollient 'Atlantic Declaration' was issued reassuring the allies that they were all on the same side. In Britain a Labour government returned to power whose mismanagement of the national economy made them more dependent than ever on American goodwill. More pragmatic administrations came into power in France under Valéry d'Estaing and Jacques Mitterand. As for the Germans, their *Ostpolitik* initiative, initially viewed in Washington with extreme mistrust, had resulted in the settlement of Central European frontiers over which wars had been fought for generations, and had ripened into the Helsinki conferences that were gradually to transform relations between East and West Europe, if not the Soviet.Union itself. By the end of the decade the European weather at last seemed set fair; which made the onset of the crisis years, 1979–84, all the more traumatic.

This new period of tension was precipitated, like the first, by a crisis in American self-confidence. The steady build-up of the Soviet military arsenal throughout the 1970s, including the modernization of nuclear weapons targeted on Western Europe, had caused concern on both sides of the Atlantic, and members of the Alliance agreed to increase their defence expenditure to deal with it. In American eyes this build-up appeared all the more sinister in the light of increasingly bold Soviet interventions in Southern and East Africa, the dreadful humiliations suffered by the United States in the course of the Iranian revolution, and, worst of all, the Soviet invasion of Afghanistan in December 1979. The apparent lack of interest by their European allies in these developments enraged the Americans, as did the insouciance with which the Europeans continued to exploit the opening trade opportunities with the Soviet Union and Eastern Europe. The incoming Reagan administration treated its allies with a brusqueness bordering on brutality that infuriated their governments, and adopted towards the Soviets a posture of rhetorical hostility that alarmed their peoples.

Once again the fear of imminent nuclear war (felt as strongly this time in Moscow as anywhere else) created political turmoil in Europe. In spite of their other differences with Washington, European governments recognized the strategic necessity of accepting the installation of American missiles to counter the Soviet SS20s aimed at their own territory, but they had huge difficulty in persuading their own peoples to do the same. Hardly had this crisis been resolved than a further problem was created by President Reagan's unilateral proclamation of a Strategic Defense Initiative that seemed likely to destroy all hope of serious arms-control agreements, appeared to undermine the entire strategic doctrine on which the Alliance was based, and made even America's friends fear a return to a doctrine of 'Fortress America'. To many in Europe, Reagan seemed a greater threat to peace than did the geriatric leadership of the Soviet Union; while it was widely believed in the United States that the Europeans had been cowed by Soviet strength into a servile condition of 'Finlandization'.

Then suddenly it all ended. Like Kennedy before him, President Reagan had mastered the crisis, not only by a massive arms build-up that restored the self-confidence (if it wrecked the economy) of the United States, but also by maintaining contact, in spite of all his rhetoric, with the Soviet leadership. In 1985 there emerged a leader, Mikhail Gorbachev, that he could do business with, and Reagan, to his eternal credit, seized the opportunity. Within five years the Cold War was at an end, Germany was reunited, the Warsaw Pact had dissolved, and Soviet troops were withdrawing to their own frontiers.

Historians will long debate whether the collapse of the Soviet Union owed more to the unremitting pressure of American arms build-ups which forced her to spend herself into bankruptcy, or to the gentle but irresistible growth of popular expectations behind the Iron Curtain as the *détente* by which the Europeans set so much store gradually took effect; much as George Kennan had predicted it would a generation earlier. But what is beyond doubt is that the Alliance never worked so effectively in conducting the Cold War as it did in bringing it to an end. Had Gorbachev been less complaisant matters might have been different. As it was, the excellent rapport established between the American and Soviet leadership was complemented by that between a German Chancellor, Helmuth Kohl, who knew exactly what he wanted – German unification – and an American president who firmly supported him in spite of the doubts of his other alliance partners. The French under President Chirac were unwontedly co-operative: whatever their feelings about the Americans, they dared not antagonize a Germany whose friendship was essential in creating an effective European Union. The British under Margaret Thatcher were initially reluctant; but whatever their feelings about Germany, they did not dare do anything to upset the 'special relationship' with the United States that had paid such excellent dividends over the Falklands. The treaty signed in Paris in November 1990 not only brought the Cold War to an end, but established a new structure of international relations among scenes of international amity barely witnessed since the Congress of Vienna in 1815.

Now we celebrate the Golden Anniversary of a highly successful marriage. A *successful* marriage, be it noted: not a happy one. As with the arranged marriages of earlier generations, it was entered into with a specific purpose. Such marriages had been intended to unite properties, appease enmities, and, above all, produce and bring up children. Whatever the spouses felt about each other, they stuck together to achieve these ends. The Alliance had been created, in Lord Ismay's famous words, 'to keep the Americans in, the Russians out, and ...' (to tactfully paraphrase his undiplomatic words) to solve the German problem. All this had happened. The Europeans had repeatedly found the Americans overbearing, self-righteous, and hysterically alarmist. The Americans often regarded the Europeans as a 'soft' (a peculiarly American term of abuse), short-sighted, mean and self-centred bunch of freeloaders. Familiarity made possible a *modus vivendi*, but bred no great affection. But the marriage worked, and the more problems it overcame, the stronger were the bonds that bound it together.

Now that the object has been achieved, voices are being raised suggesting that the marriage should be dissolved and its partners left free to look elsewhere for their security. But another characteristic of arranged marriages was that they did not dissolve even after the children had grown up. For one thing, a household had been created which remained the family home. For another, the spouses had grown used to one another, and even if there was still little affection, they had learned to make allowances for each other's infirmities. For a third, they could think of no other arrangement that was equally convenient to both. Most important of all, a separation was likely to have serious repercussions for their extended families and the society that surrounded them. So it is with the Alliance. It has built up a politico-military infrastructure that integrates the armed forces of much of Europe and provides the United States with a unique capacity to influence the policy of its allies and vice-versa. It remains, astonishingly and perhaps absurdly, the only forum where the Europeans and the Americans can meet to discuss their politico-military problems and make provision for them; and if earlier hopes that these discussions might cover broader socio-economic problems have so far borne little fruit, it is because so many other more appropriate institutions now exist to deal with them. Sheer inertia may keep the show on the road. But is that enough?

There is nothing wrong with inertia so long as it keeps the object moving in the right direction, and few would deny that continuing solidarity and co-operation between the United States and the nations of Europe remains an unexceptional goal. It might be argued that a military alliance is no longer the appropriate mechanism for preserving that solidarity now that there is no longer a military threat, but it should be remembered that NATO was not just a military alliance in the first place. Today the threat that made its members emphasize their obligations under Article 5 at the expense of those under Article 2 no longer exists. So far as Article 2 is concerned, there is no reason why the membership of the Alliance should not be indefinitely extended, and the more widely the better. Who could possibly object to 'the further development of peaceful and friendly international relations by strengthening ... free institutions, by bringing about a better understanding of the principles upon which these institutions are founded and by pro-moting conditions of stability and well-being'? If that were all that was involved, the partners could extend their family indefinitely and rub along for ever. Even the obligations undertaken under Article 5, to regard an armed attack against one or more of them as an attack against them all, are not especially rigorous: all that the parties undertake to do to assist the parties so attacked is to take 'such action as [they] deem necessary, including the use of armed force, to restore and maintain international peace and security'. What action *is* deemed necessary is left to the discretion of each party, and armed force is seen only as a possible option.

All might thus be well if the Alliance could revert to the limited arrangements and expectations of its early months. But as was discovered in 1950, a credible guarantee that 'includes the use of armed force' involves making joint military arrangements, designating and if necessary deploying forces well in advance; not just making paper promises. That was the unforgettable lesson of the 1930s, and presumably that is what aspiring candidates for membership of the Alliance now expect. Any guarantee to defend an ally now involves making the military arrangements necessary to implement it. Ambassador Robert Hunter expressed the hope that the difference between a 'partner for peace' and membership of the Alliance might become 'razor-thin', but it can be made so only by destroying the military credibility of the alliance itself. A huge gulf remains between, on the one hand, expressing ideological sympathy with another state and providing it with political support and economic help, and, on the other, committing one's armed forces, and risking the lives of one's civilians – and in the nuclear age the very survival of one's own society – for its physical defence.

Disagreements over the desirability of NATO extension have not so much divided the Alliance, as run through every NATO member state. The decision to extend was forced through by the United States, yet opposition to this step has been more extensive and vociferous in America than anywhere else. It has come not only from those who see it as an extension of the battle lines and the mind-set of the Cold War, but from those most concerned with the effectiveness and integrity of NATO as a functioning military entity. It has come also from those concerned for the political effectiveness of the Alliance. It has been hard enough to create and maintain consensus among the original fifteen members of the Alliance on any issue beyond defence against the immediate threat to their territorial independence, if indeed on that. The advent of a group of members from Central and Eastern Europe, with a quite distinct geopolitical outlook, could make the task virtually impossible. And that should be borne in mind by those who now argue that NATO can only justify itself by assisting the United States in policing or preempting regional disputes 'out of area or out of business'.

For of the four major subjects of discord among the allies – nuclear deterrence, *détente*, out-of-area commitment and burden-sharing – only the last two remain. Burden-sharing is, and will continue to be, an unavoidable fact of life, but it has never been, and need not become unmanageable. 'Out of area', however, is now widely seen as the only justification for NATO's continuing existence by many in the United States who are still conscious, rightly or wrongly, of her responsibilities for the preservation of some kind of world order. With the disappearance of the Soviet threat it is not clear what other purpose the Alliance can still serve if not to share this burden. But there are two major problems about this. The first is that only by a most imaginative interpretation of the text of the treaty can alliance partners be held to have any 'out-of-area' obligations at all. The second is that such operations demand a high degree of military co-operation and expertise such as can be expected only from a very few members of the alliance; whose intervention would probably be far more rapid and effective if it did not have to be sanctioned by a dozen or more reluctant allies and take place under the cumbrous umbrella of a NATO command structure.

Finally there is the problem created by the evolution of the European Union itself. What territory will it cover, what powers will it have, and what attitude will it adopt towards the United States?

With the adoption of the euro the European Union today seems to be developing a degree of economic cohesion that once seemed barely possible, and this will inevitably bring a certain degree of political unity in its train. Even the goal of a common foreign and defence policy, a European 'Security and Defence Identity' now seems sufficiently attainable for NATO to be making provision for it within its own organization. Yet to many in Europe this goal still seems a distant one, and the more members that are admitted both to the Union and to the Alliance, the more distant it appears. It has been difficult enough during the past half-century to hammer out some kind of consensus about world events between London, Paris, Bonn, Rome and Copenhagen, to say nothing of Ankara and Athens. Add Vilnius and Bucharest, and the imagination begins to boggle. The most that can be expected is some kind of lowest common denominator that will always incline towards the kind of passivity with which the Europeans have infuriated their American allies ever since the 1950s. If the members of an enlarged European Union were ever to develop a single coherent defence and foreign policy, it would be as likely to find itself in opposition to that of the United States as in support of it.

None of this means that the alliance should be dissolved. It remains a uniquely appropriate framework within which the United States and the states of Europe can collaborate where collaboration is possible and co-ordinate their policies when collaboration is not on the cards. But it might be as well to define very much more closely what the alliance is now for. If it is to be just a community of like-minded states peacefully co-operating with and consulting each other as foreseen under Article 2, and in addition providing facilities for military co-operation by those members who wish to take part in out-of-area operations, well and good. It would continue to serve a valuable function for all its members, and be a stabilizing factor for the world as a whole. Then much of the huge and expensive infrastructure built up to implement the mutual military guarantees under Article 5 could be dismantled, and membership extended almost indefinitely to like-minded and contiguous nations. But let us no longer pretend that this would be an effective military alliance as previously understood, whose members offer credible reciprocal guarantees to come to the defence of one another. The Alliance would still serve the goals set out in its original text, and even the wording of Article 5 would not be entirely invalid. The Alliance can certainly continue as a successful marriage, but only if the partners know what they may now reasonably expect of one another.

IV

Europe after the Cold War

13

Oslo 1995

What is 'Europe'? (For the Norwegians)

Johan Holst will be properly remembered in his own country as a great Norwegian. He will be remembered in the West, and indeed the world as a whole for his contribution to the unravelling of the knot of hatred and suspicion in the Middle East. But within the smaller circle of the international 'security community' he had long been a voice speaking continually for balance and sanity – and a voice quite distinctively European. It is thus as a great European that I prefer to remember him; so it seems appropriate that I should devote this lecture to explaining what I mean by that term. What, and where, is 'Europe'? What could and should it be? How should we be thinking about its place in the world in the aftermath of the Cold War?

The phrase 'a Great European' is rather misleading. In my own country it is not a term that commands instant and universal approval. It is normally used to describe such statesmen and thinkers as Jean Monnet or Jean-Paul Spaak, who had some kind of vision of a politically united Europe and worked for its implementation. To the best of my knowledge Johan had no such vision. If he had, he certainly did not allow it to dominate his writing and his political activities. But in my usage the term means someone whose whole life and personality was so shaped by European culture that they unconsciously embodied it wherever they went; whose ideas, presuppositions and turns of phrase betrayed them as Europeans in whatever company they found themselves. It does not imply some kind of supra-national, pan-continental European 'culture'. There is no contradiction between being a Norwegian or an Englishman and being a 'European'. Indeed one cannot be a European unless one is first thoroughly and consciously a Norwegian or an Englishman, and proud of it. But it does mean that when a Norwegian and an Englishman find themselves in company outside their own continent, even in so open and friendly environment as the United States, they recognize one another as being kindred spirits, sharing attitudes and concepts – unformulated and perhaps unformulable – that set them apart from their hosts.

Let me first try to define what has gone into the making of Europeans, and then see what it is that *has* been made. We must start with geography, and go on to history.

In the first place, Europe, unlike its fellow-continents Africa, Australia, the Americas, and the bulk of Asia, is not a discrete land-mass. It is a knotty, convoluted peninsula sticking out from the body of what geopoliticians call 'The World Island' – Eurasia. Its land frontier is embarrassingly indeterminate. Whether the peoples in the marchlands to the East are 'European' is normally discussed in terms of their culture rather than their geographical location. That culture has been determined by waves of conquest and counter-conquest stretching over two millennia. These have been bloodily continued into the twentieth century with the conflicts between Christian and Turks in the Balkan peninsula and between German and Slav in the huge plain bounded by the Vistula and the Volga; struggles that have left peoples whose nationality is still indeterminate. Whether Ukrainians or Belorussians are 'European', for example, is likely to be considered in terms of what they believe and how they behave rather than by the degrees of longitude on the map within which they live.

But that does not mean that we expect from Europeans some kind of conformity of culture. It is the very diversity of our cultures that makes up Europe. None the less it is a paradoxical diversity in unity. One of the geographical factors that has gone to the making of Europe has been the accessibility of the greater part of the continent by sea or by navigable rivers running deep into the heart of the mainland – conduits that for 2,000 years have served for communication, for conquest and for trade. Nobody exploited those conduits more effectively than did your own ancestors who traded, conquered and settled in regions as diverse as North-West France, England, Sicily and – come to think of it – the Ukraine as well. So although European cultures matured in the early Middle Ages as distinct entities, in France, in Scandinavia, Italy, Spain, Germany, Poland, each moulded by different historical and geographical circumstances, they were constantly in contact with one another as adversaries or trading partners, and could be brought together under the overarching authority of the Christian Church.

For the best part of a thousand years, indeed, the boundaries of Europe were those of 'Christendom'. The status of that alternative Christendom based on Constantinople in the eastern marchlands remained as embarrassingly indeterminate as did its political orientation. Europe was *Western* Christendom, even when Western Christendom divided and fought itself for a long and bloody century. Those religious wars further divided and defined European cultures and their effects are still with us today. The cultural distinction between the regions of South Europe where the Catholic Church remained dominant until this century and our own northern regions whose emancipation under various forms of Protestantism have determined not only our religious but our political structures was at least as significant as the division between Western and Eastern Europe during the Cold War, and lasted far longer.

Those wars developed into dynastic conflicts, during which there emerged the distinctive structure of the European states-system. It was a structure that not only created political order within national borders, but preserved a balance between the states that prevented any of them from becoming dominant and creating, at any rate for more than a few years, a continent-wide Empire. But these conflicts were as much bonding as they were divisive. Immanuel Kant saw how war could create a degree of intimacy between adversaries that led to ever closer integration between them, and might in due course lead to perpetual peace. Certainly it was these frequent wars – which before this century were not utterly destructive – and the intervals of peace that interrupted them, that created among Europeans a distinctive attitude towards each other, and indeed to the great issues of war and peace. We learned to live in a system of states, each embodying a distinct culture and probably a different language, and to co-exist with neighbours whose language we did not understand very well and whose habits we did not like very much; neighbours with whom peace was highly desirable but whose power and ambitions might sometimes make war necessary. War was not the ultimate catastrophe. The ultimate catastrophe was the elimination of our independent identity, and to prevent that wars had sometimes to be fought. But after war peace had to be made and a new balance created to make stability possible. Thus enmity was never total, nor friendship perpetual. We all lived surrounded by foreigners, with whom friendship was desirable but whose activities had to be watched with wary caution.

It is this historic relationship, one that accepted cultural diversity and recognized the existence of divergent and sometimes incompatible interests, this realization of the immanent and perhaps ineradicable possibility of conflict even when relations were at their most friendly, that has shaped the attitude of Europeans to one another and to the world as a whole. It has made our expectations limited and given us an outlook on the world that is, if not tragic, then certainly cautious and ironic. It has taught us to live with problems that we cannot solve and paradoxes we cannot resolve. And it distinguishes us very sharply from the Americans, who instinctively believe that if a problem exists, they can fix it. Quite often they can.

The fundamental values shared between Europe and the United States – the values, originally, of a common Christendom – are so great, and our alliance during the half-century between 1941 and 1991 was so vital to our survival, that the differences of attitude and approach derived from our diverse histories could be seen as irritants to be accepted and dismissed. But they constantly surfaced at every level, both in the conduct of war and in the preservation of peace. To the jaded European eye the Americans always seemed to believe that there were technological solutions to political problems; but since quite often the Europeans could not devise any other kind of solution, we were hardly in a position to criticize. Americans, in European eyes, seemed always to underrate the fundamental importance of cultural differences; understandable enough in view of their amazing success in forging a single nation out of innumerable diverse immigrant communities. There seemed to be, in the United States, an implicit belief in the universal applicability of American values, and the expectation that once these had been universalized history would come to an end. And, partly arising out of these differences, there was a very deep division of attitudes over the nature of the Cold War.

For the United States, the Cold War was a religious war; a global crusade against communism wherever it raised its head, with little distinction between the various forms that communism, or Marxist-Leninism, might take in different societies. It took that most European and un-American of American statesmen, Henry Kissinger, a man who saw it as his mission to temper American idealism with some sober European wisdom, to teach his countrymen to think in terms of power-politics (or geopolitics) and to accept the Peoples Republic of China as a valid and acceptable ally against Soviet power. But the European attitude was always more pragmatic and more parochial. For us, or most of us, the Cold War was from the beginning a simple struggle to contain Soviet power, as earlier generations had found it necessary to contain the power of Germany, or France, or Spain, or indeed Sweden. It was an unwelcome but not unexpected continuation of the traditional pattern of European politics, though now extended on a global scale. The confrontation was serious, but hardly cosmic. We knew the Russians, or thought that we did, and realized that the calculus of their power and intentions had to take into account a great deal more than an inventory of their missiles and the text-books of Marxist-Leninism. They were difficult neighbours but neighbours none the less, and they were not going to go away. They had been enemies before and they had been allies before. For two hundred years they had been actors in the European system, even if not precisely Europeans (a matter that I shall come back to in a moment). 'The Soviet Threat' was real enough, even if one posed rather by Soviet power than immediate Soviet intentions. We needed American support to enable us to confront it; but we needed to keep it in some kind of perspective.

That was where Johan was so good. He was as expert as anyone in the lore and calculations of the strategic community. He knew the importance of retaining American support to maintain the independence of Western Europe. He never subsided into the flaccid neutralism that seemed sometimes to provide a deceptively easy answer. He fully shared American alarm at the dangers posed by the successive generations of Soviet missile technology and military strength. But he knew that that was not all there was to it. Relations between Great Powers, even hostile Superpowers, consist, or ought to consist, of a great deal more than military confrontation, and Johan sometimes quite frankly gave voice to European doubts as to the direction in which military technology seemed to be leading American foreign policy. He was himself to define the problem of trans-Atlantic relations as well as I have ever seen it done; the difference in political culture, as he put it, 'between European acceptance of vulnerability and interdependent security as a result of sharing a continent among adversaries and American nostalgia for invulnerability and independent security on a continent without rivals'.[1]

Thus however deep our shared interests and values, and however close our personal friendships, the Americans are not Europeans, and do not see the world as Europeans do. But how about the Russians? Are *they* Europeans?

This is a question that the Russians themselves find profoundly problematic. It is a problem with which we British should have sympathy. We are both peoples on the margins of Europe, whose history and culture has been deeply shaped by our involvement in European affairs but who have been tempted, as communications made it possible, to turn our backs on a troublesome continent and create new worlds in our own image; the British beyond the oceans, the Russians beyond the steppes. The events of the twentieth century have shown the British that we cannot escape our European destiny: there is no longer an option overseas. But the position of the Russians is far more complex. For them Western Europe has always been culturally alien in a way that it has not been for the British, if only because Russian culture is rooted in a different kind of Christendom and because they have been open throughout their history to influences and threats from Central Asia that have given their political and social structure a quite different form from any common to their Western neighbours. Their history has oscillated between imitating and seeking integration into Western European culture – a culture to which they have made such magnificent musical and literary contributions – and rejecting it as corrupting and decadent. At the beginning of this century the 'Westernization' of Russia

[1] 'Arms Control Thirty Years On', *Daedalus: Journal of the American Academy of Arts and Sciences* Vol. 120, No. 1 (Winter 1991), p. 88.

seemed well under way. Then came the great rejection of the Bolshevik Revolution, the elimination of the entire class of Western *Kulturträger*, and a self-isolation that has only ended during the last five years. Once again the Russians and their associated peoples are hungrily opening themselves to Western influences. But will this turn them into 'Europeans'?

Frankly I doubt it. Westernization, or 'modernization' is quite as likely to turn them into Americans, but it is more likely to run along channels deeply etched by their own history and geography; a history of authoritarian rule; the geography of a huge land-mass of which Europe constitutes only one flank. Russia cannot shed her Asiatic conquests so easily as did Britain. Even if she ceases to rule them, they remain there as uneasy and probably dependent neighbours. And her greatest and most difficult neighbour is a China with whom relations are likely at best to be ones of uneasy suspicion and are likely to grow worse as the Chinese population grows and their economy expands. Russia may no longer be a Superpower, if she ever was one, but she remains a continental power, with all the problems and responsibilities which that involves.

This places the Russians in the category of the United States rather than of Europe, as does another characteristic that is likely to be of increasing importance during the coming century. She is a *Pacific* power; and one of the defining characteristics of European states at the end of the twentieth century is that none of us is any longer a Pacific power. We are now, as American political scientists kindly remind us, simply regional powers, though some of us retain vestigial interests in Africa, the Middle East and the Indian sub-Continent. But both for Russia and for the United States the Pacific bulks as large as does Europe; indeed with the end of the Cold War and the growing importance of China, considerably larger. For the United States, Europe is suddenly ceasing to be very important, and perhaps it is not very important for the Russians either. If that is so, we are faced by an interesting new situation. No longer do we have to manage the con-frontation of the Superpowers over our territory. Perhaps in the twenty-first century we shall face a situation in which both of them will increasingly ignore us and focus on developments in the Pacific. Europe may become a backwater on the world scene as Italy did after the fall of the Roman Empire; a Mecca for tourism, and that's about all.

For those who remember and have lived through the frightful history of this continent in the twentieth century, this might seem a very satisfactory outcome. Europe can be pensioned off and put out to grass, becoming perhaps an enlarged version of Switzerland. But enough of us will, I hope, remain sufficiently energetic and self-confident to resent such a destiny and object to the affairs of the world being settled without our playing any major part in the process. As Europeans we know that the wind may change in unexpected directions, and that history is not kind to those who try to opt out of it. The Russians may not always be friendly; nor indeed may the Americans. Disasters in the Pacific may have major repercussions on our own continent, as they did in 1941 at Pearl Harbor and again in 1950 in Korea. Decisions, and perhaps the wrong decisions, affecting our interests may be made over our heads. What can we do to ensure that this does not happen?

First, we must retain the closest possible links with the United States, even *1.* if we cannot expect the warmth of reciprocation that we enjoyed during the Cold War. It remains, and will long remain, the most powerful nation on earth, and its decision-making process remains the most open in the world. Although I believe that they are increasingly likely to act unilaterally, the Americans are concerned about their image in the world and by what friendly associates have to say about their behaviour. The channels of influence so effectively developed by Johan himself must be kept open, and Europe must continue to provide for the United States something that can not be provided by any other people in the world, however powerful, neither the Japanese nor the Chinese nor the Russians: an effective *interlocuteur valable*, whose opinion American leaders respect, and whose advice they sometimes take.

Second – and on this the Americans themselves are increasingly insistent *2.* – this is best done by *Europe* as such, rather than by separate European powers. The British have long felt that we have had, if not a 'special relationship' with the United States, then at least an inside track provided by our common language and close wartime alliance. But we have increasingly found that unless we speak for Europe as well, our voice carries very little weight, and that of our friends the Germans is likely to carry very much more. The Americans want to deal as one continental power with another, rather than getting themselves involved in the filigree-work of intra-European relationships, and they show increasing and understandable impatience at our apparent inability to get our act together.

I know that the question of a closer European Union is as divisive an issue in Norway as it is in Britain. We can all see the advantages, administrative, commercial, and financial, involved in a closer European Union, but none of us wishes to lose our political or cultural autonomy in the process. (It is I think no accident that it is in traditionally 'Protestant' countries like yours and mine that people protest most vociferously against a union based on a treaty signed in Rome.) The search for the right balance between autonomy and integration will inevitably be controversial and prolonged. But the longer that process goes on, the less will Europe be taken seriously as a factor in world politics. Some of us – Britain, France and Germany in particular – may still play world-parts as minor actors, but our internecine conflicts are likely to neutralize such little influence as we might corporately exert. A common European defence and foreign policy may still be little more than an aspiration, but unless we achieve it the world is likely to be governed for us by others, over our heads and not necessarily to our benefit.

Third, the Russians. Now that they are *Russians* again rather than 'Soviets' (a term without history and largely without meaning), we know where we are with them. We are familiar with their traditional problem of *Zwei Seelen in einem Brust,* a European soul embodied by St Petersburg and a Slavic whose home is in Moscow. We understand their historic difficulties with their western neighbours from the Baltic to the Black Sea. We can sympathize with their expectation to be treated as a major actor in any questions affecting Northern and Eastern Europe. In their relations with Europe, we can treat them as Europeans; that is, with the cautious goodwill and respect for their legitimate interests that we did before they effectively declared permanent war on us as they did in 1918. To that limited extent they are inescapably part of the European system. But as a continental power – to say nothing of a major nuclear power – they are part of another, global system to which we do not and cannot belong. All the more reason to keep our links with the United States in the best possible repair.

Finally, the marchlands of East and South-East Europe which have been liberated by the end of the Cold War. How far east does Europe extend?

This question, I suggest, must be determined not by geography but by history. In spite of sporadic Russian conquest and occupation, the eastern littoral of the Baltic has been part of Western Christendom for the best part of a millennium. The same applies to Poland, even though the absence of natural frontiers and confusion of cultures has always left her eastern borderlands indeterminate. The same applies to the historic lands of the former Habsburg Empire, Hungary, Slovakia and the Czech Republic. The admission, or rather re-admission, of these 'Visegrad' states into the community of Western Europe should only be a matter of time, and not very much time.

But beyond that, we are in a different cultural world. The destinies of Belorus and the Ukraine have always been bound up with that of Russia, and must continue to be. As for South-East Europe, we find ourselves in an active volcanic region whose continuous conflicts before 1914 were blotted from our sight only by the far greater ones that followed them; conflicts which should, in my own view, have been left to work themselves out and which well-meant outside intervention has done little or nothing to resolve.

'Yugoslavia' was a gallant attempt to reconcile incompatible cultures that failed. The nations formed by generations of insurrection against the Ottoman Empire, under the leadership of the Greek Orthodox Church and the support, usually, of Imperial Russia, have a different orientation from those that were absorbed for two centuries into the Western Catholic culture of the Habsburg Empire. The new frontiers of this unhappy region are not settled yet, and may not be in this century. When they are, we shall probably accept Slovenia into the community of Western Europe with little difficulty; possibly, though under a very different leadership, Croatia. Beyond that, I think we must wait and see.

I have spoken about accepting these countries into the 'community' of Europe, and perhaps indeed into the European Union. But what, finally, of NATO; that organization to whose preservation and effectiveness Johan Holst dedicated so much of his life, and which today so badly misses his wise counsel and leadership?

About NATO I shall say only two things, both I hope true, but each difficult to reconcile with the other.

The first is that, although the original situation that brought it into existence no longer exists, NATO should be preserved for two reasons. First, it is the embodiment of a supra-national 'security community' whose members have dedicated themselves to the proposition that they will never fight one another again, and have integrated their defence structures so closely that it has become virtually impossible for them to do so. I say 'virtually impossible', and the reservation is, unfortunately, necessary: we have recently seen another 'security community', that of Yugoslavia, unravel with disastrous results. But the 're-nationalization' of European defence that would follow the dissolution of NATO could only be a catastrophe for our continent. The creation of a 'European Defence and Security Identity' may be a necessary element in the growing integration of Europe, but it will not in itself command much credibility unless the components at present supplied to the alliance by the United States are replicated at huge and unacceptable expense.

That is the second reason for the preservation of NATO: the continued involvement of the United States in the affairs of our continent. The United States not only furnishes us with a kind of military support possible only to a very wealthy Superpower: she also provides an element of leadership that we are still very bad at providing for ourselves. NATO is still the only major international organization through which Europe is intimately and bilaterally linked with the United States and thus able in a unique fashion to influence her policy. I am afraid that the mishandling of the Bosnian crisis – for which there is plenty of blame to spare for everyone – has done nothing to improve American confidence in NATO as a mechanism for handling our common 'out-of-area' problems, but that is reason to do better next time, rather than to despair.

The other, and contradictory, point that I would make about NATO is this. Military alliances should and need no longer be seen as a normal feature of international relations in peacetime. We have become so used to their existence over the past century, and have sometimes suffered so badly because of their absence, that we now take them for granted in a way that is no longer necessary. Normally in international relations military alliances come into existence only to counter perceived and imminent military threats, and if there is no such threat, there should be no necessity for them. Today there is no such threat in Eastern Europe. No one can guarantee that a new one may not one day arise. As Europeans we know only too well that we have to take such a possibility into account. But to pre-empt it by an immediate extension of military guarantees to former members of the Warsaw Pact and their integration into the existing alliance structure would be not only unnecessary but probably counter-productive. The problems confronted by our new partners in Central and Eastern Europe are no longer the traditional ones of disputed frontiers or threatened invasion. They are the internal social, economic and ecological challenges common to the entire developed world, and the help they require in solving them is social and economic; not military.

I know that the logic of this proposition should dictate the dissolution of NATO itself, but logic has as little place in international as it has in intra-marital relations. Few of us govern our lives by strict logic. I have given my reasons why I hope that NATO may survive, and the existence of a 'Threat' is not one of them. We need NATO today neither to keep the Germans down nor the Russians out, but to keep the Americans in. This does mean that within the community of Europe there will for some time be two categories of states – those who are members of NATO and those who are not – but this is being handled by the various measures initiated under the Partnership for Peace. NATO needs to become something at once more and less than a military alliance before it can be enlarged without risk of causing the recurrence of tensions that it is meant to appease.

Whether Johan would have agreed with me about this I do not know. He was taken from us at a moment when we needed his wisdom perhaps more than ever before. Had he lived, there can be no doubt that he would have been one of the leading architects in the construction of the new Europe, and there is no one quite able to take his place. But if we bear in mind his example, and the principles that governed his writings and his actions, I think that we shall not go very far wrong.

14

Berlin 1995

The European States-System in an Era of Change (For the Germans)

The concept of a 'system of states' as an organizing principle of international relations has for centuries been taken for granted both by statesmen and by theorists – or, as Kant put it, both by bureaucrats and by philosophers. Developing as it did in Western Europe during the seventeenth and eighteenth centuries – most historians would date it from the Peace of Westphalia in 1648 – the system reached its apogee in the nineteenth century and became a paradigm for international organization. In the twentieth century, as new political entities fought themselves free from the dominance of disintegrating Empires – first in Eastern Europe, then overseas – they established themselves as 'states' on the European model. They were sovereign over their internal concerns; demanding from their citizens a total loyalty which where possible was justified by ethnic or other historic bonds of identity; co-operating with one another in a limited fashion under the auspices of various international organizations; but retaining at least a semblance of control over their own destinies by the maintenance of armed forces not only for self-defence, but as instruments in the conduct of their national policies. It is somewhat ironic that at the moment when this 'European model' has become globally accepted as the organizing principle of international relations, we should within Europe be trying to move away from it and find a broader focus of loyalty that might be more appropriate to the social and economic needs of peoples living in a post-industrial society. It is also significant that we are finding very great difficulty in doing so.

* * * * *

The State as it developed in the eighteenth century was very much a child of the Enlightenment. In contrast to the feudal, quasi-sacerdotal system out of which it evolved in which obedience was mandated by Divine Command, it postulated a purely secular concept of loyalty. Domestically it was based, even in its most authoritarian guises, on a principle of mutal obligation between rulers and ruled. In the conduct of international relations, both in peace and in war, 'statesmen' (and the very word is significant) worked within limits defined by Reason; the very specific kind of reason known as *raison d'état*. The governing principle of their mutual relations was that of 'balance'. They tried to maintain, in the part of the world that lay within their own control, the stability that Isaac Newton had discerned in the cosmic order of the universe. It was a system that assumed, among the elites responsible for its management, a common value-system and a common culture; and between the seventeenth and the nineteenth centuries such a culture did indeed bind together the aristocracy of Europe from which those elites were recruited.

With the advent of democracy that monopoly was broken and stability was less easy to maintain. Populist governments could swing between extremes of hegemonial ambition – witness the example of the French Revolution in 1793 and the Nazis a century and a half later – and the kind of self-absorbed lethargy that characterized Britain and the United States between the wars, to mention no more recent examples. As de Tocqueville observed, the conduct of foreign affairs demands a kind of concentrated attention, a blend of watchfulness, boldness and moderation, such as is seldom found in democracies.

The supreme exemplar of those virtues was Herbert von Bismarck. Bismarck, a conservative Prussian aristocrat, was the reluctant architect of a Germany whose potential he himself distrusted. Having created it, he devoted the remaining two decades of his career to managing the European balance that the very existence of Germany tended to upset. The Second Reich was a giant, but Bismarck was concerned to see that she did not behave like one. His successors were not so careful. Through the clumsiness of their policy they created exactly the balance against them that Bismarck had worked to avoid. A lethal combination of apprehension and ambition created by 1914 a situation in which, for the ruling circles in Berlin, war seemed the most acceptable – for some, even the most welcome – solution of problems that were largely imaginary, if not wholly self-created.

For Germany's adversaries, the First World War was, at least in part, a struggle to destroy what they saw as the threat of German hegemonialism, and to restore the balance of power. In the course of that war they discovered that Germany was too strong for such a balance to be recreated within Europe alone. It could be done only with the aid of the United States. After the war, once the United States withdrew its weight from the balance and so long as the Soviet Union was pre-occupied with its own affairs, the scales dipped inevitably towards the establishment of a German hegemony; a hegemony which, but for Hitler – and it must be said, even with Hitler – many influential figures both in Britain and in France would have been very inclined to accept.

The eventual solution to the problem of the European balance was of course brutal: the division of Germany, the abandonment of Central and Eastern Europe to Soviet domination, and the militarization of Western Europe under the leadership of the United States. For half a century the traditional states-system of Europe disappeared; or rather, it survived only in the truncated form of the states of Western Europe, including a now much diminished Germany, seeking a new *modus vivendi* under the protection of the United States. For some of its members, particularly those defeated in the Second World War, the solution seemed to lie in the creation of a new European entity that would transcend state rivalries and open a new and happier chapter in the history of the Continent. Others, notably Britain, attempted to maintain their traditional national sovereignty, in spite of increasingly adverse strategic and economic circumstances. The French contributed to both schools of thought, and found surprisingly little difficulty in doing so. But all tacitly agreed that war between them was no longer an option for the settlement of their differences – an agreement all the more convincing because it *was* tacit rather than formalized in a new Kellogg-Briand Pact. Still, the peoples of Europe, however shrunken and pacific, could not escape their history. Even within the framework of the North Atlantic Alliance and the evolving European Community the outlines of the traditional states-system, with its inbuilt suspicions and rivalries, still remained intact.

At the beginning of this last decade of our century, the Cold War has come suddenly and dramatically to an end, and with it the transformation it had effected in the European balance. The collapse of the Soviet Union liberated East and Central Europe and made possible the reunification of Germany. The end of the 'Soviet Threat' reduced American interest in European affairs. A chastened Russia demanded re-admission to 'the common European House'. The frontiers of Europe, in fact, reverted to what they had been in 1914. After nearly half a century there has re-emerged a unified Germany at the centre of a European Continent which by her position, her power and her wealth she is bound to dominate, whether she wants to or not. It is a situation that has made Germany's neighbours understandably apprehensive, and one which the Germans themselves certainly do not welcome.

If the traditional pattern of *Staatspolitik* were to be renewed and European statesmen were to take up the game where it was left before the two World Wars, there would be good cause for apprehension. By all the normal indicators of power a German hegemony over the Continent would once again seem inevitable, unless once more checked by an alliance of her neighbours that would again have to include Russia. (And we tend to forget the extent to which, in the immediate aftermath of the Second World War, fear of German revival fuelled the attempts of the Western allies to remain on good terms with Stalin in spite of his treatment of Eastern Europe.) There is indeed a school of international theorists in the United States calling themselves 'Structural Determinists' who believe that such a development is inevitable, and that Germany is bound to emerge as a nuclear power. But I have met nobody in Europe, either inside Germany or outside, who believes anything of the kind. There is a general sense that, although the European states-system has survived both World Wars and the Cold War, it has radically changed its nature, and European statesmen cannot take up the game where they left off in 1914, or 1939, or 1945, even if they wanted to.

* * * * *

To understand why this should be so, we need to consider another dimension of the international system and examine another historical development complementary to that of the State; that of the Nation. Thanks to some of its more unpleasant recent manifestations in South-Eastern Europe, nationalism has for the past few years been subjected to a hostile, almost pathological scrutiny, and in general its historical record has not been good. But national sentiment has served, and can continue to serve, a very necessary function.

As has been very generally observed, the fundamental difference between the nationalism of Western and of Eastern Europe is that in the former case states created nations and in the latter nations created, or attempted to create, states. The European states of the eighteenth century were the creation of dynasties, and dynastic loyalty was initially sufficient to legitimize them. Their inhabitants were subjects of a monarch, not citizens of a country. Then as populations grew and became better educated, and as an increasing proportion became involved in political affairs, a more effective link was needed to bind them together. There developed a greater or lesser degree of 'national self-consciousness', and with it the sense that loyalty to the state was the consequence of membership of a 'nation' or a 'people'; a unique and comprehensive community defined by its language and its historic culture. In some cases this happened slowly and incrementally. In others it was the result of deliberate indoctrination. It was normally strengthened by international conflict, but was often the consequence of domestic developments as well. In Britain national self-consciousness, and self-confidence, had already become sufficiently strong by the eighteenth century for an unpopular dynasty to be expelled and a more docile one imported from Germany. In France an even more precise concept of the

Nation was to legitimize the overthrow of the dynasty and its purely conditional, ultimately unsuccessful restoration. In both, the nation, or the people, defined themselves in opposition to a monarchy whose legitimacy they rejected. The same occurred, even more explicitly, beyond the Atlantic with the emergence of the United States.

But in Germany things worked out differently. In Prussia the Hohenzollern dynasty was to use the concept of the Nation, not only to legitimize its own rule, but to extend its authority over the peoples of a newly united Germany. Whereas in Britain and France – and even more so in the United States – the concept of the Nation was closely associated with that of self-rule exercised through a balanced constitution guaranteeing the rule of law, in Germany the opposite was to be the case. Western concepts of self-government, individual freedom and human rights such as developed – from the English through the American to the French Revolution, found little place in the Germany created by the Hohenzollerns. Those who professed them were all too often suspected as *reichsfeindlich*, un-German.

In all nationalism there is an element of primitive tribalism; that is, pride in the peculiarities of one's society just because it *is* peculiar, and hostility to exogenous societies just because they *are* different. In the two World Wars, for the bulk of the combatants, it was enough to know that they were fighting for their country – Britain, Germany, France, America, Russia – against a foreign threat to their 'way of life'. But in the nationalism of the British, the French, and most of all the Americans, there was also an element of universalism. They believed that their national loyalties embodied values that were applicable to the whole of mankind, and that their victory would involve the liberation of their adversaries rather than their conquest. It was a universalism that had had its drawbacks. It was after all the universalism of the French Revolution that had provoked the nationalism of Germans who did not appreciate the liberties brought to them on the points of French bayonets. Nor was the 'Rule of Law' by which the British justified the maintenance of their overseas Empire or the *mission civilisatrice* by which the French justified theirs always fully appreciated by those on whom these benefits were imposed. None the less these nationalisms were not simply tribal. They had, and still have, a supranational resonance, and can still be professed without embarrassment or guilt.

It was the tragedy of German nationalism that it was never able to transcend its tribal origins. Indeed it was largely rooted in a reaction against precisely the cosmopolitan values of the Enlightenment embodied in the American and the French revolutions. In the First World War the German people saw themselves as fighting to defend a *Kultur* of unique richness and profundity against the decadent commercialism of the West and the primitive barbarism of the East. It was, it must be said, a culture that strongly emphasized the values of what the dominant groups within it liked to regard as a warrior society, one of heroes as opposed to business-men, *Helden* against *Händler*; one that regarded struggle as ennobling and war as the finest test of moral virtues. But in the Second World War traditional German patriotism became so adulterated by the hegemonial racism of the Nazi Revolution as to be almost unrecognizable and unrescuable. As a result of that terrible experience the very concept of 'the nation' has become for many thoughtful Germans entirely unacceptable.

It is this elimination of traditional nationalist sentiment from contemporary German culture that makes the prospect of the restoration of German power acceptable to her neighbours, as well as making Germany the most enthusiastic among the leading powers in Europe for the creation of a effective European Union. But again, it places Germany in a rather different position from her European neighbours, notably Britain. For the British, the experience of the two World Wars did not discredit national sentiment: on the contrary, it validated it. Both wars, but especially the second, could be credibly depicted as struggles not simply between Britain and Germany, but between two concepts of international order, between Freedom and Tyranny; and the concept for which Britain and her allies had fought emerged triumphant. It was possible to see Winston Churchill, not only as a great national leader, but as a statesman embodying universal principles of freedom and self-government. Further, the role of national sentiment in creating solidarity within a society deeply divided along lines of class is now recalled with a certain nostalgia. Whatever the rational arguments in favour of submerging national identity in a greater European Union, there is among the British people a stubborn reluctance to abandon loyalties and to submerge an identity that have hitherto served them very well. For the British, the Second World War was not, as it was for the Germans, a terrible trauma that seemed to discredit all their historical values and loyalties. On the contrary, it seemed to justify them, as much for the idealistic internationalists of the Left as for the traditional patriots of the Right.

The French have less difficulty in reconciling national sentiment with the concept of Europe. The terrible sacrifices of the First World War and the humiliations of the Second have led to a proud reassertion of national identity, but unlike the case of the British that reassertion has not led them away from the European idea. Rather, it has led them towards it. In the days of her grandeur, France was always the cultural and political leader of Europe. In so far as the Continent has a political and cultural unity, one might say that it has been the creation, first of the French culture of the *ancien régime* and then of the Napoleonic conquests that extended throughout Western Europe a common system of administration and law. Both the admirers and the critics of France can see in 'the European Idea' an extension of French universalism, and judge it accordingly. For many in Britain it has reinforced their hostility to the whole concept of European unity. For as many Germans the goal of European unity was sufficiently desirable to make its French flavour tolerable; especially since there was every reason to suppose that French political dominance would be more than counter-balanced by German wealth.

*   *   *   *   *

For those who wish to see the creation of a European entity that will replace the old national rivalries, traditional nationalism is of course an obstacle that needs to be transcended and if possible eliminated entirely. For them, contemporary Germany with its subdued sense of nationality is a model, and the national self-consciousness of Britain an archaic survival from an earlier and less fortunate age. This is a judgement that has to be examined very carefully. Arguably, there has to be an element of irrationality and emotion in any loyalty if it is to be effective. The relationship between citizens and the state cannot be purely contractual. If the desire for some kind of emotional bonding could be removed from the human psyche, the world would obviously be a much more reasonable, if a somewhat duller place; but it seems to be part of our nature, and if it is not focused upon the state, it tends to find an outlet in other, often more destructive group-loyalties. Hitler mobilized this sentiment to such terrible effect that in Germany the very memory of it has now been shunned. I must confess to some sympathy with those who wish to see the concept of *Deutschland* once again inspiring the same sense of pride and commitment that I can feel for the concept of Britain or my French and American friends feel for their own countries. But if it is not to be purely tribal, an extension of loyalty to one's football team, that concept must be linked to a world of moral imperatives that have at least some aspiration towards universalism. Nothing is more repellent than the abuse of national symbols and the hijacking of national loyalty in the service of xenophobic racism. But unless nationalism is seen, and taught, as the bonding together of a community in the higher service of mankind, that is how it is likely to end up.

Further, unless a people have some consciousness of themselves as a people (and by 'people' I do not mean that emotive and untranslatable term, *Volk*) they are unlikely to be effective in the world of international affairs. Here again, I would draw a contrast between Britain and Germany. In spite of their undeniable and in many respects humiliating decline, the

British retain a degree of national cohesion and self-confidence that has enabled them, in the words of the present Foreign Secretary, to 'box above their weight' in international affairs, and to be regarded as a far more significant participant than their purely economic power would warrant. Their readiness to commit armed forces to international enterprises, and to use them in defence of their interests in remote corners of the world – a readiness that would be impossible without a very wide measure of popular support – has been a quite important element in this. To a large extent, the same holds true of France. It is, as I have said, the absence of any such spirit of national pride and self-assertiveness that makes Germany so acceptable in Europe, not only as a partner, but as a very senior partner. It is only a dwindling band of ageing xenophobes who see in the Germany of Chancellor Kohl a revival of the threat posed by that of Kaiser Wilhelm II or Adolf Hitler. But it does mean that Germany still boxes rather below her weight; and Germany has, from the enormous resources of her cultural and historical experience, a great deal more to offer the world than her wealth and her technological expertise. The richness of a culture that can claim some of the greatest names in European civilization; and, perhaps even more, the amazing achievement of the past half-century in building up, from the rubble of total destruction, a democratic, prosperous and peaceful community that is a model to the world; all this should be a cause for proper national pride.

It is, however, quite possible that Germany is pointing a way to the future in which the historic national sentiments of her neighbours will also have disappeared, and the states of Europe will negotiate with one another as dispassionately – or no more passionately – as do business enterprises; *Gesellschaften* rather than *Gemeinschaften*. But that the European Union can ever replace the old nation-states as a comparable focus of loyalty seems to me highly improbable. Differences in culture, of which linguistic diversity is only a symptom, mean that only a small, sophisticated and highly unrepresentative proportion of the population of any European state (with the possible exception of the Benelux countries) can regard the European Union as anything more than a convenient medium of international co-operation; certainly not as a cohesive and finite community that has nurtured them, to which they owe their primary loyalty, and at whose bidding they would be willing to go to war. On the contrary: the more the European Union tries to extend its powers, the greater degree of *national* resistance it encounters; that is, the more it revives national sentiments that were previously dormant, and indeed believed to be dead. Reactions to the Maastricht Treaty have shown that Britain was not exceptional in her resistance to the trend towards federalism, and that Mrs Thatcher had considerably more allies than had generally been supposed.

Political scientists and economists may predict that a combination of economic necessity and transnational flows will in the long run erode the states-system of Europe and bring into being a federation that will transcend it as totally as the creation of the German Reich in 1870 transcended the old *Kleinstaaterei*. My own belief is that this will not happen until we have a common linguistic culture. Even then we would need a statesman of the stature of Bismarck, and probably, I am afraid, a war. Bismarck needed at least two; one to assert Prussian dominance in Germany, and one to unite all Germans against a common adversary. For Europe, such a means of forging unity is as undesirable as it is improbable. Who, after all, would we fight? If we fought the Russians, it would be as junior allies of the Americans. If we fought the United States, we would lose. As for the nightmare scenario sometimes projected of a European unity being forged in the crucible of a race conflict against the Muslim world, this would seem to me a cure infinitely worse than the disease.

A slightly less improbable eventuality would be evolution into a kind of Helvetic Union, a prosperous, self-governing multi-lingual confederation; but the Swiss have achieved this only at the cost of abandoning any foreign or military policy, and sympathetic though some elements in Germany may feel towards such a solution, the French and British are likely to find this too high a price to pay. The idea of a centre of wealth and potential power on the scale of a united Europe abandoning to the United States and Japan all influence on the affairs of the world is one that I myself find it very hard to visualize. For that perhaps we really *would* need a war, and one in which we were defeated.

So for the foreseeable future the historic system of European states is likely to survive. Within the European Union traditional rivalries will remain, perhaps reinforced by new ones as further interests and involvements develop. But that system has always been one of co-operation as well as rivalry, and the habit of co-operation has now become second nature to European statesmen. If it remains a *Europe des patries* as de Gaulle foresaw, so much the better. That means that its institutions will continue to be rooted in the basic loyalties of the still highly diverse peoples of which Europe is still made up. And if I may express a purely personal and irrational preference, I hope that we may remain highly diverse, for it is that which constitutes the real strength of European civilization. As the French put it in a somewhat different context: *Vive la différence!*

Britain, France, and the Making of Europe
(For the French)

Twice during the past ten years I have been invited by Europhile British statesmen, one from each of our leading political parties, to provide them with historical arguments to use in their campaigns to 'get Britain into Europe'. Is it not the case, they asked, that Britain's whole culture is European? That our roots are identical with those of our neighbours across the Channel and the North Sea? That our cultures have constantly interpenetrated, and the sea, so far from being a barrier, has in fact been a link fostering a continual interchange of trade and ideas? Could I not, they asked, draft a few persuasive sentences that would help them persuade their sceptical audiences that, as Britain's past has lain in Europe, so must her future; and the logic of history lies in her becoming a core member of the European Community, or Union?

To both of them I had reluctantly to reply that, in spite of being myself an enthusiastic Europhile, I could do nothing of the kind. There was no comfort to be found in the past, and the Europhobes were right in arguing that to merge ourselves in any European entity would be to turn our backs on five hundred years of our history. Certainly Britain, or most of it, was part of the Roman Empire, although there is nothing left of that but roads and ruins. Certainly we were colonized, in the days of the *Völkerwanderung*, by successive Teutonic and Scandinavian tribes, the last of these being the Normans whose Empire embraced also Western France and much of the Mediterranean. Certainly the ambitions of our Norman rulers and their cousins involved us in dynastic conflicts which were to culminate in the Hundred Years' War that was to do so much to shape both the English and the French identities. And most important of all, for five hundred years we were part of an undifferentiated Western Christendom, a truly Catholic Church that not only shaped our thinking but bequeathed to us, as it did to you, an architectural legacy whose splendour still leaves us awestruck. Did not all this make us 'part of Europe'?

At the time it did. But that time was five hundred years ago. From the beginning of the sixteenth century until our own lifetime, Britain has followed a path of development, a *Sonderweg*, that has increasingly separated us from our European neighbours. Let me start by outlining the main reasons why British historical and cultural consciousness is so different from that of Continental Europe, and why our history is an obstacle rather than a bridge to our entry into any kind of European Union.

History is important if we are to understand ourselves. We are all shaped by our past; not so much by what we learn of it at school as by the way that it has shaped our institutions and cultural attitudes. Communities are built up by shared needs and shared experiences, and during the past five centuries Britain has been influenced much more by experiences that she did not share with her European neighbours than by those that she did.

The first great experience was of course the Reformation, the revulsion against an Italian-dominated Catholic Church. But that experience was shared by virtually the whole of Europe north of the Alps and the Pyrenees. It did not in itself differentiate Britain from her European neighbours; indeed the wars it precipitated if anything drew us closer to them. But what was really significant for our history were the consequences of the Reformation, and two in particular.

First, whereas in Europe, especially Germany, the Reformation led to a strengthening of monarchical power through the establishment of a national church, in England and Scotland it created an irresistible movement of ecclesiastical decentralization – what we would today call 'subsidiarity' – whereby individual congregations decided for themselves how they would worship. These 'Protestants', or 'Dissenters' were protesting as much against, and dissenting from, the national Anglican Church established by the Tudor sovereigns as they were against the Church of Rome. It is true that they failed to establish more than a brief political ascendancy in the aftermath of our civil wars, but they sank deep cultural roots in British society which have never been eradicated. In the United States, of course, they sunk still deeper. A large proportion of the British population, even if they no longer hold any specific religious belief, still remain deeply *Protestant*; suspicious of central government and all their doings, suspicious of the upper-class ruling elites, and deeply suspicious of foreigners, especially Roman Catholic foreigners. From the point of view of the Europhiles, it is a great pity that the European Community was established by a treaty signed in Rome.

The second consequence of the Reformation that separated us from our European neighbours was the Counter-Reformation; an event of enormous importance in the cultural and political history of Continental Europe, but one that Britain escaped. The Catholic Church and the great European dynasties sank their differences, crushed religious dissent as far as their armies could reach, enforced a pattern of obedience to a powerful central authority and confirmed their triumph by building the great baroque churches and palaces which are the glories of European culture but are so conspicuous by their absence in England. If the Stuarts had won the civil wars, our artistic heritage might have been considerably improved, but at the expense of our political development. As it was, the Stuarts were banished in 1689 by a landed oligarchy who celebrated *their* ascendancy by building country houses far grander than anything our unfortunate monarchs were able to afford. The power and popularity of the new regime was confirmed by another Hundred Years' War against France – a war fought initially for the preservation of the Protestant Settlement against the forces of absolutism and catholicism embodied in the regime of Louis XIV, but one that developed into a competition for global hegemony. It was in the course of that conflict, which filled the entire eighteenth century, that the self-image of the British people became crystallized: Protestant as against Catholic (which caused, and still causes us, so much trouble with the Irish); libertarian as against absolutist; and above all oceanic as against Continental, so long as the Royal Navy ruled the waves. Conversely the image of Continental Europe became equally confirmed, especially that of the French: impoverished, sunk in superstition, eating frogs. These stereotypes remained dominant in England, I regret to say, until well into the twentieth century.

Then came the next great defining experience for Continental Europe that we did not share; the French Revolution, and its extension throughout Western Europe through the Napoleonic conquests. Welcomed at first as the destruction of tyranny and superstition, the Revolution rapidly appeared to be the imposition of a new and yet more dangerous kind of tyranny, as well as bringing about a formidable renaissance of French military power. There were those in England, as there were throughout Europe, who whole-heartedly admired the Napoleonic achievements; the destruction of aristocratic and ecclesiastical privilege, the replacement of archaic survivals by legal and political institutions based on reason, equality, and human rights; the translation of the ideas of the Enlightenment into political actuality. Had Napoleon successfully invaded us, he might really have made Britain part of Europe, sharing those great legal and administrative codes that still provide the basis for so many West-European institutions; even perhaps making us drive on the right-hand side of the road. But for better or worse, it was an experience that Britain escaped. We retained our own archaic laws and social structure, priding ourselves on their irrationality. Our victories in those wars increased our alienation from the continent, and, be it said, our hubris; and both were to be yet further increased by the wealth and prestige that accrued during the nineteenth century through the development of the British Empire overseas and the global expansion of the Anglophone world. For the British the Continent remained 'abroad' and foreign in a way that Canada, Australia, the United States – even India – did not. French was taught in schools, rather half-heartedly, but only aspiring diplomats seriously bothered to learn it.

Finally we come to our own disastrous century. The First World War should have taught us that our involvement in the Continent was inescapable. Unfortunately the experience was so appalling that afterwards we did our best to ignore that lesson and again turned our backs on 'quarrels between far-away peoples of whom we knew nothing'. As a result we bear a terrible responsibility for the rise of Hitler. As for the Second World War, this was widely seen in Britain as a kind of re-run of the Napoleonic wars, to which, from the British point of view, it did indeed bear a superficial similarity. Once again there was an attempt forcibly to create a 'New Order' in Europe, though one based this time not on reason and the rights of man but on irrationality, cruelty, and racial hegemony. Once again, the Channel saved us from an experience that, ghastly as it was, would be a further bond of unity among the peoples of Continental Europe. Once again we were victorious, if this time by courtesy of the United States. And once again, victory gave us a sense of superiority over continental neighbours whom we had either liberated or conquered. It was in this mood of hubris that our rulers rejected the chance to take part in the Messina conference ten years later. Within five years we were to be knocking at the door of Europe, as humble petitioners asking to be let in.

* * * * *

This is the baggage that we have brought from the past, and which still encumbers us. Had we lost the war, we might have been as anxious to shed these encumbrances as the Germans have been anxious to shed theirs, and, like them, welcomed a European identity as a way of making a fresh start. But history decided otherwise.

The French, happily, have no such encumbrances. Its course has been such that you can see European Union as a continuation, a culmination even, of your own history rather than as an interruption. The history of France has always been one of successful centralization. Your monarchs had their problems, as had ours, with religious dissension and aristocratic separatism, but they overcame their Huguenots and their *frondeurs* in a way that the Stuarts could not. Louis XIV brought his *noblesse* to Versailles, where he could keep an eye on them, and thus decapitated provincial revolt. Colbert created the machinery of the first modern state, while Vauban rationalized its frontier defences. The Revolution completed the work of state-building, destroying those provincial, class and ecclesiastical immunities that had survived into the *ancien régime*. The extension of those reforms, the spread of liberty, equality and fraternity to France's less fortunate neighbours then appeared as a duty: the *tricoleur* was a symbol, not of national conquest, but of liberation, and for many Europeans Napoleon *was* indeed seen as a liberator – Hegel's 'World Spirit on Horseback'. The work of liberation and rationalization that the Revolution had done for France, France must now do for Europe. And it seems to the eyes of a sympathetic Englishman that the same sense of *mission civilisatrice* has inspired French sponsorship and support for the European Union. It lies in the logic of your history, as it does not in ours.

It is a fair argument, whether Britain helped to liberate Europe from Napoleonic despotism or frustrated the creation of a new, fair and rational European order based upon the rights of man. The basic problem for the British, however, was that the creation of that order, however fair and rational, involved the kind of accumulation and centralization of power of which they had become congenitally suspicious, whether within their own country or outside it. Processes and institutions accepted in France as necessary mechanisms of order, efficiency and civilization were – and often still are – regarded in England with instinctive suspicion and dislike. Montesquieu's picture of the division of powers in eighteenth-century England was an idealization, but the role of Parliament – and increasingly, interestingly enough, the judiciary – as a watch-dog over the executive is still taken very seriously indeed. I would certainly not say that the British are anarchic; indeed we pride ourselves, rightly or wrongly, on being a great deal more law-abiding than you are. But we are *Protestant* in a way that you are not; suspicious of government, disliking the accumulation of power wherever it may be held, and resenting its use. And if that power is held by 'foreigners', so much the worse.

No one realized this more clearly than that great statesman, Charles de Gaulle. The four years that he spent in London did little to make him Anglophile but they gave him a deep understanding of the strengths and limitations of the British character. These were not a European people: their sympathies and inclinations, he perceived, lay elsewhere. He had observed the sense almost of relief with which the British reacted to the disasters of the summer of 1940 which severed their continental entanglements and left them on their own. When twenty years later a chastened British Prime Minister came as a suppliant to request membership of the new European Community, de Gaulle's refusal was based, not on pique, but on a well-founded appreciation that in that Community, whatever the good intentions of her governments, Britain was always likely to be a *mauvais coucheur*. I doubt, however, whether even he anticipated what restless nights were to be experienced by anyone who found themselves in bed with Mrs Thatcher.

For by the 1960s the British government had realized that there was nowhere left for them to go. The Suez fiasco had shown that we did not belong to the 'top table', and that the United States had no interest in keeping us there. The Commonwealth was dissolving as a military, political and economic entity. Continental Europe, on the other hand, was beginning to boom: not only West Germany but France and Italy were experiencing an economic miracle that left Britain far behind. British financial and commercial circles and the governmnent departments they dealt with became increasingly 'Europhile' and very slowly the electorate followed them; but how far those elites were prepared to go, and how far the country was prepared to follow them, remained, and still remains, an open question.

I am not qualified to discuss the small print of the 'making of Europe', or the large print either: like most of my countrymen, I find much of it bewildering and unintelligible. But that bewilderment and unintelligibility is itself significant. The making of Europe, as Clemenceau said of the making of war, is too serious a matter to be left to the experts. Mrs Thatcher observed the experts at work throughout the 1980s, and although even she could never out-argue them, she had a gut feeling that it was *all wrong* – a feeling, it must be said, that was shared by a large proportion of the British electorate. And not only the *British* electorate: when the experts produced at Maastricht a document quite unintelligible to anyone except themselves, the Danish electorate (another Protestant country, be it noted) rejected it quite unequivocally. Even the people of France, when they were consulted, showed themselves to be far from enthusiastic.[1] This gap between the experts and the electorates on whose behalf they were negotiating became known, in Eurojargon, as 'the democratic deficit', and it is one that we are still trying to make up.

'It is no accident', as the Marxists used to say, that the democratic deficit is taken more seriously in Britain than in any other major European country, or that those continental states where it *is* taken seriously share Britain's Protestant culture, if not her insularity. Their political culture – in which both the Counter-Reformation and the Napoleonic Enlightenment have played such a major part – has made the peoples of Continental

---

[1] I was, at the time of the Danish referendum, at a conference attended by a number of officials from the European Commission. They were *indignant* that the text of the treaty had been circulated to the Danish electorate at all!

Europe more acquiescent and perhaps more indifferent to the activities of their leaders – an acquiescence that sometimes seems based on a bland determination to ignore any agreements that those leaders sign on their behalf. The British, however, extend to Brussels the inherent mistrust that they have always felt towards the focus of their own administrative system in Whitehall. The activities of Whitehall are legitimized only because they are, at least in principle, controlled by Westminster, that is to say, by Parliament; and Parliament is, again in principle, accountable to the British electorate – in principle, and, every five years, in practice. In fact the executive, in Britain as elsewhere, has enormous powers not strictly limited by the constitution, and necessarily so. But the principle of *accountability* is absolutely central to the British political culture. It is the apparent absence of this in the operations of the European Union that causes so much disquiet in Britain, and lends itself to exploitation by those who instinctively mistrust the whole European idea.

Again I say 'apparent'. In principle, of course, the European Commission is as accountable to the Council of Ministers as in England the Whitehall machine is responsible through its ministers to an elected Parliament; while there is in addition a European Parliament to monitor its actions. In practice those ministers are very busy people who meet seldom, and many decisions are necessarily taken by the *fonctionnaires* in Brussels – as in domestic matters they are necessarily taken by the *fonctionnaires* in Whitehall. But in these matters perceptions are all-important. It is the belief in the real accountability of government to Parliament and of Parliament to people that legitimizes the actions of the British government, however widely separated the image is from the reality. As yet, no such belief has been created about the operations of the European Commission, and it may take many years to create it. These are not matters, alas, of constitutional formulae, but of political cultures that are compounded as much of irrational as of rational elements, as much of perceptions as they are of realities.

We have our own problems with this within the so-called United Kingdom. We totally failed to assimilate the Irish, for whom the English have always been seen as alien oppressors, and have continual problems with the Scots and the Welsh. Fundamentally governments are legitimized only if they are perceived to represent and embody a cohesive and self-conscious political *community*. That community may have originally been created by conquest and sustained by prescription, as both France and Britain were created by the conflicts and the sometimes oppressive power of their ruling dynasties. They may still have to be nourished by the propagation of historical and social myth. But it is only this consciousness of community that enables people freely and willingly to entrust the responsibilities of government to one another in the belief that the decisions taken on their behalf, however disagreeable, are in their best interests, and to accept and carry them out however much they may disagree. Communities are not created by simple acts of will or the signature of treaties – least of all nations, the highest communities of all. They need to have grown together, even if they were originally forced together. Treaties, acts of independence, constitutions, declarations of rights, are effective only in so far as they confirm what is already there.

What is already there, however, is usually at first only a community of elites. The Act of Union between England and Scotland that created our United Kingdom, logical as it appeared to both governments, was for many years deeply unpopular in both countries. Only a minority in the American colonies desired independence from Britain, and they dealt with their dissidents rather brutally. In France, in spite of the draconian measures of the Revolution and the mobilizing effect of the Napoleonic wars, at least a century was needed to turn the peasants of the provinces (in the words of an American historian) into Frenchmen, and it will take at least as long to turn the British into Europeans. The treaty establishing the European Community was similarly aspirational. It was the work of a community of elites – French, Germans, Italians, Belgian, Dutch – whose cultural background and historical experience had shaped a community of minds. They were creating a framework for a community rather than the community itself; and they were doing so without what is normally regarded as the first requirement of any community, a common language. And if the members of the community retained the distinct cultural identities embodied in their language, then, however common their historical experience and however compatible their interests, can such a *Europe des patries* ever be more than the kind of high-level *Zollverein* in which even the British could feel themselves at home?

*   *   *   *   *

It is difficult to create a community without a common language but a common language is not in itself sufficient to create a community. This brings me to a further problem faced by the British in assimilating themselves to the community of Europe; the lingering belief that our language and political culture link us more closely to the United States than to our continental neighbours – the so-called 'special relationship'. This is not to be dismissed. The protestant political culture that differentiates Britain from the Continent exists in even greater intensity in the United States, settled as they were initially by people who found even British protestantism too conformist. Their emphasis on local self-government and mistrust of central authority is sometimes carried to bizarre if not lethal extremes. Their legal system derives directly from English roots. But we must go a long way back to find the shared experiences that make a true, as opposed to an imagined, political community. If Britain began growing away from Continental Europe in the sixteenth century, the Americans began growing away from Britain in the seventeenth, and the gap widened still faster. From its very origins, the American historical experience and the culture that it shaped has been as different from that of the British as from that of the rest of Europe. Even before the great immigrations of the nineteenth century swamped the original Anglophone settlers, American dislike and mistrust of the British was one of the most powerful factors in shaping their foreign policy. The concept of a 'special relationship' only began to develop at the turn of the century as the American East-Coast elite felt increasingly ill at ease in its own polyglot community, and it has survived only so long as that elite has been able to retain its political and cultural dominance. Winston Churchill, Harold Macmillan, and perhaps Margaret Thatcher were the only British statesmen who successfully exploited it in such a way as to influence American foreign policy. There are still Americans and British of the older generation – who feel that they have more in common with one another than they have with their own countrymen; but it is not a healthy situation, nor one likely to last for very much longer.

It has very largely been the growing understanding of the fragility of the 'special relationship' that has spread the realization among the British political classes, and increasingly the electorate as a whole, that unless we accept our membership of the European community we are on our own in a competitive and hostile world. As I have indicated, the realization began with the Suez debacle. Nevertheless the effects of that disaster were mitigated, if not totally counteracted, by the continuation of the Cold War. The Americans still saw Britain as their most reliable ally against the Soviet Union and they therefore maintained a close, if not special relationship, the preservation of which became the guiding principle of British foreign policy. Future historians may question the wisdom of that policy. In so far as it prevented us from accepting whole-heartedly our membership of the European Community I believe that their criticisms will be justified. But I must admit that I myself have worked throughout my life to preserve that relationship, believing, first, that the stability and prosperity of the world depended on decisions taken in Washington, and, second, that the best way to affect those decisions was to be accepted as a friend rather than mistrusted as an adversary.

Yet I am afraid that, with the end of the Cold War, that relationship, and the relationship of the United States to Europe as a whole, will be difficult to sustain. Our statesmen, our diplomats, our journalists, our foreign-affairs specialists, will continue to interact as easily with their American opposite numbers as they ever did. We will still find kindred spirits whose analysis of the international situation, and prescriptions for dealing with it, are identical with our own; but although these people may continue to steer American foreign policy, the fuel that drove the vessel, the fundamental sentiment that kept the American people united behind their governments, was a visceral anti-communism. Their primary interest in Europe, as it was in Britain, was as allies in the Cold War. Now that has gone. There is no longer any overriding issue to unite the Americans behind a single foreign policy, and there are many to divide them. Their elites may continue to urge on them the responsibilities of world leadership, but they themselves are divided over the direction in which to lead, and their electorates show no enthusiasm about following. There is a real danger that the international-affairs community among which we have so many friends and which has done such good service to the world will become talking heads divorced from their body.

Which brings me back to the European Community. Although we must do all we can to sustain a close and friendly relationship with the United States, we have to accept that an era that opened in 1940, with the American entry into the Second World War and their decision to give priority to the European over the Pacific war theatre, is finally ended. Europe was rescued by the United States during the war and nourished after it, but that period of dependence is over and we must cope on our own. NATO I hope will survive, but its purposes are likely to be increasingly political rather than military, and the evolution within it of a distinct European entity is only a recognition of political reality.

As for the making of Europe, the difficulties I have outlined do not make me believe that it is any the less possible, or any the less necessary. The British difficulties with the concept cannot be blamed on any particular statesman – or stateswoman – or political party or group within a party. The anti-Europeanism of our Europhobes would be unimportant if it did not resonate within a broader political consciousness, and however clear-sighted – and far-sighted – the intellectual elites may be, political leaders in Britain cannot afford to move too far ahead of popular sentiment. For us the questions 'how fast?' and 'how far?' can only be resolved pragmatically – an attitude, I know, that is maddening to our Cartesian neighbours. To force the issue, whether over a common currency, a common foreign policy, or most of all a common defence policy, could wreck even such progress as has already been made. Since we cannot be forced into the Community, much less into a political Union, we must be given time to grow into it.

The younger generation in Britain are encumbered with far less historical baggage than their parents and grandparents. For better or worse, they have far less reverence for our historic institutions. They travel easily and frequently throughout the continent, and will do so more easily and more frequently as the tunnel establishes itself as a normal mode of transport. They share a 'youth culture' that, for better or worse, transcends national boundaries. And above all, they are encouraged to become Europeans by the most paradoxical feature of the European Union: its *lingua franca* is English. They will I hope have inherited at least the scepticism of authority and the demand for accountability that characterized their Protestant ancestors; but I am enough of a Protestant myself to believe that this may be the most important contribution that the British can make to the evolution of European political culture.

V

The 'War against Terror'

Royal United Services Institute
2001

War against Terrorism (October 2001)

When in the immediate aftermath of the attack on the World Trade Center the American Secretary of State Colin Powell declared that America was 'at war', he made a very natural but a terrible and irrevocable error. Leaders of the Administration have been trying to put it right ever since.

What Colin Powell said made sense if one uses the term 'war' in the sense of war against crime or against drug-trafficking: that is, the mobilization of all available resources against a dangerous anti-social activity; one that can never be entirely eliminated but can be reduced to, and kept at, a level that does not threaten social stability. The British in their time have fought many such 'wars'; in Palestine, in Ireland, in Cyprus and in Malaya, to mention only a few. But we never called them 'wars': we called them 'emergencies'. This meant that the police and intelligence services were provided with exceptional powers, and were reinforced where necessary by the armed forces, but all continued to operate within a peacetime framework of civil authority. If force had to be used, it was at a minimal level and so far as possible did not interrupt the normal tenor of civil life. The object was to isolate the terrorists from the rest of the community, and to cut them off from external sources of supply. They were not dignified with the status of belligerents: they were criminals, to be regarded as such by the general public and treated as such by the authorities.

To 'declare war' on terrorists, or even more illiterately, on 'terrorism' is at once to accord them a status and dignity that they seek and which they do not deserve. It confers on them a kind of legitimacy. Do they qualify as 'belligerents'? If so, should they not receive the protection of the laws of war? This was something that Irish terrorists always demanded, and was quite properly refused. But their demands helped to muddy the waters, and were given wide credence among their supporters in the United States.

But to use, or rather to misuse the term 'war' is not simply a matter of legality, or pedantic semantics. It has deeper and more dangerous consequences. To declare that one is 'at war' is immediately to create a war psychosis that may be totally counter-productive for the objective that we seek. It will arouse an immediate expectation, and demand, for spectacular military action against some easily identifiable adversary, preferably a hostile state; action leading to decisive results. The use of force is no longer seen as a last resort, to be avoided if humanly possible, but as the first, and the sooner it is used the better. The press demands immediate stories of derring-do, filling their pages with pictures of weapons, ingenious graphics, and contributions from service officers long, and probably deservedly, retired. Any suggestion that the best strategy is not to use military force at all, but more subtle if less heroic means of destroying the adversary are dismissed as 'appeasement' by ministers whose knowledge of history is about on a par with their skill at political management. Figures on the Right, seeing themselves cheated of what the Germans used to call a *frisch, fröhliche Krieg*, a short, jolly war in Afghanistan, demand one against a more satisfying adversary, Iraq; which is rather like the drunk who lost his watch in a dark alley but looked for it under a lamp post because there was more light there. As for their counterparts on the Left, the very word 'war' brings them out on the streets to protest as a matter of principle. The qualities needed in a serious campaign against terrorists – secrecy, intelligence, political sagacity, quiet ruthlessness, covert actions that remain covert, above all infinite patience – all these are forgotten or overriden in a media-stoked frenzy for immediate results, and nagging complaints if they do not get them.

All this is what we have been witnessing over the past three or four weeks. Could it have been avoided? Certainly; rather than what President Bush so unfortunately termed 'a crusade against evil', that is, a military campaign conducted by an alliance dominated by the United States, many people would have preferred a police operation conducted under the auspices of the United Nations on behalf of the international community as a whole, against a criminal conspiracy; whose members should be hunted down and brought before an international court, where they would receive a fair trial and, if found guilty, awarded an appropriate sentence. In an ideal world that is no doubt what would have happened. But we do not live in an ideal world. The destruction of the Twin Towers and the massacre of several thousand innocent New York office-workers was not seen in the United States as a crime against 'the international community' to be appropriately dealt with by the United Nations; a body for which Americans have little respect when they have heard of it at all. For them it was an outrage against the people of America, one far surpassing in infamy even the Japanese attack on Pearl Harbor. Such an insult to their honour was not to be dealt with by a long and meticulous police investigation conducted by international authorities, culminating in an even longer court case in some foreign capital, with sentences that would then no doubt be suspended to allow for further appeals. It cried for immediate and spectacular vengeance to be inflicted by their own armed forces. And who can blame them? In their position we would have felt exactly the same. The wisdom of President Bush in resisting the call for a strategy of vendetta has been admirable, but the pressure is still there, both within and beyond the Administration. It is a demand that can be satisfied only by military action – if possible, rapid and decisive military action. There must be catharsis: the blood of three thousand innocent civilians demands it.

Again, President Bush deserves credit for his attempt to implement the alternative paradigm. He has abjured unilateral action. He has sought, and received, a United Nations mandate. He has built up a wide-ranging coalition that truly does embody 'the international community' so far as such an entity exists. Within a matter of days, almost, the United States has turned her back on the unilateralism and isolationism towards which she seemed to be steering, and resumed her former position as leader of a world community far more extensive than the so-called 'free world' of the old Cold War. Almost equally important, the President and his colleagues have done their best to explain to the American people that this will be a war unlike any other, and they must adjust their expectations accordingly. But it is still a war. The 'w' word has been used, and now cannot be withdrawn; and its use has brought inevitable and irresistible pressure to use military force as soon, and as decisively as possible.

Now a struggle against terrorism, as we have discovered over the past century and not least in Northern Ireland, is unlike a war against drugs or a war against crime in one vital respect. It is fundamentally a 'battle for hearts and minds'; and it is worth remembering that that phrase was first coined in the context of the most successful campaign of the kind that the British Armed Forces have ever fought – the Malayan Emergency in the 1950s (a campaign incidentally that it took some fifteen years to bring to an end). Without hearts and minds one cannot obtain intelligence, and without intelligence terrorists can never be defeated. There is not much of a constituency for criminals or drug-traffickers, and in a campaign against them the government can be reasonably certain that the mass of the public will be on its side. But as we all know, one man's terrorist is another man's freedom-fighter. Terrorists can be successfully destroyed only if public opinion, both at home and abroad, supports the authorities in regarding them as criminals rather than heroes. In the intricate game of skill played between terrorists and the authorities, as we discovered in both Palestine and Ireland, the terrorists have already won an important battle if they can provoke the authorities into using overt armed force against them. They will then be in a win–win situation. Either they will escape to fight another day, or they will be defeated and celebrated as martyrs. In the process of fighting them a lot of innocent civilians will certainly be hurt, which will further erode the moral authority of the government. Who will ever forget Black Sunday in Northern Ireland, when a few salvos of small-arms fire by the British Army gave the IRA a propaganda victory from which the British government was never to recover? And if so much harm can be done by rifle fire, what is one to say about bombing? I can only suggest that it is like trying to eradicate cancer cells with a blow-torch. Whatever its military justification, the bombing of Afghanistan, with the inevitable 'collateral damage' it causes, will gradually whittle away the immense moral ascendancy that we enjoyed as a result of the bombing of the World Trade Center. I hate having to say this, but in six months' time for much of the world that atrocity will be, if not forgotten, then remembered only as history; while every fresh picture on television of a hospital hit, or children crippled by land-mines, or refugees driven from their homes by Western military action, will strengthen the hatred of our adversaries, recruit the ranks of the terrorists and sow fresh doubts in the minds of our supporters.

I have little doubt that the campaign in Afghanistan was undertaken only on the best available political and military advice, in full realization of its military difficulties and political dangers, and in the sincere belief that there was no alternative. It was, as the Americans so nicely put it, an AOS situation: 'All Options Stink'. But in compelling us to undertake it at all, the terrorists had taken the first and all-important trick. I can also understand the military reasoning that drives the campaign. It is based on the political assumption that the terrorist network must be destroyed as quickly as possible before it can do any more damage. It further assumes that the network is master-minded by a single evil genius, Osama bin Laden, whose elimination will demoralize if not destroy his organization. Bin Laden operates out of a country whose rulers refuse to yield him up to the forces of international justice. Those rulers must be compelled to change their minds. The quickest way to break their will is by aerial bombardment, especially since a physical invasion of their territory presents such huge if not insoluble logistical problems. Given these assumptions, what alternative did we have?

But the best reasoning, and the most flawless logic, is of little value if it starts from false assumptions. I have no doubt that voices were raised both in Washington and in Whitehall questioning the need and pointing out the dangers of immediate military action; but if they were, they were at once drowned out by the thunderous political imperative: Something Must be Done. The same voices no doubt also questioned the wisdom, if not the accuracy, of identifying bin Laden as the central and indispensable figure in the terrorist network; demonizing him for some people, but for others giving him the heroic status enjoyed by 'freedom-fighters' throughout the ages. We are now in a horrible dilemma. If we 'bring him to justice' and put him on trial, we will provide him with a platform for global propaganda. If we assassinate him – perhaps 'shot while trying to escape' – he will be a martyr. If he escapes, he will be a Robin Hood. He can't lose. And even if he is eliminated, it is hard to believe that a global network that apparently consists of people as intelligent and well-educated as they are dedicated and ruthless will not continue to function effectively until they are traced and dug out by patient and long-term operations of police and intelligence forces, whose activities will not, and certainly should not, hit the headlines. Such a process may well take decades.

Now that the operation in Afghanistan has begun it must be pressed to a successful conclusion; successful enough for us to be able to disengage with a reasonable amount of honour and for the benefit of the tabloid headlines to claim 'victory' (though the very demand for 'victory' and the sub-Churchillian rhetoric that accompanies it shows how profoundly press and politicians still misunderstand the nature of the problem that confronts us). Only after we have done that will it be possible to continue with the real struggle that I have described above; one in which there will be no spectacular battles, and no clear victory.

The analogy with the Cold War is valuable in another respect. Not only did it go on for a very long time: it had to be kept cold. There was a constant danger that it would be inadvertently toppled into a hot nuclear war, which everyone would catastrophically lose. The danger of nuclear war, at least on a global scale, has now ebbed, if only for the moment, but it has been replaced by another, and one no less alarming; the likelihood of an on-going and continuous confrontation of cultures, that will not only divide the world but shatter the internal cohesion of our increasingly multi-cultural societies. And the longer the overt war continues against 'terrorism', in Afghanistan or anywhere else, the greater is the danger of that happening.

There is no reason to suppose that Osama bin Laden enjoys any more sympathy in the Islamic world than, say, Ian Paisley does in that of Christendom. He is a phenomenon that has cropped up several times in our history – a charismatic religious leader fanatically hostile to the West leading a cult that has sometimes gripped an entire nation. There was the Mahdi in the Sudan in the late nineteenth century, and the so-called 'Mad Mullah' in Somaliland in the early twentieth. Admittedly they presented purely local problems, although a substantial proportion of the British Army had to be mobilized to deal with the Mahdi and his followers. The difference today is that such leaders can recruit followers from all over the world, and can strike back anywhere in the world. They are neither representative of Islam nor approved by Islam, but the roots of their appeal lie in a peculiarly Islamic predicament that has only intensified over the last half of the twentieth century: the challenge to Islamic culture and values posed by the secular and materialistic culture of the West, and their inability to come to terms with it.

This is a vast subject on which I have few qualifications to speak, but which we must understand if we are to have any hope, not so much of 'winning' the new 'Cold War', but of preventing it from becoming hot. In retrospect, it is quite astonishing how little we have understood, or empathized with, the huge crisis that has faced that vast and populous section of the world stretching from the Mahgreb through the Middle East and central Asia into South and South-East Asia and beyond to the Philippines: overpopulated, underdeveloped, being dragged headlong by the West into the post-modern age before they have come to terms with modernity. This is not a problem of poverty as against wealth, and I am afraid that it is symptomatic of our Western materialism to suppose that it is. It is the far more profound and intractable confrontation between a theistic, land-based and traditional culture, in places little different from the Europe of the Middle Ages, and the secular material values of the Enlightenment. I would like to think that, thanks to our imperial experience, the British understand these problems – or we certainly ought to – better than many others. So, perhaps even more so, do our neighbours the French. But for most Americans it must be said that Islam remains one vast *terra incognita* – and one, like all such blank areas on medieval maps, inhabited very largely by dragons.

This is the region where we have to wage the struggle for hearts and minds and win it if the struggle against terrorism is to succeed. The front line in the struggle is not Afghanistan. It is in the Islamic states where modernizing governments are threatened by a traditionalist backlash: Turkey, Egypt, Pakistan, to name only the most obvious. And as we know very well, the front line also runs through our own streets. For these people the events of September 11th were terrible, but they happened a long way away and in another world. Those whose sufferings as a result of Western air raids or of Israeli incursions are nightly depicted on television are people, however geographically distant, with whom they can easily identify.

That is why prolongation of the war is likely to be so disastrous. Even more disastrous would be its extension, as American opinion seems increasingly to demand, in a 'Long March' through other 'rogue states' beginning with Iraq, in order to eradicate terrorism for good and all so that the world can live at peace. I can think of no policy more likely, not only to indefinitely prolong the war, but to ensure that we can never win it.

September 11 and After (February 2002)

In a lecture I gave a few months ago I expressed doubts about the efficacy of bombing as an instrument in 'the war against terrorism'. I suggested that it would be 'like trying to eradicate cancer cells with a blow-torch'. At that moment it was not at all clear that the bombing of Taliban and el-Qaeda targets in Afghanistan was in fact preliminary to a carefully orchestrated ground attack that would destroy enemy resistance within a matter of days. In fact this bombing, directed from an intelligence and communications network masterminded from a command centre in the United States, proved to be an essential element in a brilliant campaign that could mark a turning point in the history of war, and for which the United States Armed Forces deserve high praise. There was, alas, 'collateral damage'. Innocent Afghan civilians were certainly killed, but far fewer than in previous comparable campaigns. In winning the campaign in Afghanistan bombing 'worked', and without it the war would probably still be dragging on with far greater losses on both sides. Like many others better informed than myself, I got it wrong.

But I said rather more than that. I suggested that it was a mistake to regard this as a 'war' at all, except by analogy with the war against other kinds of crime or against disease. 'Wars' as generally understood are armed conflicts fought between finite political entities which normally end in a clear outcome: victory, defeat, or compromise. In dealing with 'terrorism' as such, none of those results can be expected. One cannot wage war against an abstract noun or a strategy. What we are dealing with is an exceptionally dangerous transnational network of political conspirators who employ 'terrorism' as a strategy: that is, they strike at non-military targets so as to gain publicity for their cause, to demoralize and discredit governments, and gain popular support by provoking the authorities into overreaction. These are the classic tactics of the weak, and have been so ever since they were invented in the late nineteenth century. They will continue to be used long after el-Qaeda and its associates have become ancient history.

So a war against 'terror' as such can no more be won than can a war against disease. But with patience and skill particular diseases can be controlled and even eliminated, and so can particular terrorist organizations.

The main instruments in dealing with them will be the intelligence services and the police, backed where necessary by specialist paramilitary units. Military forces, if used, should be a last resort. Their use not only involves the kind of 'collateral damage' that plays into the hands of the terrorists, but more important, it gives them the status and publicity they need. That has certainly been one by-product of the war in Afghanistan: whether or not Osama bin Laden is eventually captured or killed, he will now be a cult figure for an entire generation of radical Muslim youth, and not only Muslim; much as Che Guevara was for the revolting young in the West a generation ago.

None the less, the use of military force becomes unavoidable when a terrorist organization can operate on too large a scale to be dealt with by normal methods, or has established itself in a base beyond their reach. It may do this by creating 'no go areas' as the IRA attempted in Northern Ireland; or by establishing a base in territory that is virtually 'no man's land', as pirates did in the Caribbean in the seventeenth century, on the north coast of Africa in the eighteenth, or in the South China Seas in the nineteenth and twentieth. Such a situation may prevail today on the territory of such 'failed states' as Somaliland. Finally it may enjoy the protection and support of another sovereign state. Where this happens it certainly provides a legitimate *casus belli*. That was the case with Afghanistan.

Even where there is such a *casus belli*, it is not always wise to exploit it. India claims it with respect to Pakistan's alleged protection of Kashmiri terrorists (or 'freedom-fighters') as does Israel in respect of Palestinian protection of suicide bombers. Both cases are problematic, to put it no more strongly. Britain prudently did not regard the support and protection accorded in the United States to IRA terrorists as good reason to bomb Washington, but we might well have done two centuries ago. But the most memorable example is that of Serbia *vis-à-vis* Austria-Hungary in 1914. Then a Bosnian terrorist organization, covertly armed and masterminded by elements in the Serb Army with the 'benign neglect' of the Serbian government, assassinated the heir to the Austrian throne, provoking an unacceptable ultimatum that led not only to war, which they expected, but to world war, which they did not. Harbouring terrorists may provide a legitimate excuse for declaring war, but that is not always a wise way to respond.

None the less, when a terrorist organization does succeed in establishing itself on the territory of a foreign state, with or without the consent of its government, then a serious war may be necessary to bring the criminals to justice. In undertaking such a war a government has to treat its adversaries as belligerents, and assume the obligations and constraints that have been accepted by civilized nations when conducting armed conflicts. This presents all the problems that the United States faces today with respect to prisoners taken on the battlefield. If they belong to the regular armed forces of the enemy they should in principle be treated as prisoners of war. But we should remember that at the end of the Second World War the Allied armies denied that status to surrendered German forces because of the administrative problems this would have involved. They were termed 'Disarmed Enemy Forces' or 'Surrendered Enemy Personnel', and it was left to the discretion of the military authorities to decide into which category they fell. There is thus nothing new in the difficulties that confront the government of the United States today. In principle members of terrorist organizations who do not belong to the armed forces of the enemy should be treated as criminals, not as prisoners of war, and handed over to the civil courts for trial and sentencing. But if one has declared war on them, can they not then claim the status of belligerents? I think it is fair to suggest that the Americans had not thought through these problems when they undertook the war in Afghanistan, and I doubt whether our own government had either. Certainly they still seem rather confused about it.

Be that as it may, when the campaign against a terrorist conspiracy involves a distinct war, as it did in Afghanistan, it must be won, and in short order. A victory such as that won by American forces, even if it is still not entirely complete, not only breaks up the terrorist network but discourages other states from offering it hospitality, and makes its subsequent operations much more difficult. A prolonged campaign, with the inevitability of further civilian casualties, would itself be a victory for the terrorists. Yet however complete the victory, the war in Afghanistan is only the beginning of a long and complicated process of destroying the terrorist network. Unless that is conducted with skill, patience and restraint, the victory in Afghanistan could in retrospect be remembered much as are the spectacular victories that the German armies won at the beginning of the two World Wars; military triumphs that were later to be squandered through the rashness and insensitivity of their governments.

There are, however, two features of the situation we now face that makes historical analogies at best inadequate, at worst misleading. The first is the vulnerability of our complex and interdependent societies; something of which specialists both inside and outside governments have for long been aware, and on which there is already a sizeable literature. The destruction of the Twin Towers was horrific and spectacular, but the actual damage it caused was finite. The massacre of some three thousand people was appalling, but with nuclear or biological weapons the death toll would have been at least ten times as great. The disruption of world trade was traumatic, but it was temporary and minimal; whereas skilful intoxication of global computer-networks could magnify and prolong that disruption indefinitely. It was a single if terrible act; but a linked series of such catastrophes could cause widespread panic, economic crisis and political turbulence on a scale that might make democratic government almost impossible. Dystopian scenarios of the kind popularized by H.G. Wells a hundred years ago have now become possibilities, if not yet probabilities. And they could all be caused, like the destruction of the Twin Towers itself, by conspiratorial networks that needed no state-sponsorship to provide them with weapons, expertise, finance, or motivation; 'non-state actors', to use the jargon of political science, nourished and supported by the very societies they are attempting to destroy; their members educated in Western universities, trained in Western laboratories, financed, however unwittingly, by global consortia. It was in dealing with such people – the actual people who destroyed the Twin Towers – that I used the analogy of cancer cells and a blow-torch. I am afraid that in the long run it may appear more appropriate than it does today.

2   The second feature is even more disquieting – the motivation of the terrorists. Normally terrorism has been a method used to achieve a specific political objective. In nineteenth-century Russia, it was the overthrow of the Czarist regime. In the Bosnia of Gavril Princip or the Ireland of Sinn Fein, it was liberation from alien rule. In British Palestine in the 1940s it was the establishment of a Jewish State. Once their objective was achieved the terrorists – now transformed into 'freedom-fighters' – were welcomed into the community of nations and became respected heads of state. The terrorist activities of contemporary Islamic extremists are certainly linked to one particular political struggle – the attempt of the Palestinians to achieve independent statehood and recognition; but even if that were successful they would not necessarily come to an end. Their roots go far deeper and their objectives are infinitely more ambitious. They are rooted in a visceral hatred and contempt for Western civilization as such and resentment at its global ascendancy, and their object is to destroy it altogether.

There is nothing new about this hatred, and it is not peculiar to Islam. All historians of nineteenth- and twentieth-century Europe will be familiar with it. It originated in the reaction against the whole process of what is loosely known as 'the Enlightenment' and is almost as old as the Enlightenment itself. It is a protest against the erosion of traditional values and authorities by the rationalism, secularism and free-thinking that both underlay and were empowered by the American and French Revolutions. It gained further strength from the disorientation and alienation that developed as industrialization and modernization transformed European society in the nineteenth century; a phenomenon that was not only analysed and exploited by

Karl Marx and his followers on the left, but, more significantly, was condemned by the Roman Catholic Church, for whose leaders the word 'Modern' became as much a term of abuse as it is for the mullahs today. (A nineteenth-century Pope famously refused to allow the building of railways in the Papal States on the grounds that 'railways beget commerce, and commerce begets sin'.) By the beginning of the twentieth century there was mounting alarm at the development of a global economy that, in spite of the growth of democracy, placed the destinies of millions in the hands of impersonal and irresponsible forces beyond the control of national governments. It is, in short, a cry of rage and despair against the whole seemingly irresistible process resulting from the dissolution of traditional constraints on thought and enterprise and the release of the dynamic forces of industrial development known as 'capitalism'. Mankind may have been freed from the feudal servitude and superstition of the old order, but was left to find his way in a new world without landmarks. His freedom was all too often freedom to starve.

The reaction took diverse forms not easily categorized into left or right. Communism was one, providing the certainties of an international Church with an infallible priesthood to proclaim them. Another was the intense tribal nationalism exemplified by Imperial Germany in the First World War and Japan in the Second that was to mutate into Fascism and National Socialism; heroic cultures protesting against the decadence of Western materialism and preaching redemption through war. Ultimately these movements were defeated and driven to the fringes of the political spectrum, but only after two World Wars and the intervention of the United States; a nation where the values of the Enlightenment remained intact, and capitalism, on the whole, worked.

But the experience of Europe in the nineteenth century was to be repeated in the twentieth throughout what is still, for want of a better label, described as 'the Third World'. There also industrialization led to urbanization, with the resulting breakdown of traditional authorities and the destruction of cultures rooted in tribal rule or land-tenure. There also medical advances, by reducing the death-rate, led to unprecedented increases in population. There also there occurred a flight of surplus population from the countryside to the overcrowded cities, and from the cities where possible overseas. But there the similarity ends. In the nineteenth century there was a New World prepared to accept immigrants on an unlimited scale. In the late twentieth century there was not. The Third World has to absorb its own surplus populations as best it can.

In nineteenth-century Europe the immiseration of the Industrial Revolution was certainly eased by emigration, but it was eventually conquered by the very economic development that had originally caused it. Market economies overcame their teething troubles and converted their hungry masses into consumers with money in their pockets. State activities expanded to curb the excesses of the market and to care for its casualties. Ultimately the success of free-enterprise societies in increasing and sharing wealth among their members (what disgruntled socialists sourly termed 'consumerism') was to outdistance their Soviet competitors as decisively as their capacity to wage war had destroyed Fascism. Today the assumption, spoken or unspoken, is that the problems of the Third World will ultimately be solved by the same process; the creation of thriving national economies that will absorb surplus labour and transform the unemployed masses into prosperous consumers, within a stable infrastructure provided by an efficient and uncorrupt state.

The trouble is that this very goal, that of a prosperous materialist society with religion an optional extra, is itself as unwelcome to Islamic fundamentalists today as it was to the opponents of the Enlightenment in nineteenth-century Europe. They do not offer, as did the communists, an alternative path to the creation and diffusion of wealth. Rather, like the Fascists, they reject this as a goal and regard Western society not as a model to be imitated and surpassed but as an awful warning, a Sodom and Gomorrah, an example of how mankind should not live. They embrace instead a heroic anti-culture, one that has more in common with Fascism, and hold it with a fanaticism possible only to those who believe that they will receive their reward in an after-life. Like both Fascism and Communism their creed is one that appeals to the idealistic young; especially those who feel rejected by the society around them as do all too many immigrants in the societies of the West. Like Fascism and Communism it attracts all who are disillusioned with the promises of liberal capitalism, or are suffering from its defects.

This appeal is yet greater among cultures for whom the world of Western capitalism is not only profoundly alien and offensive in itself, with its godlessness, its shamelessness, its materialism and its blatant vulgarity; but worse, seems to be *winning*; bulldozing away the world of their ancestors and the values that have held their societies together for aeons, much as it did in Europe a century ago. For such people the enemy is not just 'Western capitalism' as such – an adversary as ill-defined as 'terrorism' itself – but, inevitably, the power-house of Western capitalism, the United States; and more immediately, those forces within Islamic societies that appear to be co-operating with it. These are the conditions that breed terrorist organizations; and when American statesmen speak of 'draining the swamps' I doubt whether they understand the scale of the task that they are setting themselves.

Let me continue in this gloomy vein for a little longer. For some, 'draining the swamps' means tackling the huge inequalities of wealth between the West and the Third World. But historical precedent suggests that poverty itself is not the problem. As has been frequently emphasized, it is not among the poorest Islamic states that el-Qaeda find its recruits, but the richest. Alexis de Tocqueville pointed out a century and a half ago that revolutions are caused not by poverty but by rising expectations; by the very process of development without which poverty cannot be eliminated. The French Revolution was made, not by the indigent 'masses', but by prosperous peasants and wealthy bourgeoisie who resented the unearned privileges of a Church in whose dogmas they had ceased to believe and an aristocracy whose members were often considerably poorer than they were themselves. Growing wealth does not make people more docile, but more restive and resentful. This is not an argument against alleviating poverty and inequality, which for Christians at least is a categorical imperative, but against the belief that such alleviation will make for a more peaceful and manageable world. It is more likely to do exactly the opposite.

Nevertheless, there is as little sympathy in the Islamic world for the methods and objectives of the terrorists as there is in the West. Whatever their self-appointed spokesmen may say, the rising expectations of the Islamic peoples are almost certainly focused on achieving the kind of material well-being that the West ultimately promises and the terrorists reject, and the mullahs can be no more effective than were the cardinals of the nineteenth-century Catholic Church in holding them in check. El-Qaeda and its associates are exactly the kind of puritanical iconoclasts who come to the fore in all revolutionary situations and try to remould humanity to fit in with their own ideal world. We had ours in Britain at the time of the civil wars. The French had Robespierre with his reign of 'virtue and terror'. The Russians had Lenin and the Bolsheviks. In stable societies these people remain a conspiratorial nuisance that can be monitored and controlled by the police. In unstable ones, their ruthlessness and fanaticism enable them, however briefly, to seize power and do an untold amount of harm.

So the global reach of contemporary terrorists should not blind us to the fact that their strength derives from the instability of contemporary *Islamic* societies, and that ultimately the problem is one for Islam. We can deal with its manifestations within our own countries, but this is no more than cutting down weeds whose roots continue to flourish underground. If there is indeed a 'war' against terrorism, it has to be fought and won within Islam itself. The role of the West is to support and encourage those who are fighting that war, and we must take care that our actions do not make their task more difficult. This will not be easy. How can we support our friends in the Islamic world without giving them appearance of being Western stooges betraying their own cultures? How should we treat leaders who are as hostile to Islamic fundamentalism as we are but use what we regard as unacceptable measures to suppress it? How can we avoid being associated with the elements that are most resistant to social changes that will make the growth of 'enlightenment' most acceptable?

These are all problems for the long run. What about the short?

There are two paradigms for dealing with 'international terrorism'. One is the liberal ideal: a police action conducted under the auspices of the United Nations, with any necessary military action carried out by an alliance acting strictly in accordance with the Geneva Conventions to apprehend suspects and bring them to trial before an international court where they would be treated according to strict process of law. The other is that popular in the United States today. For many, perhaps most Americans, this is simply 'America's War', and is so described by all the American mass media: a private fight conducted by the armed forces of the United States against the forces of evil. In this narrative Afghanistan was only the first round. It must be continued with hot pursuit to Somaliland, Iraq, Iran, Libya, any state that gives aid and comfort to the enemy until the plague of terrorism has been extirpated. In this conflict no holds are barred, and America must do 'whatever it takes'. The support of the outside world is welcome and indeed expected – as President Bush himself put it, 'those who are not with us are against us' – but the war itself will be waged and won by the United States without any interference by well-intentioned but wimpish allies or condemnation by woolly minded do-gooders.

The first of these paradigms – the liberal idea – may be desirable, but it is quite unrealistic. In their present mood the American people are simply not prepared to subject themselves to any international authority or hand over the perpetrators of the Twin Towers massacre to any foreign jurisdiction. There is throughout the United States a visceral demand for vengeance that may be deplored but has to be accepted. In any case the record shows that the international community as such is quite unable to get its act together for any serious military intervention unless the United States not only supports it but plays a leading role. Whether we like it or not, the campaign against international terrorism must be conducted on terms acceptable to, though not necessarily dictated by, the United States, and in waging it American resources will be indispensable.

But if this liberal paradigm is desirable but unrealistic, the other, 'America's War', may be realistic but is highly undesirable. In the first place this is not simply 'America's War'. Leaving aside for a moment the question whether it is a war at all, it is a conflict that concerns the entire civilized world. El-Qaeda may have struck at targets that are unquestionably on the territory of the United States, but New York is an international city; perhaps the most international that the world has ever seen, and its status as such is symbolized by the presence of the United Nations. The global significance of the outrage was recognized by the virtual unanimity with which the world's leaders declared their support for the United States within twenty-four hours. To regard it as 'America's War' is to belittle and parochialize it.

Further, for whatever reason, the United States has many enemies in the world; some for good reason, some for ludicrously trivial. By appropriating this conflict the United States unnecessarily alienates many potential supporters from what should be a truly global alliance, even if it does not ensure that their sympathies will be on the other side. Even in this country the degree of knee-jerk Americanophobia was evident within a few days of the Twin Tower atrocity in the correspondence-columns, if not the editorials, of some newspapers, and among the audiences, if not the presenters, of certain radio programmes. There are those who, if the United States is on one side in a conflict, will automatically take the other or subside into sullen neutrality. Perhaps this is inevitable – the price any nation has to pay for being wealthy, powerful and successful. But in thus appropriating the conflict – nationalizing rather than internationalizing it – the United States has weakened her own capacity to wage it.

Worse, the American Administration is in danger of spoiling a historic opportunity such as occurs at best once in a generation, of using its power to mould a better world. In 1945 the United States was able to convert a wartime alliance into a framework for world governance capable of embracing her wartime enemies. In 1990 her rapid liquidation of the Cold War and generosity to her former adversaries held out genuine promise of 'A New World Order' – if only the world were capable of being so ordered. The events of September 2001 seemed to offer just such another catalytic moment when America's traditional rivals and adversaries fell over one another in offering support that was eagerly accepted, and it looked as if a genuine world community was being forged of entirely new range and depth. Out of the evil done on September 11th it looked as if unprecedented good might come. It still might, and it still should.

But it will only come about if the United States abandons her unilateral approach to the handling of terrorism and recognizes that she can only effectively be dealt with by the international community that she has herself done so much to create, but which still needs American leadership if it is to function effectively. I would hope that talk of war, and particularly 'America's War' will end with the victorious campaign in Afghanistan. It is an end messier and less conclusive than we would have wished, but one in which the United States may justifiably take pride. Now the eradication of el-Qaeda and its associates will be the task of co-operative action by national police and intelligence services; a task comparable to, and closely linked with, the eradication of the drug traffic: dirty, unglamorous, unheroic, and mainly conducted in the shadows. If a further 'war' against a sovereign State does become necessary to root out the terrorist network, let us be clear that it *is* a war; one undertaken after all peaceful alternatives have been clearly exhausted with full understanding of its regional and international repercussions and consequences, waged with the support if not the participation of the bulk of the international community, sanctioned by the United Nations, and conducted so far as possible in accordance with civilized conventions, and with the least possible collateral damage. Even then we must not be surprised if it gets a bad press throughout the Islamic world.

That brings me back to the main point I made in my original lecture. Our object in combating terrorists must be not to exact revenge but to bring them to justice for the crimes they have committed and prevent them from committing any more. They are criminals, and must be seen as such and treated as such; not accorded the heroic status to which they aspire. Like all such previous campaigns, this is a battle for hearts and minds; and the hearts and minds that matter are those in the Islamic world.

Keeping Order in a Global Society: Pax Americana or Global Policing? (June 2003)

Until the middle of the twentieth century, the idea of a 'global society' was little more than an aspiration, and the problem of policing it barely arose. The world – or at least the European world – had since the eighteenth century been divided among sovereign states, who kept order within their own territories, and among themselves by a balance of power adjusted by periodic wars. The wars of the twentieth century were so devastating that the balance dwindled to one between two Superpowers who did not dare go to war with one another, but maintained an effective hegemony within their own spheres of influence. In the last decade of the century the Soviet pillar of world order collapsed and the West, under American leadership, was able to extend its hegemony throughout the world. The world became a single market, bound together by a global language – English – and by the instant communications provided by the internet. A true 'international community' came into being, a transnational 'civil society' independent of the states in which its members were rooted and often hostile to their own governments. By the end of the twentieth century the dream of the eighteenth-century Enlightenment seemed to have come true.

Who now threatened the peace in this new Utopia? Certainly not the former communist states, who, led by the Peoples' Republic of China, were scrambling to get onto the capitalist band-wagon. Of those that were not doing the same, only North Korea seemed to offer a serious threat to regional stability. There were indeed other 'failed states', including most of the post-colonial governments in Africa, whose incapacity to keep order within their own territories threatened regional stability, or resulted in situations of famine, disease or genocide that the international community found morally disquieting, if not intolerable. Then there were 'rogue states' whose rulers were on principle hostile to Western domination but were unable to do much about it except encourage and harbour terrorist organizations. Finally there were the terrorists themselves: transnational rebels with different agendas, but all basically hostile to the whole process of modernization that gave the West such power. Many of these were drawn from extremist Muslim groups, whose activity was fuelled by the confrontation between Israel and its Arab neighbours; a tragic and festering sore that has spread to infect the entire world.

Troublesome as these were, none of them (with the possible exception of North Korea) seemed to offer the kind of threat that had led the nation-states of the twentieth century to maintain large defence establishments, including where feasible nuclear weapons, to deter and if necessary deal with threats to their very survival. The United States continued to do so as the guarantor of last resort. Even so their defence establishment adjusted reluctantly to the quasi-military tasks of peace-making and peace-keeping that the new world order demanded of them.

In principle the maintenance of global order was the responsibility of the United Nations, that had been created half a century earlier with precisely this in mind. But the world had changed a great deal since 1945. Then the UN had consisted of some fifty members, loosely attached to, if not dominated by, one or other of the two 'Superpowers'. By the end of the century there were getting on for two hundred, ranging from microstates to the sole remaining Superpower, the United States of America; possessing nothing in common with each other but the nominal sovereignty that was their admission ticket. Each, however minuscule, had its own agenda. None was any longer disciplined by a common threat. Events in Yugoslavia during the 1990s showed the difficulty of achieving a consensus within the UN when it needed to act, and the ineffectiveness of action once it was taken. They showed also that action was likely to be taken and be effective only under the leadership of the United States.

But the Americans had their own agenda as had everyone else. And like everyone else, the United States no longer felt itself constrained by the existential threat to her own security that had forced her out of her isolation in the earlier part of the century. Huge, self-contained, wealthy, with vast problems of their own, the American people had always found it difficult to see themselves as part of a wider 'international community'. It had always needed a major direct threat to their homeland to make the American people accept that they were 'involved in mankind'. In the twentieth century there had been two such threats. The first had been in 1917. Then it was not so much Germany's attack on their trade that aroused American public opinion as her intention revealed in the infamous 'Zimmerman telegram' to break up the Union and restore its South-Western states to Mexican rule. In 1941 there had been the attack on Pearl Harbor. When such a direct threat did reveal itself, American reaction was two-fold: first, the total mobilization of American power to destroy the adversary; and second, the use of that power, not just to compel the unconditional surrender of their enemy, but to reshape the world to create a new order based on 'American values'; or as Woodrow Wilson put it, 'to make the world safe for democracy', as the only way to guarantee peace. For paradoxically, ever since the end of the nineteenth century, American isolationism had been closely associated with cultural imperialism; the belief, inherited from the Enlightenment, that stable peace could be ensured only by the universal establishment of democratic values, which America had the right and the duty to underwrite.

So in 1919 the United States established a League of Nations, in 1945 the United Nations, and thereafter during the Cold War, a 'Free World', in which American values were identified with anti-communism throughout the world and defended with American military power. During these years American crusading anti-communism co-existed uneasily with the necessity of tolerating 'evil' regimes with which she did not dare go to war, and linking herself with allies whose ideals and interests she did not necessarily share.

But by the end of the twentieth century the Cold War was over. The American homeland no longer appeared to be threatened, and there seemed no need to subordinate American policy to those of a broader community embracing diverse interests. American support for the co-operative institutions she had established after the Second World War sharply declined. The Republican Party in particular, always suspicious of 'entangling alliances', fell under the influence of a group who termed themselves 'neo-conservative' but can be more accurately called Radical Right, that combined isolationism and cultural imperialism in equal measure. They saw the United Nations almost as an alliance of their enemies. They regarded with contempt international efforts to strengthen the global community by establishing an International Criminal Court, to ward off threats to the environment by the Kyoto agreement, and to check the further proliferation of nuclear weapons. George W. Bush, when campaigning for the presidency, explicitly distanced himself from the thankless tasks of 'peace-keeping' and 'nation-building' that had no appeal either to the American people or the American armed forces. The United States seemed bent on returning to the isolationism of the 1920s.

Then came '9/11'; certainly the most appalling and effective act of terror in modern, if not world history, in which 3,000 Americans died horribly under the eyes of television audiences all over the world.

This action was perpetrated by a terrorist group, el-Qaeda. Their immediate target was certainly the United States, whose military presence in Saudi Arabia they saw as polluting the Holy Places of Islam and whose support for Israel made it an appropriate target for a *jihad*; but their mindset was rooted in a more profound and widespread fear and detestation of the modernization, secularization and decadence of Western societies that seemed to be undermining Islamic values throughout the world. All urbanized societies, those of Europe in particular, saw themselves as equally threatened and hastened to offer their support to the United States in a common policing effort, with military support where necessary, to eliminate criminals who were, like pirates in an earlier age or drug smugglers in this, the common enemies of mankind.

The American reaction was different. The people of the United States did not see this as a crime against a member of the international community, demanding an international response. For them it was an act of war against the United States, comparable to, though infinitely worse than, the attack on Pearl Harbor. Within hours President Bush had responded by declaring a 'War against Terror' – which rapidly became more specifically, 'America's War against Terror' – something that it still remains. This war was to be a specifically American enterprise. The support of friendly states would be welcomed; indeed anyone who was not with the United States, warned the President, would be regarded as against them. No allowance would be made for diversity of interests or perceptions. In this war American strategy would be pro-active, hunting down the enemy wherever he might be and taking no account of the sovereign immunity of states suspected of harbouring them. Domestically the American administration assumed powers of arbitrary arrest and detention unthinkable except in times of extreme crisis; and they did so with the support of a people traumatized by a shock such as they had never experienced before in their history. The 'war', they were warned, would be prolonged: no one could foretell its conclusion. Some strategic analysts went so far as to term it 'The Fourth World War'.

In this new perspective, 'the international community' as such disappeared from the screen, and so did a great deal of international law. The United States invoked self-defence to justify any pre-emptive actions they found it necessary to take.

Initially this motive was generally accepted. The manner in which el-Qaeda was tracked down to Afghanistan and its Taliban hosts were eliminated by American military power (with some assistance from the British) was universally applauded and admired.

But further American actions caused disquiet. In the first place President Bush introduced an eschatological note into his pronouncements that Europeans had not heard since its own wars of religion four hundred years earlier. This was a war, he proclaimed, not only against terror, but against Evil, and he went on to name specific foci of 'evil' for further American attack: Iraq, Iran, and North Korea. Preparations for war against Iraq were begun at once. The political rationale was not entirely clear. The regime of

Saddam Hussein was certainly evil and despotic; but it was not generally apparent that, battered as it had been by defeat in war and weakened by subsequent sanctions, it posed any threat to the world or even to its neighbours – all of whom, with the exception of Israel, made clear their belief that a renewal of the war against Iraq would be unwise and undesirable. Try as it might, Western intelligence could find no direct connection between Saddam and the events of September 11th, although nearly half of the population of the United States continued to believe this to have been the case. There was as little more evidence of a connection between the secular state of Iraq and the fanatical Islamic sect of el-Qaeda; far less evidence indeed than of support for them by America's close ally Saudi Arabia.

In the absence of more plausible *casus belli* than these, even American public opinion remained deeply divided over the wisdom of such a war, while international opinion was overwhelmingly hostile. Only the support provided by the British Prime Minister, itself not yet endorsed by a majority of British public opinion, provided a token of international solidarity. Wisely, the Bush administration shelved its plans for a unilateral attack on Iraq, and sought international legitimacy from the United Nations on the grounds that Saddam was in default of his obligations to destroy all his 'weapons of mass destruction' – nuclear, chemical, biological. Whether he still possessed any still remains to be seen:[1] the Americans and their British supporters were reluctant to allow UN inspectors the time they needed to verify the accusation. The United States obtained sufficient support to legitimize an action that it was now generally believed she intended to undertake anyhow; but in the process she stretched relations with her closest friends and allies to, if not beyond, breaking point.

By the time the war began, however, the Bush administration had settled on a new *casus belli*: the liberation of the Iraqi people, 'Operation Iraqi Freedom'. This had all too little validity in international law but a great deal in Western public opinion, and even America's harshest critics now find it hard to deny that the intervention to overthrow Saddam's oppressive regime was morally if not legally justified. Many people remain puzzled as to America's real motives in going to war, but, as is usually the case, these were probably mixed. American public opinion as a whole demanded revenge against someone for September 11th. Saddam Hussein was a hard target who, if not directly responsible for those events, was a powerful link in the global 'axis of evil', and as such American security demanded that he should be disarmed by a pre-emptive strike. Further, the defeat of Saddam would 'liberate' the Iraqi people and allow them to develop a democracy that

[1] He did not.

would embrace American values and support American policy throughout the Middle East. For more sophisticated policy-makers in Washington, especially members of the Radical Right, it was probably these latter considerations that carried most weight. This group, as we now know, had been urging an attack on Iraq even before September 11th, on the grounds that 'Regime Change' in Iraq and a resultant American dominance in that country, whether it created democracy or not, would transform the geopolitics of the whole of that region. The terrorist cells in Palestine, Syria and Iran could be flushed out. Israel would no longer be under threat. The Western-oriented regimes of Jordan, Saudi Arabia, Kuwait and the Gulf States would feel free to relax their authoritarian regimes and themselves evolve towards democracies. Western oil supplies would be secured. American military power, in short, could be used not only to support but to extend American values by pacifying the Middle East and destroying the roots of terrorism.

It was a truly dazzling prospect, though the Bush administration felt it wiser not to unveil it as their underlying 'Grand Strategy'. But it is hardly surprising that even in Washington the word *hubris* made itself increasingly heard. Nobody doubted that the United States and her coalition partners would win the war, and win it fast, though few expected that Saddam's regime would crumble quite so rapidly. But it was generally foreseen that the real trouble would begin once the war was over – and so it has.

The Bush administration had planned on the assumption that with the removal of the Saddam regime the Iraqi people could take charge of their own destinies and, under a period of American tutelage measurable in months rather than years, could develop a working democracy that would thereafter be a dependable ally of the United States. But they had not foreseen that it would be necessary first to recreate the basic essentials of a state – order, and law – before going on to build a democratic regime to govern it. It is now clear that without a great deal of outside help this will involve a heavy and prolonged military occupation that is likely to be as unwelcome to the American electorate as it will be to the Iraqi people. Such an American presence is at least as likely to exacerbate Islamic terrorism and Iraqi xenophobia as it is to overawe it. There is in fact a terrible possibility that, so far from being the kind of benevolent and successful expansion of American power that followed the Spanish American War of 1898, this could be a 'quagmire' as unpopular and demanding as that which followed the intervention in Vietnam.[2] It need hardly be said that such an outcome would be a disaster for us all.

[2] It is.

The United States is already moving on to the second stage of its pro-gramme; using its military presence to overawe Iraq's neighbours, Syria and Iran, into withholding support from the terrorist organizations they have been hosting, and to reassure the Israelis that they can now safely make concessions to the Palestinians that would assuage their grievances. This is admirable, but all depends on the success of their policy in Iraq. If American forces have to remain there for a matter of years to maintain order and sustain an American-approved regime against a sullen Shiite opposition, then Iraq will be yet another breeding-ground for terrorism. Things will be little better if the American electorate loses patience and insists on a pre-mature withdrawal before the foundations of a new Iraqi state have been established, leaving behind an incipient civil war. The United States will have to exercise enormous wisdom if her new dominance in the Middle East is to usher in, not a new Pax Americana, but a new and yet more bitter phase of their 'War against Terror'.

Should this happen, there will be a great temptation for America's critics in Europe and elsewhere to indulge in an orgy of *Schadenfreude*, but it is one to which we must not yield. Somehow the fences must be mended. If the American project in the Middle East succeeds, we must applaud and be generous in our gratitude. If it falters, we must do what we can to help rescue it. I think that the Iraq experience is making it clear in Washington to all but the most violent 'hawks' that even in an age of unchallengeable American military power, the United States is no less dependent than before on the support and co-operation of the wider international community to achieve their goals, and that they can command that support only if they listen to critical voices and occasionally yield to them. Without it, their unilateral action is likely to intensify an isolation that can only reduce their effectiveness in influencing world affairs.

Conversely the rest of us still need to accept that the United States is the only nation that has both the capacity and the will to project military power when it is needed to maintain order in what is still a very turbulent world. The United Nations cannot provide an alternative, and any attempt by European powers to do so can only increase that turbulence.

So the problem for world order today is, how the rest of the world can relate to American power. My own country may have accepted American dominance too readily, and allowed itself to be involved in operations from which it might have done well to distance itself. The governments of France and Germany, in withholding support from the American war in Iraq, certainly reflected public opinion in their own and many other countries. They, and Russia, are historic powers ('Old Europe') with a dignity and self-respect of their own who resent having their support being taken for granted in someone else's war, and being insulted when it is not forthcoming. Legitimate disagreement is not 'treachery'.

American power is indispensable for the preservation of global order, and as such it must be recognised, accommodated, and where possible supported. But if it is to be effective, it needs to be seen and legitimized as such by the international community. If it is perceived rather as an instrument serving a unilateral conception of national security that amounts to a claim to world domination – pursuing, in fact a purely 'American War against Terror' – that is unlikely to happen*.

Frederick the Great once said that diplomacy without arms was like music without instruments. One could reverse this and say that arms without diplomacy is like instruments without a score.

* The phrase was later amended to 'Global War Against Terror'.

The chapters of this book are all adapted from lectures given at the following times and locations:

Chapter 1. The Emden Lecture at St Edmund Hall, Oxford 1998.

Chapter 2. The Ramsay Murray Lecture, Selwyn College, Cambridge, 1997.

Chapter 3. The Leverhulme Lecture, University of Liverpool, 1996.

Chapter 4. Lecture at Yale University, 1994.

Chapter 5. The Bindoff Memorial Lecture, Queen Mary College, London, 1991.

Chapter 6. The Gallipoli Memorial Lecture, 1997.

Chapter 7. The Prothero Lecture to the Royal Historical Society, 1992.

Chapter 8. The Dacre Lecture, Peterhouse, Cambridge, 1993.

Chapter 9. The Klaus Knorr Lecture, Princeton University, 1997.

Chapter 10. Lecture for the Foreign and Commonwealth Office, 1995.

Chapter 11. The Ditchley Lecture, 1993.

Chapter 12. Article in 'Foreign Affairs', 1999.

Chapter 13. The Johan Jurgen Holst Memorial Lecture, Oslo, 1995.

Chapter 14. Lecture for the Deutsche Gesellschaft fur Auswartige Politik, Berlin, 1995.

Chapter 15. Lecture for the Institut Français pour Relations Internationales, Paris, 1995.

Chapter 16. Lecture for the Royal United Services Institution, 2001.

Chapter 17. Lecture at University College London, 2002.

Chapter 18. Lecture for the Swiss Institute for International Studies, Zurich, 2003.

Index

American v. European culture

"between European acceptance of vulnerability,
and interdependent security as a result of sharing
a continent among adversaries and American
nostalgia for invulnerability & independent
security on a continent without rivals " p 147

E uropei's 21 shC . ①, ②, ③ ④   p 149/150
role in]

p180. America & Islam
  " for most Americans - - -

p115 " mood & philosophy in German society ".-
  — ' unfashionable for us to admit "